DESIGNING TRANSFORMATIVE MULTICULTURAL INITIATIVES

DESIGNING TRANSFORMATIVE MULTICULTURAL INITIATIVES

Theoretical Foundations, Practical Applications,
and Facilitator Considerations

EDITED BY

Sherry K. Watt

Foreword by
Marybeth Gasman

STERLING, VIRGINIA

Published by Stylus Publishing, LLC
22883 Quicksilver Drive
Sterling, Virginia 20166-2102

Library of Congress Cataloging-in-Publication Data
Designing transformative multicultural initiatives : theoretical
foundations, practical applications, and facilitator considerations /
edited by Sherry K. Watt.
    pages cm
Includes index.
ISBN 978-1-62036-060-6 (pbk. : alk. paper)
ISBN 978-1-62036-059-0 (cloth : alk. paper)
ISBN 978-1-62036-061-3 (library networkable e-edition)
ISBN 978-1-62036-062-0 (consumer e-edition)
1. Education, Higher. 2. Multicultural education. I. Watt, Sherry
Kay, 1968-
  LB2322.2.D47 2015
  378--dc23

                                                                    2014047171
13-digit ISBN: 978-1-62036-059-0 (cloth)
13-digit ISBN: 978-1-62036-060-6 (paperback)
13-digit ISBN: 978-1-62036-061-3 (library networkable e-edition)
13-digit ISBN: 978-1-62036-062-0 (consumer e-edition)

Printed in the United States of America

All first editions printed on acid-free paper
that meets the American National Standards Institute
Z39-48 Standard.

Bulk Purchases

Quantity discounts are available for use in workshops and for
staff development.
Call 1-800-232-0223

First Edition, 2015

10   9   8   7   6   5   4   3   2   1

To my family

To Beulah Ruth Watt and Earl Altamont Watt (my parents); to Kelly India Snow-Watt (my sister), Brandy Watt-Hardy, Clyde F. Snow III (to whom I am both parent and aunt), and Cameron (my great nephew); and to Guy Snow (my nephew/son)—my sage and personal comedian—for all the light he brings with him wherever he goes.

"Ever tried. Ever failed. No matter. Try again. Fail again. Fail Better."
—Samuel Beckett

CONTENTS

**PART FOUR: CONSCIOUS SCHOLAR PRACTITIONERS'
REFLECTIONS ON IDENTITY, POWER, AND
PRIVILEGE**
How do conscious scholar practitioners face the challenges
within the convergence of identity, power, and privilege
that are inherent to multicultural initiatives and campus
organizational change?

Errata notice: The following acknowledgments were regretfully omitted from the first printing of *Designing Transformative Multicultural Initiatives*, but will be included in all subsequent printings.

ACKNOWLEDGMENTS

Excerpt from "For the New Year"

And if you hear my music, praising the mornings of the world, then in that other time, in the blackness of my night, sing it back to me.
—Barbara Rohde (1994), *In The Simple Morning Light: A Meditation Manual*

To all the chapter authors, I say a heartfelt "thank you." I appreciate your time, insights, and commitment to the project. As a verbal processor, I am most grateful to have such great listeners surrounding me. I am so thankful for how all things fell into place to create an environment that focused me on the task. I would like to express gratitude to my colleagues at the University of Iowa: HESA faculty (Christopher Morphew, Chris Ogren, Mike Paulsen, and Cassie Barnhardt) and especially to Ernie Pascarella for being a truth-teller and to Deb Liddell for her long-standing support. I am thankful for Katrina M. Sanders not only listening for, but also for helping me to hear my own voice.

I would like to thank my mentors and friends Tracy Robinson-Wood and Mary Howard-Hamilton for their unwavering support and belief in my potential, and for engaging my endless streams of thought.

Thank you to other guides in this journey such as Jan Arminio and John Schuh, whose feedback on early versions of the idea in previous publications propelled it forward.

Words cannot adequately express how blessed I feel to have John von Knorring as an editor. I appreciate the ease and precision with which you work and all of your helpful feedback.

To Elizabeth Whitt, who always, always asks me such great questions. Even when she is not physically present, I imagine what she might ask. I am thankful that she shares her gift of fearless and thoughtful critique with me. This without question elevates the quality of my scholarly work.

I am forever grateful for awakening discussions with my students both inside and outside of the classroom, especially the ones I had with the 2011–2012 Leadership and Public Service class and the HESA MA Class of 2014. To my current and past Privileged Identity Exploration (PIE) research team members (Noel Harmon, Kristi Mindrup, Kathleen M. Goodman, Jodi Linley, Ren Stinson, Elham Bagheri, Michael Venzon, Greg Curtis, Jerri Drummond, Angela Kellogg, Adele Lozano, Gina Tagliapietra Nicoli, Marisela Rosas, Eugene Parker III, Cindy Kilgo, Nicholas Katopol, Kira Pasquesi, Richard Barajas, Jarvis McCowin, Will Liu, and John Mueller), I am thankful for a steady stream of lively and intellectually stimulating discussions.

I do not know what I would do without my friends and campus partners who continuously vet my ideas in the "real world": Georgina Dodge, Heidi Arbisi-Kelm, Kristi Mindrup, Coreen Frank, Lindsay Jarratt, Jonathan Poullard, and Sherri Erkel.

I am thankful for my writing accountability group and the community that we have built to support each other's productivity.

And lastly, to my friends—Chriscynethia Floyd, Kate Rumley, Ethel and Gene Madison, Barb Van Gorp, Kathy Mattes, Beth Briddle, Jennifer Masada, Amy Grahs, Jen Greer, Roy Mayfield, and John and Jean Spitzer—for believing in the promise of these ideas. And to my Courage Family members, Beverly Coleman, Gloria Gostnell, Terry Chadsey, David Henderson, John Fenner, Sally Hare, Parker Palmer, Veta Goler, Donna Bivens, Estrus Tucker, Anita Morales, and Rick and Marcy Jackson, I thank you for "singing it back to me," particularly during the darker days.

FOREWORD

In *Designing Transformative Multicultural Initiatives*, Sherry K. Watt and the contributors to her edited book present the concept of diversity as a value that higher education institutions should hold dear and promote. They also provide readers with concrete steps toward moving diversity to a more central place in organizations.

The authors provide clear definitions of *diversity* from varying perspectives and for various settings within higher education. They also include poignant theoretical frameworks for both exploring and pushing against dominant understandings of diversity. Unlike many other works on multicultural initiatives within the higher education setting that are only theoretical, Watt and her contributors include many strategies with real possibilities for change; they also anticipate the roadblocks that often strangle much needed change in the area of diversity.

Perhaps what I enjoyed most about *Designing Transformative Multicultural Initiatives*, are the multitude of perspectives under one cover. Watt includes the voices of those that approach diversity efforts theoretically—for example, those that use Critical Race Theory—but also includes voices from the National Science Foundation, where diversity is a significant challenge and has vital importance but is far from theoretical. Likewise, Watt presents the perspectives of student affairs professionals as well as those teaching—helping readers to understand how diversity manifests, and more importantly, could manifest within, a multitude of settings.

Designing Transformative Multicultural Initiatives is a book for many audiences and if the strategies are adopted has the potential to make meaningful change in our colleges and universities. Thank you to Sherry K. Watt and her colleagues for a thoughtful book, and also for providing fresh perspectives to move all of us forward in our understanding and valuing of diversity.

Marybeth Gasman, Professor
University of Pennsylvania

INTRODUCTION

A *perfect storm* is "a term used by meteorologists to describe, in the North Atlantic Ocean, the simultaneous effects of several weather systems in creating extremely violent conditions that threaten any vessels unfortunate enough to encounter them" (Moss, 2014, p. 23). Higher education as an institution is experiencing a set of specific challenges: changing demographics, varying perceptions of campus climate, shrinking operating budgets, and the voices of campus community members demanding changes to structural inequities (National Center for Education Statistics, 2010; Veletsianos, Kimmons, & French, 2013). This convergence of events in this particular time in the history of education is a perfect storm of sorts. Recent local and national news outlets report stories about persons or groups with privileged identities unintentionally acting in ways that are hurtful and demeaning to marginalized groups (e.g., people of color, women, and the impoverished). For instance, a sorority at Penn State held a theme party where guests dressed-up as Mexican migrant workers complete with stereotypical slogans on signs. Photographs of the event were plastered on social media sites (Basu, 2012). These sorority members were primarily White women from affluent economic backgrounds projecting on the experience of lower income Mexican migrant workers. The university recognized the offensive nature of this derogatory theme party and publicly denounced the behavior. This news story highlights a lack of awareness of privileged identities, relational conflicts of individuals who experience the world from different power positions, and how cultural misunderstandings ultimately interfere with students' educational experiences and outcomes. The objectification of the migrant workers rendered them less than human. The sorority members behaved in such a way that dehumanized those who are Mexican and grew up as migrant farmers by trivializing their experience. Such conditions can fuel unhealthy organizations and damage relationships between community members. Ultimately, this example identifies that both on an individual as well as at an institutional level there is a lack of fidelity with engaging Difference in productive ways. For the purposes of this book, "Difference is having dissimilar opinions, experiences, ideologies, epistemologies and/or constructions of reality about self, society, and/or identity" (Watt, 2013, p. 6). How

1

can institutions of higher education find ways to gird up their community with the skills to engage Difference effectively in order to live within this perfect storm?

This book introduces a theoretical framework that assumes institutions of higher education are in a never-ending storm. The intention of the book is to suggest that colleges and universities must employ a set of strategies that are widely enacted on multiple levels of institutional practice in order to centralize the value of diversity and inclusion. Viewing individual and institutional change efforts through the lens of "diversity as a value" means to embrace social change efforts as a central and additive component versus episodic and required. These required initiatives primarily focus on the altering of marginalized groups to fit with a dominant structure as "diversity as a good" posits (Watt, 2011).

This book merges the ideas of Paulo Freire's *Pedagogy of the Oppressed* (1970) and his idea of using education as a practice of freedom elaborated on by bell hooks (1994) to inform an approach to social change efforts on campus. A higher education institution that views multicultural initiatives as a practice of freedom enacts a process of deconstructing dehumanizing environments and reconstructing them for optimal inclusion. This process is a civic, political, and moral act (Giroux, 2010) that promotes change from inside an organization by transforming both how people situate themselves in the context of the Difference, how the environment values Difference, and how campus community members relate to one another. Focusing constructively on the process and the skills needed to face Difference can lead to positive community relations. This approach depends on the leadership of conscious scholar practitioners that intentionally and knowingly deconstruct and reconstruct environments to transform a campus community. The community transforms in ways that increase the possibility that its members can be more fully human while getting their education. Being human entails community members living within a welcoming environment where they are respected and freer of the physical or psychological burdens that define a cultural reality that limits their capability to realize fully their identity and potential.

A conscious scholar practitioner needs to manage this process with care in order for dialogue to result in participants taking action to change social inequity. This requires action on an organizational level that is "grounded in theory and research, informed by experiential knowledge, and motivated by personal values, political commitments, and ethical conduct" (McClintock, 2004, p. 393). Taking action as a conscious scholar practitioner involves deconstructing aspects of a challenge such as underlying meaning, historical context, and relational power. This deconstruction process extends practices that also call for reconstructing the environment intentionally to include in respectful ways experiences of historically marginalized groups and non-dominant ways of being in the world. For the purposes of this book, *conscious scholar practitioner* is an umbrella term. Any faculty, administrator, or student affairs professional can develop and deploy the skills of a conscious scholar practitioner to manage these types of conflicts on campus.

Conscious scholar practitioners may work to address these issues through their teaching, by providing programming, and/or through creating policy. The purpose of higher education is to not only to learn an academic discipline and/or a trade, but also to develop personally (Knefelkamp, Widick, & Parker, 1978; Sanford, 1967). Therefore, the work of college administrators, staff, and student affairs practitioners along with faculty is to create effective, holistic learning environments that facilitate the development of college students. The aim is to engage students in ways that prepare them to function as good citizens in society and to teach them how to engage Difference in ways that expand their capacity for making a positive contribution to the environments that they inhabit during and after college.

Scholars in higher education increasingly emphasize that developing good citizens involves engaging college students in their community through the development of skills to interact in meaningful and responsible ways around Difference (people, ideas, identities, experiences, and so on) (Ravitch & Viteritti, 2001). As a result, many institutions are designing programs and policies to cultivate environments where college students can actively engage in social and political change. These types of diversity efforts have taken many forms over the years including curricular (i.e., culture and ethnic studies coursework) and co-curricular activities (i.e., service learning projects and Tunnel of Oppression). Many of these activities focus on raising awareness with some focus on knowledge and skills. For the purposes of this book, "a multicultural initiative is any type of program and/or a set of strategies that promotes skill development to better manage difference on a personal, institutional, community, or societal level" (Watt, 2013, p. 7). This definition assumes that skill development for community members to engage Difference aims to prepare the individual with the stamina to participate in social change efforts. It also assumes in focusing on skill development, the goal of institutional efforts for diversity and inclusion is to shift and focus on a process for managing change versus simply imparting knowledge about cultural differences.

Adopting a campus ethos that embraces Freire's concept of education as a practice of freedom means that a campus behaves as an organization that fundamentally believes and operates as if teaching and learning is for all campus community members. This includes not only its students, but also its staff, administrators, student affairs practitioners, and faculty. Education as a practice of freedom in this context is process-focused, not outcomes-focused. Shifting not only what we do (away from studying to embracing Difference), but also how we do it (outcomes- to process-focused) is using multicultural initiatives as a practice of freedom. By intentionally exploring Difference as a practice, an entire campus and/or segment of campus can take action together that deconstructs dominant culture and reconstructs environments where those with non-centralized identities can be more fully human in those spaces.

Many college campus administrators appoint individuals to do diversity work without giving much thought to the required skills and expertise needed to design and facilitate successful multicultural initiatives. This limited focus can result in designating campus community members because of their passion about social activism and personal experience with managing social and political conflict due to their own marginalized identities. Higher education institutions need to recognize that facilitating these types of initiatives includes both skill and scholarly expertise.

Multicultural education is both a field of study and a mode of practice. Banks and Banks (1995) define *multiculturalism* as "a field of study and an emerging discipline whose major aim is to create equal educational opportunities for students from diverse racial, ethnic, social-class, and cultural groups" (p. xi). They extend their definition by defining multicultural education as a mode of practice. They state "we may define multicultural education as a field of study designed to increase educational equity for all students that incorporates, for this purpose, content, concepts, principles, theories, and paradigms from history, the social and behavioral sciences, and particularly from ethnic studies and women studies" (Banks & Banks, 1995, p. xii). Ideally, a greater understanding that multicultural education is both a discipline and a practice will influence the hiring practices of the field of higher education and student affairs. Minimally, campus administrators need to select intentionally campus community members to lead multicultural initiatives who practice being a conscious scholar practitioner. Whereas any campus staff, administrator, or student affairs professional can become a conscious scholar practitioner, they have to commit intentionally to self-explore as well as to learn the behaviors, disposition, and scholarship of the discipline. Conscious scholar practitioners understand the nuances of the theory, research, and practice needed to create effective learning experiences for college students to engage Difference productively. Most importantly, they recognize that as conscious scholar practitioners that they are always in a process of becoming effective as they learn about Difference from self, others, and community rather than claiming to be all knowing and instead focus on being experts in facilitating process to traverse these unpredictable "storms."

Currently, the research and theory of multicultural education is widely dispersed in the literature. This edited book introduces a structured approach, and refers to as well as applies the relevant theoretical frameworks, research, and practices surrounding diversity initiatives in post-secondary education. Within these chapters, the authors introduce individual and organization skills needed to manage Difference effectively. The guiding principles and practical strategies presented in this book intend to inform conscious scholar practitioners whether they are academics, student affairs professionals, or administrators on college campuses.

Through sharing examples of multicultural initiatives, theory, and research as well as the reflections of facilitators of successful multicultural initiatives, the authors bring together expertise in the emergent field of multiculturalism and diversity. There are four parts and each part addresses an overarching question. The content of Part One addresses the question: *What are some useful guiding principles used by conscious scholar practitioners to design transformative multicultural initiatives?* The chapters in Part Two respond to the question: *What techniques do conscious scholar practitioners use to develop a multicultural initiative that will lead to a successful outcome?* Part Three examines the question: *What are examples of the varying types of multicultural initiatives in the field of higher education and student affairs?* The authors in Part Four ponder the question: *How do conscious scholar practitioners face the challenges that arise from the convergence of identity, power, and privilege that are inherent to multicultural initiatives and campus organizational change?*

Part One, *Guiding Principles for Transformative Multicultural Initiatives*, includes three opening chapters written by Sherry K. Watt. Chapter 1 defines *multicultural initiatives* as a practice of freedom and broadens the language to include not only programs, but also policies and practices on campuses. In addition, the chapter frames the underlying motivations of multicultural initiatives by introducing the "diversity as a value" versus "diversity as a good" lens. Chapter 2 introduces a shift in the purpose and intent of multicultural initiatives as well as a framework for applying scholarly "content, concepts, paradigms, and theories" (Bank & Banks, 1995, p. xii) relevant to multicultural education, and introduces the *authentic, action-oriented, framing for environmental shifts (AAFES) method.* The AAFES method is a process-oriented approach that uses the principles of education as a practice of freedom to disrupt social oppression in environmental settings. Finally, the chapter defines and describes behaviors and dispositions as well as frames the fundamental elements of transformational multicultural initiatives used by conscious scholar practitioners. In Chapter 3, Sherry K. Watt introduces a re-articulation of the *privileged identity exploration (PIE) model* (Watt, 2007) and explores how the ability to identify defensive reactions contributes constructively to the process of deconstructing and reconstructing environments for inclusion.

Part Two, *Designing Multicultural Initiatives: Effective Strategies,* provides a conscious scholar practitioner with some fundamental tools to use when creating a multicultural initiative. In Chapter 4, Cindy Ann Kilgo and Richard Barajas review the basic components of a multicultural initiative such as defining the problem, reviewing relevant literature, clarifying a rationale, setting goals and learning objectives, selecting a theoretical/philosophical frame, developing a strategy for action, and understanding your target population. Lacretia Johnson Flash authors Chapter 5. In this chapter, she explores the organizational context in which multicultural initiatives exist. This chapter highlights change strategies from an organizational perspective building from her *multicultural competence in student affairs organizations (MCSAO) questionnaire* (Flash, 2010). In the last chapter in this part, Chapter 6, Wayne Jacobson discusses strategies for how to prepare an evaluation plan to assess the effectiveness of a multicultural initiative. This chapter provides a rationale for the utility of terminology of distinguishing evaluation from assessment as it relates to these types of initiatives.

In Part Three, *Scholarly Examples of Multicultural Initiatives in Teaching, Higher Education Administration, and Student Affairs Practice,* the authors not only present their programs, but also offer a critical view of their experience. In Chapter 7, John P. Dugan and Daviree Velázquez resituate leadership development as grounded in transformative multiculturalism. The authors examine three core principles associated with the use of a transformative multicultural approach in a credit-bearing, leadership course: (a) infusion of conversations across difference; (b) diversification of content and interrogation of dominant narratives; and (c) cultivation of students' capacities for critical perspectives. The exploration of each of these principles includes practical examples of how they translate to specific course content and activities. Paulette Granberry Russell and Melissa McDaniels in Chapter 8 examine the implementation of new policies and aligning procedures related to diversity and inclusion from the perspective a Chief Diversity Officer and a strategic partner and program director of a five-year National Science Foundation project. The authors discuss the lessons learned from initiating change at an institutional level. In Chapter 9, Kathy Obear and Shelly Kerr review the central components of a multiyear, systemic change process in a student affairs division at a large, public institution designed to develop the organizational infrastructure and internal capacity of staff to create inclusive campus environments. The chapter outlines specific steps taken by the division's Multicultural Organizational Development Implementation Team to build the foundation for leadership and staff, and offers suggestions on how to design and implement a similar systemic change process in other student affairs divisions. In Chapter 10, Sherri Edvalson Erkel discusses how students talk about race as informed by a research project. The project offers an example of how to intentionally explore race through dialogue and raise awareness on campuses in the aftermath of challenging racial incidents. In Chapter 11, Bridget Turner Kelly and Joy Gaston Gayles take a closer look at the uses of power within multicultural initiatives within classroom environments. The authors reflect on their experiences as teachers of a course on social issues as well as research they have conducted that explores student responses. The intent of this chapter is to discuss the dynamics of power within classroom environments. This chapter concludes with suggestions for practical strategies for dealing with power dynamics and ways to interrupt systems of domination. Chapter 12 concludes this part and Lucy A. LePeau offers insight into partnerships between academic affairs and student affairs that aim to promote diversity and inclusion as a means to social change. The author examines how campus community members view "the way we do things here" and how it can determine the progress the campus environment makes toward its goals of managing Difference more effectively.

The authors in Part Four, *Conscious Scholar Practitioners' Reflections on Identity, Power, and Privilege*, provide reflections on challenging aspects of implementing multicultural initiatives. In Chapter 13, John A. Mueller and Craig S. Pickett discuss the role of identity in the process of designing and implementing multicultural initiatives. In particular, they unpack the politics of identity inherent in doing this work through exploring the concepts of multiple and intersecting identities. This chapter closes with recommendations for negotiating the politics of identity within multicultural initiatives. In Chapter 14, Mary F. Howard-Hamilton shares personal reflections on toxic environments within higher education organizations and in particular, the psychologically violent assaults on marginalized multicultural scholars in the academy. Jodi L. Linley and Sherry K. Watt share reflections on the various ways racism manifests in higher education settings using the metaphor of the proverbial lion in Chapter 15. In Chapter 16, Ellen E. Fairchild reflects on the struggles of teaching about power, privilege, and oppression to college students in the current generation. Finally, in Chapter 17 Tracy L. Robinson-Wood, long-time mentor and friend to Sherry K. Watt, responds critically to this conceptual and practical approach to multicultural initiatives.

References

Banks, J. A., & Banks, C. A. M. (1995). *Handbook of research on multicultural education.* New York: Macmillan.

Basu, M. (2012, December 6). Penn State sorority sisters denigrate Mexicans in party photo. *CNN.* Retrieved from http://inamerica.blogs.cnn.com/2012/12/05/penn-state-in-spotlight-again-with-sorority-photo-mocking-latinos/

Flash, L. J. (2010). *Developing a measure of multicultural competence in student affairs organizations* (Unpublished doctoral dissertation). University of Vermont, Burlington, VT.

Freire, P. (1970). *Pedagogy of the oppressed.* New York: Continuum.

Giroux, H. (2010, October 17). Lessons from Paulo Freire. *Chronicle of Higher Education.* Retrieved from http://chronicle.com/article/Lessons-From-Paulo-Freire/124910/

hooks, b. (1994). *Teaching to transgress.* New York: Routledge.

Knefelkamp, L. L., Widick, C., & Parker, C. A. (1978). Editor's notes: Why bother with theory? In L. L. Knefelkamp, C. Widick, & C. A. Parker (Eds.). *Applying new developmental findings* (pp. vii–xvii). San Francisco: Jossey-Bass.

McClintock, C. (2004). The scholar–practitioner model. In A. DiStefano, K. Rudestam, & R. Silverman (Eds.), *Encyclopedia of distributed learning* (pp. 393–397). Thousand Oaks, CA: Sage.

Moss, B. (2014). Models from ecohydrology and hydrobiology can inform our human future. *Ecohydrology & Hydrobiology, 14*(1), 21–32.

National Center for Education Statistics. (2010). *Status and trends in the education of racial and ethnic groups* (NCES 2010-015). Retrieved from http://nces.ed.gov/pubs2010/2010015.pdf

Ravitch, D., & Viteritti, J. P. (Eds.). (2001). *Making good citizens: Education and civil society.* New Haven, CT: Yale University Press.

Sanford, N. (1967). *Where colleges fail: The study of the student as a person.* San Francisco: Jossey-Bass.

Veletsianos, G., Kimmons, R., & French, K. D. (2013). Instructor experiences with a social networking site in a higher education setting: Expectations, frustrations, appropriation, and compartmentalization. *Educational Technology Research and Development, 61*(2), 255–278.

Watt, S. K. (2007). Difficult dialogues, privilege and social justice: Uses of the privileged identity exploration (PIE) model in student affairs practice. *College Student Affairs Journal, 26*(2), 114–126.

Watt, S. K. (2011). Moving beyond the talk: From difficult dialogues to action. In J. Arminio & V. Torres (Eds.), *Why aren't we there yet: Taking personal responsibility for creating an inclusive campus* (pp. 131–144). Sterling, VA: Stylus.

Watt, S. K. (2013). Designing and implementing multicultural initiatives: Guiding principles. In S. K. Watt, & J. Linley (Eds.), *Creating successful multicultural initiatives in higher education and student affairs* (pp. 5–15). San Francisco: Jossey-Bass.

PART ONE

GUIDING PRINCIPLES FOR TRANSFORMATIVE MULTICULTURAL INITIATIVES

What are some useful guiding principles that help conscious scholar practitioners design transformative multicultural initiatives?

MULTICULTURAL INITIATIVES AS A PRACTICE OF FREEDOM

Sherry K. Watt

> Education either functions as an instrument which is used to facilitate integration of the younger generation into the logic of the present system and bring about conformity to it, or it becomes "the practice of freedom," the means by which men and women deal critically and creatively with reality and discover how to participate in the transformation of their world.
> —Richard Schaull, Foreword to *Pedagogy of the Oppressed* (Freire, 1970, p. 15)

Being able to invoke strategies to effectively negotiate conflicts related to difference is essential when living in diverse society. Respectfully and productively negotiating these conflicts means that community members must relate to each other in a way that balances thoughtful dialogue with action (Watt, 2011). Due to the increasing diversity (race, gender, religion, cultural traditions, etc.) of college campuses, faculty, administrators, and student affairs professionals are constantly managing conflicts that raise questions about how to be fair and inclusive to those with marginalized identities (people of color, sexual minorities, economically disadvantaged, women, non-Christian) without limiting the rights of those with dominant identities. Higher education institutions are microcosms of our larger society where systems of oppression are perpetuated and managing difference is often mishandled, resulting in a privileging of the rights of one group over another. Due to the historical context, this system of oppression often normalizes dominant groups' ways of being in the world. Elevating dominant group values dehumanizes any other way of being in the world. This Darwinian (survival of the fittest) way of viewing human relationships and portraying difference has consequences for all groups, especially marginalized groups, but dominant ones as well. Our college campuses are in the position to practice strategies for inclusion that make a shift in the way our society relates to difference.

Leaders in post-secondary education seek ways to manage effectively these conflicts between differences. "Difference is having dissimilar opinions, experiences, ideologies, epistemologies and/or constructions of reality about self, society, and/or identity" (Watt, 2013, p. 6). Many administrators, faculty, and student affairs professionals as well as students realize how structural inequities undergird how institutions operate as well as inform how individuals within a community relate to one another. Although our society has made some recognizable progress in some areas, such as obvious race discrimination laws, there is still blatant legislation that represents the systemic problems that limit how individuals live if they are gay, lesbian, and bisexual evidenced in recent cases (Cummings & NeJaime, 2010; Herek, 2011) and massive subtle systematic exclusion of people of color. For instance, the 1996 Defense of Marriage Act legislates that a legal union is one between one man and one woman only. This legal crusade protests that same-sex couples should wait indefinitely for recognition of their marriages under state and federal law. People of color are only marginally represented among senior administrators (16% are people of color) and among presidents (14% are people of color) (American Council on Education, 2008). The efforts to recruit people of color to these positions are often thwarted by subtleties such as the hiring committee's perception of whether or not that person will be a good fit for the organization. These perceptions can be based on a lack of awareness of what it feels like to endure change, including alternate experiences, and relating to one another in ways that go against traditional practices. Many campus community members are rightfully demanding a deconstruction of the structural inequities and are taking steps to name the restricting ways that U.S. culture defines an individual's existence by a dominant culture norm (i.e., marriage is between a man and a woman; White and Anglo-Saxon ways of being in the world; Christianity is the accepted religion). Approaching these demands in ways that are systemic rather than individually focused can bring about change that is fundamental to the operations of an organization. The American Council on Education (1998) describes fundamental organizational change that is "deep, pervasive, intentional, and long term; it is organic and requires holistic and integrated thinking; and it entails new approaches to student affairs, faculty development, pedagogy, assessment, and community involvement" (as cited in Woodard, Love, & Komives, 2000, p. 61). *How can an organization hone the skills of its community members to facilitate a process that results in deep, pervasive, intentional and long-term change?*

As pedagogy informed by Freire's (1970) work suggests, education as a practice of freedom means learning new methods of practice that are inclusive. Hooks (1994) describes this process of deconstruction as surrendering to "the wonder of re-learning and learning ways of knowing that go against the grain" (p. 44). Even though Freire's theory focuses on education, this idea of education as a practice of freedom is useful to reframe relationships between those with centralized identities (Whites, men, heterosexuals) and non-centralized identities (people of color, women, homosexuals) as well as institutional-level operations. *How can a community on institutional and personal levels embrace an ethos whereby the act of deconstructing and reconstructing environments is a practice of inclusion?* To make this type of organizational shift, higher education institutions need to employ a set of strategies that are widely enacted on multiple levels of institutional practice, and that centralize the value of diversity and inclusion. This chapter explores the question: *How can an institution embrace multicultural initiatives as a practice of freedom?*

This chapter presents the fundamentals for multicultural initiatives as a practice of freedom. A *multicultural initiative* "is any type of program and/or a set of strategies that promotes skill development to better manage Difference on a personal, institutional, community, or societal level" (Watt, 2013, p. 7). I present relevant definitions and a rationale for approaching multicultural initiatives as a skill development effort. Second, I align Freire's (1970) concept of education as a practice of freedom with actions and efforts to promote skill development for productive engagement with Difference. Third, I expound upon the definition of *multicultural initiatives* by reframing their intent and purpose. I explore how to use multicultural initiatives to shape not only programs for marginalized groups, but also to inform the way a post-secondary institution arrives at policies and practices for the larger campus community. This includes revisiting the underlying motivations of multicultural initiatives through the lens of Diversity as a Value versus Diversity as a Good (Watt, 2011, 2013). Finally, I raise critical questions around why the shift to valuing diversity and inclusion matters by exploring its benefits and challenges.

Relevant Terms and Definitions

Many relevant interrelated terms address the complexities of socio-cultural histories, social identities, and the way individuals of marginalized and privileged groups exist within a society. This section defines the terms *social oppression, privileged identity*, and *diversity inclusion and exclusion*, as well as *social change*, within the context of higher educational environments.

Higher education institutions perpetuate systems of oppression because they are microcosms of the larger society. Due to the increasing diversity and educational mission of college campuses, higher education institutions are constantly managing conflicts that raise questions about how to be fair and inclusive to the marginalized without limiting the rights of the dominant groups. The privileged or centralized identities (male, heterosexual, White, able-bodied, upper social class) are central and dominant whereas marginalized or non-centralized identities (female, transgender, people of color, people with disabilities, lower social class) are marginal and devalued. A privileged identity is an identity historically linked to social or political advantages in this society; privileged identities include not only racial (White), but also sexual (heterosexual) and ability (able-bodied) identity (Watt, 2007). Superimposing values of the privileged identity onto all is common practice in American culture.

Systemic oppression is a comprehensive set of interrelated attitudes and behaviors that are normalized that position dominant and oppressed groups in a power dynamic (Hardiman, Jackson, & Griffin, 2007; Pharr, 1997). "Systems of oppression are woven into the social fabric so that their processes and effects become normalized" (Hardiman et al., 2007, p. 37). These behaviors and attitudes are consciously and unconsciously made manifest through individual acts. However, the true nature of systemic oppression lies within the fact that these actions are carried out within an overall system of power that, embedded in social structures, operates within a society and that results in both intended and unintended outcomes that cause psychological, physical, and economic harm to its citizens.

As a microcosm of the larger society, post-secondary institutions exclude diversity. Diversity exclusion is the act of centralizing dominant culture norms and values, which dehumanizes, downplays, and shifts to the margins individuals and groups with non-centralized worldviews. An exclusive and dominant-centered worldview places difference on the margins of a society and questions the relevance of any alternate perspective. Making the shift toward diversity inclusion policies and practices requires social change. Diversity inclusion is the act of including age, national origin, religion, disability, sexual orientation, socio-economic status, education, marital status, language, and physical appearance whereby different opinions, experiences, ideologies, epistemologies and/or constructions of reality about self, society, and/or identity are equally valued and centralized. Social change refers to a systemic level shift within social structures/institutions that impacts how citizens relate to each other within a community. Social change involves acts of advocacy among individuals with shared values to transform their community's normative ways (Haferkamp & Smelser, 1992). Social change efforts are necessary because we live in a society where systemic oppression exists. Higher education institutions hold the promise that can lead to social change for the larger society by starting on a microcosmic level. The next section explains how the process of engaging Difference as an intentional practice can inform the ways a campus embraces social change efforts.

Engaging Difference and Practicing Freedom

Paulo Freire's *Pedagogy of the Oppressed* (1970) articulates that the restricting relationship between the oppressed and the oppressor causes damage to both. Altering the ways in which those with historically marginalized and dominant identities relate involves earnest reflection by all stakeholders participating in dialogue about actions an institution can take to make changes at a cultural level (Watt, 2011). Dialogue of this nature involves deconstructing personal identities (privileged and marginalized); operating modes (behaviors and attitudes); and social/institutional conditions (policy and practices). The practice of engaging in this type of dialogue is a fundamental step for a higher education institution that intently wants to shed traditions and practices that perpetuate diversity exclusion, which limits the lives of its inhabitants (Watt, 2011).

Traditionally, in the field of higher education and student affairs, there are different views on the approaches to developing the knowledge, skills, and awareness related to Difference (Watt, 2013, this volume). Some approach institutional transformation for inclusion by making changes through policy and administrative leadership, whereas others in the field focus on facilitating change by working with students and underscoring personal self-exploration. Viewing multicultural initiatives as a practice of freedom shifts the focus from this artificial house-divided approach toward an understanding that the dynamic social change process requires a complimentary multi-level transformative approach. A multi-level approach to social change recognizes the reality that the dynamic social change process requires all campus community members to work together from their particular professional roles. Multicultural initiatives that focus on skill development are process-focused. Specifically, these types of initiatives focus on how the group goes about solving the conflict by considering the group makeup, the preparedness of group members, and the quality of communication. First, this involves taking care to invite a diverse set of community members. Second, it means taking steps to support the development of the skills the group members need to contribute productively to the dialogue. Finally, it requires being sure that the group members spend time talking to understand each other and to discuss from each person's vantage point how they will go about solving the conflict together. This type of dialogue balances the head (intellect/thought), heart (emotion/spirit), and hands (practical/real world application) (Watt, 2013, this volume).

Deconstructing and reconstructing environments for inclusion requires faculty, administrators, and staff work together to change practices on the individual and community, institutional and societal, and policy and attitudinal levels. Campus community members need to work together to solve complex problems. Institutions need to make shifts toward nurturing the behaviors and dispositions for productively engaging Difference rather than only teaching a finite set of information about certain marginalized groups. Developing the skills to respond responsibly to change can sustain an institution as organizations have to adjust to cultural differences that are ever-changing and nebulous.

Adopting a campus ethos that embraces Freire's (1970) concept of education as a practice of freedom means that a campus behaves as an organization that fundamentally believes and operates as if teaching and learning is "a deeply civic, political and moral practice" (Giroux, 2010) for all campus community members including its students, staff, administrators, and faculty. Education as a practice of freedom in this context is process-focused and not outcomes-focused. In other words, campus community members work together to problem-solve and to envision ways they might improve inclusion efforts within their campus environment by using skills and ways of relating that engage Difference intentionally and responsibly (Watt, 2013). It assumes that when diverse groups of people work together and value Difference that the best solutions will be the outcome.

By intentionally exploring Difference as a practice, an entire campus and/or segment of campus can take action together that deconstructs dominant culture and reconstructs environments where there is the likelihood that more non-centralized identities can be more fully human in those spaces. The process of deconstruction and reconstruction is a social and political act that promotes change from inside an organization by transforming both how people view themselves in the context of the Difference and how community members relate to one another. Focusing constructively on the process and the skills needed to face Difference can lead to positive collective community outcomes. Centering on how to build relationships within and across Difference increases the capacity for individuals within a community to work together on complex problems. Ultimately, these effective working relationships can solve problems that can lead to structural change that results from community members relating to one another from their various identity positions and directing their energy toward changing the environment that limits not only those with non-centralized identities, but also to some degree those with centralized identities.

It is important that institutional leaders understand that how they operate as an organization is inextricably linked to what they are teaching their students. Shifting the approach to inclusion, efforts to focus on skill development enhance the institutions to maintain health as an organization and better prepare their campus for the changing future. Ultimately, this shift toward equipping the campus community with the skills to navigate Difference increases the potential that the institution will prepare students to be good citizens in an ever-changing society.

Currently, many higher education institutions are earnestly searching for effective programs that will open up mental and physical space on their campus for marginalized groups to fit within the dominant structure. The problem with this approach is that it does not aim to change fundamental structure. Therefore, these practices perpetuate marginalizing non-dominant ways of being in the world (i.e., non-White, non-male, non-heterosexual). Shifting the focus of multicultural initiatives toward skill development refocuses the responsibility for diversity work away from the margins of campus and into central functions of the organization to include not only programs, but also changing policies and practices on campuses. How does a campus community go about changing at multiple levels the culture that dehumanizes non-centralized identities? By centralizing the value of diversity, campus community members can navigate Difference with intention and use those skills to re-examine institutional practices. Multicultural initiatives as a practice of freedom purport that intentional and conscious deconstructing and reconstructing environments can transform a campus community in ways that increase the possibility that community members can be more fully human in the environment. The next section identifies a shift away from programming for diversity and inclusion and toward centralizing diversity efforts as a practice of freedom.

Welcome to "Our" Home: Moving From Diversity and Inclusion Programs to Valuing Diversity and Inclusion

There are two basic principles that motivate institutional efforts related to diversity and inclusion. One motivating principle is Diversity as a Good

(Watt, 2011, 2013, this volume) which only requires a surface level understanding of systematic oppression. This principle seeks to maintain the societal status quo of dominant group membership and cultural practices (i.e., White, heterosexual, male, Christian). At the same time, practices motivated by this principle intentionally seek to create some necessary supports to marginalized communities on campus. For instance, many predominantly White and openly heterosexual college campuses hold an additional graduation ceremony for students of color and one for gay, lesbian, transgender students. This is a necessary support to provide a safe space for marginalized students to celebrate accomplishments. Otherwise, their experience and voice might get lost in the larger celebration when dominant culture messages override.

Another motivating principle is Diversity as a Value (Watt, 2011, 2013, this volume). This underlying ideology seeks to create inclusive environments by embracing strategies to disrupt systematic oppression on a deeper level. In other words, matters of diversity and inclusion are central and additive versus episodic, required, and marginalized parts of the college experience. Campus community members who aim to operate with this underlying value system ponder and act on ways to change traditions that do not reflect a clear representation of diverse experiences, voices, and perspectives. Fundamentally, these post-secondary institutions operate with an ethos that healthy engagement with Difference is not only welcomed, but also is an essential part of the optimal development of the campus as an organization as well as the individuals within it.

For many years, higher education institutions that operate within the dominant societal value have taken steps toward increasing minority representation in faculty, staff, and students. As a woman of color, I attended predominantly White institutions for primary, secondary, and post-secondary as well as graduate school. The welcome extended by those who inhabit these institutions had a conflicting and often unspoken message. In deciphering this unspoken message repeatedly, I have come to this metaphor using furniture in a home (Turner & Myers, 2000). I share this furniture analogy not to "call out" my colleagues nor any of my former or current institutions. I use this analogy to exemplify one of the "strange fruits" (Margolick & Hilton, 2001) of Diversity as a Good.

Upon arrival, open arms welcome me. I receive outward gestures that say welcome to "our" house, please come in and have a seat on the furniture. Please be comfortable and make yourself at home. I receive an office, a computer, and resources to do my research. Colleagues, administrators, and senior faculty invite me out for meals and for visits to their homes. Simultaneously, there is an unspoken and subtle message that accompanies these courtesies. For instance, I hear about traditions of the institution expressly.

Successful faculty members share examples of how they made it. Senior faculty members mentor me on "how things are done here." Although all of these acts of socialization seem positive and innocuous, oftentimes the traditions do not include my heritage and the practices go against my experiences and expressions of my identity. Therefore, the subtle and unspoken message that I receive is that I must learn the traditions (not create my own) and I must understand how "things are done here" (not inspire change) to be successful. In other words, you can sit on the furniture and enjoy the comforts, but the house and its accoutrements do not belong to you.

Once tenured, I received more messages about the house and the furniture. The assumption is that promoted associate professors earn tenure based on the merits of their work. My scholarship on diversity and multiculturalism is relevant and important research for the higher education field. The outward message is that the institutional gatekeepers want me to believe the furniture is sturdy, comfortable, and that I now own part of the house and the furniture within. Inviting an institution to change, fundamentally, "how things are done here" requires intentional shifts in curricular, co-curricular, and administrative practices to infuse diversity and multiculturalism ideology. Even though my research informs these kinds of shifts, I observe various types of barriers erected to deconstruct the creation of an inclusive environment and to embracing this ideology. The partnering message I receive is "do not move the furniture." If you try to move the furniture, we will tell you very quickly and with the most neutral, slightly patronizing, and non-emotional tone, "enough already." This attitude has an air of "who do you think you are to disrupt how things are done here?" In other words, institutional gatekeepers resist deconstructing the traditions and changing its practices to address structural inequities.

An institution that truly embraces Diversity as a Value commits to not only moving the furniture, but also remodeling the entire structure if necessary. Few college presidents are women (23%), and there are even fewer non-White senior administrators (16%) leading post-secondary institutions (American Council on Education, 2008). For example, if an institution wants to increase intentionally female senior administrator leadership on their campus, it needs to make a shift toward structural change and begin by deconstructing how male leadership and the pathways to it are valued. Further, the institution needs to actively observe the subtle messages that assume masculine ways of leading are a normal practice at higher education institutions. The institution also needs to conduct a careful assessment of how female leaders are treated by examining the subtle messages that are not only rampant in the larger society, but more specifically on its campus. A shift away from Good toward Value principles might mean that in the process of these intentional efforts to hire more women leaders that the campus also consciously enters into dialogue about how systemic oppression shapes our perceptions of the leadership styles and the use of power. A campus can extend that dialogue into actions that change practices on campus on both a macro-level (e.g., admission policy) and micro-level (e.g., respectful relations between community members). These actions can move the campus away from restricted views of leadership that shape the perception that ultimately diminishes the effectiveness of women to lead a campus. In this example, the effort to increase women leaders turns the focus on the environment and requires that the campus take action to move the furniture and change the fixtures by reimagining leadership. This creates space for a female senior administrator to find her personal way of leading rather than requiring her to fit into the particular style of leadership. This shift creates a pathway where a person with a non-centralized identity can be more fully human within a campus environment. Notice that this type of shift does not focus on what the female leaders can do to fit into "how things are done" but instead requires a shift in the environment, practices, and possibilities for expression of oneself.

Making this shift requires a focus on developing the skills to engage in difficult dialogue in productive and principled ways. These types of difficult dialogues happen within the context of relationships that campus community members develop with each other. These relationships are both professional in the context of a campus community as well as authentic whereby individual identities, values, and beliefs are considered. And through these relationships the aim is to actively and critically interrogate the historical and contemporary roots of traditions and practices (head), to explore self in relation to context of the point of conflict in authentic and self-awakening ways (heart), and that balance reflection of the former with taking collectively thoughtful and socially-just action (hands) to change the environment. This shift means adopting a campus ethos that embraces Paulo Freire's (1970) concept of education as a practice of freedom.

Conclusion

Why does the shift to valuing diversity and inclusion matter? One might ask with the rising costs of post-secondary education, how the higher education industry can put resources—both financial and human—toward improving skill development for managing difference in these lean budgetary times. On the other hand, how can a campus not prioritize developing these essential skills when not only higher education but also our larger world faces so many challenges? Our higher education institutions aim to develop good citizens and this requires an intentional forward thinking strategy to wisely use budgetary resources to maneuver this perfect storm effectively.

Overall, public school enrollment is projected to increase from 49.5 to 52.1 million by 2023. This includes a shift in the racial/ethnic makeup of public schools (U.S. Department of Education, 2013). The larger society will be predominantly non-White, representing a major shift vastly different from recent history (U.S. Census Bureau, 2012). Higher education needs to keep pace with the changing world. It is important that the leaders in post-secondary institutions adopt and replicate positive and intentional strategies for dealing with these changes both in terms of creating campus community as well as preparing students for a future that will undoubtedly be rife with Difference. Faculty, administrators, staff, and student affairs professionals can take on this perfect storm by proactively nurturing the skills to engage Difference effectively. Collectively engaging can lead to thoughtful decision-making processes whereby a perfect storm becomes an opportunity to elevate the experience of all community members. Leveraging the skills and creativity of the whole population on a campus maximizes the potential for efficiency in solving problems, which has economic benefits for the institution. Nurturing the skills to balance reflection and action to guide explorations of Difference can transform higher education institutions into environments where perfect storms create opportunities for faculty, administrators, student affairs practitioners, and staff to be a part of real social transformation.

References

American Council on Education (1998). *On change: En route to transformation.* American Council on Education Occasional Paper Series. Washington, D.C.: Author.

American Council on Education (2008). On the pathway to presidency: In brief. *On Campus with Women, 37*(1). Retrieved May 11, 2011 from http://www.aacu.org/ocww/volume37_1/inbrief.cfm

Cummings, S. L., & NeJaime, D. (2010). Lawyering for marriage equality. *UCLA Law Review, 57,* 1235.

Freire, P. (1970). *Pedagogy of the oppressed.* New York: Continuum.

Giroux, H. (2010, January 17). Lessons from Paulo Freire. *Chronicle of Higher Education.* Retrieved from http://www.truth-out.org/archive/item/87456:rethinking-education-as-the-practice-of-freedom-paulo-freire-and-the-promise-of-critical-pedagogy/

Haferkamp, H., & Smelser, N. J. (Eds.). (1992). *Social change and modernity.* Berkeley, CA: University of California Press.

Hardiman, R., Jackson, B., & Griffin, P. (2007). Conceptual foundations for social justice. In M. Adams, L. Bell, & P. Griffin (Eds.), *Teaching diversity for social justice* (2nd ed.; pp. 35–66). New York: Routledge.

Herek, G. M. (2011). Anti-equality marriage amendments and sexual stigma. *Journal of Social Issues, 67*(2), 413–426.

hooks, b. (1994). *Teaching to transgress.* New York: Routledge.

Margolick, D., & Hilton Als (2001). *Strange fruit: The biography of a song.* New York: Harper Collins.

Pharr, S. (1997). *Homophobia: A weapon of sexism.* Berkeley, CA: Chardon Press.

Turner, C. V., & Myers, S. L, Jr. (2000). *Faculty of color in academe: Bittersweet success.* Needham Heights, MA: Allyn and Bacon.

U.S. Census Bureau. (2012). *U.S. Census Bureau projections show a slower growing, older, more diverse nation a half century from now.* News Release CB12-243. Retrieved from http://www.census.gov/newsroom/releases/archives/population/cb12-243.html

U.S. Department of Education, National Center for Education Statistics, Common Core of Data (CCD). (2013). State Nonfiscal Survey of Public Elementary and Secondary Education, 2001–02 and 2011–12. See *Digest of Education Statistics 2013*, table 203.50.

Watt, S. K. (2007). Difficult dialogues, privilege and social justice: Uses of the privileged identity exploration (PIE) model in student affairs practice. *College Student Affairs Journal, 26*(2), 114–126.

Watt, S. K. (2011). Moving beyond the talk: From difficult dialogues to action. In J. Arminio, V. Torres, & R. L. Pope (Eds.), *Why aren't we there yet? Taking personal responsibility for creating an inclusive campus* (pp. 131–144). Sterling, VA: Stylus.

Watt, S. K. (2013). Designing and implementing multicultural initiatives: Guiding principles. In S. K. Watt, & J. Linley (Eds.), *Creating successful multicultural initiatives in higher education and student affairs* (pp. 5–15). San Francisco: Jossey-Bass.

Woodard Jr., D. B., Love, P. G., & Komives, S. R. (Eds.). (2000). *Leadership and management issues for a new century.* San Francisco: Jossey-Bass.

2

AUTHENTIC, ACTION-ORIENTED, FRAMING FOR ENVIRONMENTAL SHIFTS (AAFES) METHOD

Sherry K. Watt

> The academy is not paradise. But learning is a place where paradise can be created. The classroom, with all its limitations, remains a location of possibility. In that field of possibility, we have the opportunity to labor for freedom, to demand of ourselves and our comrades, an openness of mind and heart that allows us to face reality even as we collectively imagine ways to move beyond boundaries, to transgress. This is education as a practice of freedom.
> —bell hooks (1994), *Teaching to Transgress: Education as the Practice of Freedom* (p. 207).

I fell in love with the higher education environment when I was 9 years old. I went to visit my cousin in college. I remember that she was sitting in the lounge of her residence hall, watching soap operas, and eating potato chips.

Wow, I thought, how cool! The idea that you could live in the place that you learned ignited a fire in me. I could not wait to get to college. At the time, I did not know this love affair could turn into a career. I also did not envision the ways my relationship with higher education would replicate how I grew up.

As an army brat, I usually respond in essay form to the question "Where are you from?" I explain that for my formative years I moved every three years and sometimes every year. I lived in Belgium and Germany overseas. In the United States, I lived in California, North Carolina, and Kansas as well as three times in different parts of Virginia. Prior to Iowa, I lived the longest in North Carolina where I spent my high school, college, and graduate school years. Although I could say I am "from" North Carolina, I know when people pose that question they mean, "Where are your roots?" Therefore, I am not "from" North Carolina or Iowa; my roots are nomadic and I am from army life. Higher educational settings provide me with some familiar structures similar to growing up in army life. Moving from base to base, I encountered a structured community created at each army base. Although each had its own unique approach, each base had a commissary (grocery story), post exchange (department store), and youth centers (recreation facilities). Each community took on the personalities and certain social causes all shaped by who lived on the base at that time as well as whether America was in a time of war or peace. This nomadic life demanded that I learn to accept change, it created opportunities to learn about other cultures and traditions, and it transformed my way of viewing the world.

Growing up this way, Difference has been a long-standing teacher for me. *Difference* is "having dissimilar opinions, experiences, ideologies, epistemologies and/or constructions of reality about self, society, and/or identity" (Watt, 2013, p. 6). Although I have had other sages (cancer, deaths of loved ones, parenting, racism, etc.), Difference has been the teacher that walked alongside all of my life lessons. My parents, who were both African American (Jamaican naturalized U.S. citizen and American-born mother) and college educated, raised me to adjust to change. My father was an army officer and my mother was a nurse. My father was one of the few African American officers in the army at each post and we lived in assigned housing in neighborhoods that were predominantly White. I attended predominantly White institutions for my education at the primary, secondary, and post-secondary levels. I learned early on that racism defined my existence as the problem. To survive "being the problem" (Du Bois, 1903) and to make sense of Differences I encountered, I began to informally and formally research strategies for disrupting exclusions. My experiences in army life model much of the mainstays of college campuses in that each campus has its own version of dining halls, recreation centers, and lore of town and gown. In addition, each campus community has its own cultural traditions and chooses by default the matters of injustice it aims to change largely shaped by each generation of college student and their interaction with larger societal issues. Resultantly, living my life affiliated with a higher education institution has contributed to my understanding and experiences with diversity and inclusion.

I identify as a Black, female, intellectual activist who intends to live authentically in this world. Due to the convergence of my personal and educational background, my social and political identities, as well as my commitment to bringing my whole self into environments, I search for ways that education can move "beyond the life of the mind to incorporate the emotions of the learner and the needs of society" (Stevens-Long, Schapiro, & McClintock, 2012, p. 180). Although I fell in love with higher education as a 9-year-old, I began to practice as a professional in the environment in the early 1990s. I practiced as a resident director, then as career counselor, and now as a faculty member. In each of these roles, my involvement in campus life went beyond my role. I conduct research on privileged identity exploration that informs an understanding of the various ways in which people react to difficult dialogue related to social issues. In each of those roles, the fire ignited when I was a child became a full-fledge flame. I am enamored with the possibility that higher education environments can transform the levels of where oppression operates.

Over the years of my professional life, I pondered, in some form, these questions: *How can I create transformative learning experiences? How can I aid in facilitating the development of those I work with (colleagues, students, staff, administrators, etc.) in the higher education environment? How can I create spaces where people can bring their whole selves?* Moreover, I ponder the immense questions with no tangible outcome such as, *how can I put an end to oppression?* Oppression operates at the personal, interpersonal, institutional, and cultural levels (Blumenfeld, 2010). Oppression exploits, devalues, and deprives people privileges that are conferred without question to those with power (Barker, 2003; Young, 2000). This power is unearned and linked to a dominant identity. Systems perpetuate oppression by dehumanizing those without power. According to Freire (1970) "dehumanization, which marks not only those whose humanity has been stolen, but also (though in a different way) those who have stolen it, is a distortion of the vocation of becoming more fully human" (p. 28). People with marginalized identities are restricted in the ways they can be more fully human in an environment through limited choices of space where they can see positive representations of self. Taking away choices constricts personal expressions to a strict gender binary and neutralizes ethnic/racial representations so that they replicate dominant cultural ways of being in the world. *How can higher education intentionally create inclusive environments where its community members have the possibility of being more fully human?*

A *multicultural initiative* "is any type of program and/or a set of strat-egies that promotes skill development to better manage Difference on a personal, institutional, community, or societal level" (Watt, 2013, p. 7). I discovered over my years of developing multicultural initiatives that trans-formative learning experience related to higher education must engage the head (intellect), heart (emotion), and hands (practice) (Watt, 2011, 2013, this volume). This is particularly relevant when teaching around Differ-ence. Our deepest-held beliefs and values shape our understanding about self, identity, and society. At the same time, it is necessary for people to interact respectfully with those who hold different beliefs and values in order to relate in a learning community. Hooks (1994) describes *education as the practice of freedom* as a laboring that demands an open collective fac-ing of the realities of injustice and extending dialogue into unfamiliar terri-tory of learning about oppression without being limited by structures that confine questions about our socialization. To strengthen skills for engag-ing in this type of dialogue and relating around Difference, people have to know themselves and resituate themselves in relation to the dissonance that emerges from facing the complexity of the inherent paradox. This requires a transformative learning experience. "Transformative learning is the expansion of consciousness through the transformation of basic world-view and specific capacities of the self; transformative learning is facilitated through consciously directed processes such as appreciatively accessing and receiving the symbolic contents of the unconscious and critically analyzing underlying premises" (Elias, 1997, p. 3). I am introducing a method that highlights some of the key elements to creating transformative learning experiences within institutions.

Research, theory, and practice described in Chapter 1 and Chapter 3 inform this method. I apply my research in education settings by design-ing and leading educational experiences that involve strategies to engage participants in dialogue that is meaningful, passionate, and self-awakening. The authentic, action-oriented, framing for environmental shift (AAFES) method is a framework that structures a way for all campus community members (higher education administrator or student affairs professional, faculty, student, or staff) to participate in the social change process. This method approaches engaging Difference through a guided process that aims to create space for all voices to be respectfully included. As the definition for multicultural initiatives suggests (Watt, 2013), this method focuses on a process for developing the skills to withstand the controversies associ-ated with Difference. By focusing on skill development, institutional efforts for diversity and inclusion shift toward developing a process for managing change. Developing a process for managing change can sustain an institution through the transformations an organization must make in an inchoate culture. The premise of this method is that engaging in a process of deconstruction and reconstruction as a community are essential practices for creating inclusive environments where the possibility exists for people to express their humanity more completely.

Essentially, the practice of freedom through multicultural initiatives requires transformative experiences. *What are the fundamental components for creating environments fertile for transformation? What key questions can I as a conscious scholar practitioner use as a guide to help design transformative initiatives?*

This chapter describes the AAFES method. First, I share the theoretical foundation, assumptions, and components of the AAFES method. Second, I define the behaviors and dispositions of a conscious scholar practitioner. Third, I suggest ways that administrators, faculty, student affairs practitioners, and staff, as well as students, can make these commitments. In closing, I briefly highlight how to use the AAFES model in concert with other approaches to inclusion efforts.

Authentic, Action-Oriented, Framing for Environmental Shifts (AAFES) Method

The AAFES method identifies qualities of process that higher education institutions can use in dismantling systemic oppression. How is this method different from traditional programs for inclusion? Earlier approaches studied identified groups (African Americans, Women, Asian Americans, and Latinas/Latinos). Whereas these approaches to inclusion efforts are a necessary step toward raising awareness about the other and can fortify the identity group members with a sense of their value within the larger dominant culture, the underlying value is Diversity as a Good (Watt, 2011). In other words, these programs promote "structural equity and recognition of identified groups" (Sleeter & Grant, 2009, p. 123). Even though these efforts raise awareness of the social problems facing a marginalized group, they do not require deconstructing the system nor necessitate that those with dominant identities situate themselves within the social problems. The actions born out of this approach misplace the burden of responsibility for deeper change onto the marginalized and historically traumatized communities (Kaleem, 2012). The theoretical foundation to AAFES method lies in transformational learning theory (Cranton, 1994, 1996; Mezirow, 1991, 1995, 1997; Taylor, 2010) and liberatory praxis (Freire, 1970; hooks, 1994).

Theoretical Foundations

While the AAFES method emerged over my 20-year career of designing and implementing multicultural initiatives, it fundamentally connects with the theoretical principles of transformative learning (Cranton, 1994; Mezirow, 1994) and liberatory praxis (Freire, 1970; hooks, 1994). Process-oriented multicultural initiatives focus on how the group develops the skills needed to engage in difficult dialogues and the quality of the process the group uses to go about solving the conflict. *Transformative learning* is "the social process of construing and appropriating a new or revised interpretation of the meaning of one's experience as a guide to action" (Mezirow, 1994, pp. 222–223). The research findings related to transformative learning reveal that participants are not able to take action unless they learn "to identify, explore, validate, and express affect" (Sveinunggaard, 1993, p. 278). Transformative learning theory suggests that learners must "become critically reflective of the assumptions underlying intentions, values, beliefs, and feelings" (Mezirow, 1997, p. 6). In other words, it is important that participants engaged in a process of transforming their environments for inclusion reflect intellectually, affectively, and kinesthetically with the social problem that poses dissonance.

Paul Freire (1970) heavily influences my conceptual framework since my introduction to his work in the early 1990s. Paulo Freire's *Pedagogy of the Oppressed* (1970) articulates the early underpinnings of education and liberation praxis by framing the restricting relationship between the oppressed and the oppressor and the damage caused to both. My work aims to alter ways in which the historically marginalized and those with dominant identities relate to social problems by having them participate in dialogue about actions to make changes at a cultural level (Watt, 2011). As Freire's (1970) work suggests, dialogue of this nature involves deconstructing personal identities (privileged and marginalized); operating modes (behaviors and attitudes); and social/institutional conditions (policy and practices). Education as a practice of freedom is process-focused and not outcomes-focused. It focuses on using skills and ways of relating that engage Difference intentionally and responsibly (Watt, 2013). Education as a practice of freedom defines a process of deconstructing and reconstructing environments as a civic, political, and moral act. This process promotes change from inside an organization by transforming both how people view themselves in the context of the Difference and how community members relate to one another. To summarize, the AAFES method is rooted in the ideas of transformation and liberation. This method specifically guides participants through a process of critical reflection that is about fundamentally transforming dehumanizing environments and nurturing a cultural setting where people within it can be more fully human.

Six Assumptions of AAFES Method

There are six main assumptions to AAFES method to multicultural initiatives. First, this method assumes that there is a pathology manifested in our society. Social oppression is a pathology, a societal illness. Natural scientists refer to *pathology* as "biochemical and physiological abnormalities that are detected and medically labeled as disease, injury or congenital/developmental conditions" (Verbrugge & Jette, 1994, p. 3). Social scientists might define *pathology* as deviances that lead to social ills. This method assumes that the pathology formed from a history of unconscionable acts of conquering and persistent dehumanization of Blacks, Asians, women, Native Americans, and others within the United States—a pathology fed by capitalism manifest in negative consequences such as low self-esteem, increased acts of violence, homelessness, or lowered ability to afford basics of food, shelter, and clothing (Broom, 2006). An outgrowth of this pathology is that dominant cultural beliefs (e.g., White, patriarchy, Christian) are elevated and non-centralized values (Non-White, gender binary, non-Christian) are undermined. The remnants of pathology are deeply rooted in our campus culture, history, tradition, and practices. Therefore, this pathology rears up daily in how community members interact, how administrators make decisions, how faculty members teach, and how students learn in post-secondary institutions within the United States.

Second, multicultural initiatives in this framework assume that transformation occurs when individuals in the environment are participants in the deconstruction and reconstruction process. This method also assumes that this process of deconstruction and reconstruction is multi-leveled and focuses on the social and institutional conditions that restrict both the lives of those with non-centralized and centralized identities from being fully human. Therefore, communities need to be continually in a process of dialogue about deconstructing and reconstructing environments for inclusion.

Third, this approach assumes that transformation requires engagement that balances intellect (head), emotion (heart), and action (hands) (Watt, this volume). It is important to note the AAFES method posits that although emotional exploration is necessary it happens in concert with intellectual exploration and within the context of taking action for the sake of addressing a social issue that is dissonance provoking.

Fourth, this method assumes that the act of inclusion is a riveting process for community members and the institution. While inviting diverse experiences and varying points of views to deconstruct and reconstruct an environment may be uncomfortable and controversial, this method assumes that controversy has a greater potential to lead to a more just outcome, particularly for the historically oppressed.

Fifth, the AAFES method assumes that a shift in the environment and its inhabitants needs to occur rather than retrofitting individuals with non-centralized identities to fit within a pathological system. Hardiman, Jackson, and Griffin (2007) state that "our socialization into acceptance of oppressive systems, through our interactions with individuals, institutions, and cultural norms and values, constitutes a cycle of business as usual until we are able to interrupt it with information or experiences that call into question the truth of what we have learned about the power relationships among different social groups and our own position" (p. 41). This assumes a shift in how an institution considers power relationships and positionality.

Sixth, increasing the capacity of community members/citizens to engage skillfully Difference equips people with the skills to face culture that is ever-changing and nebulous. Ultimately, improving qualities of processes and developing skills equips communities with necessary capacities to create just and inclusive environments. Therefore, using the lens of a conscious scholar practitioner is essential to effectively facilitate difficult dialogues, engage participants in a meaningful experience, and avoid common pitfalls that derail multicultural initiatives. Next, I describe the behaviors and dispositions of a conscious scholar practitioner.

Behaviors and Dispositions of Conscious Scholar Practitioner

Many campuses form their diversity efforts around programs that focus on a particular goal such as creating greater self-awareness for dominant groups; increasing the enrollment of first-generation college students; and providing support for, recruiting, and retaining students of color. Campus community members who have either a commitment or a mandate work together to provide a set of experiences for faculty, staff, and/or students that might contribute to these goals. However, critics of diversity efforts often question the effectiveness of these programs (Brown, 2004; Hutchinson & Hyer, 2000; Milem, 2003; Witt, Chang, & Hakuta, 2003; Wood, 2003). Campus community members who advocate for diversity carry the burden of creating and promoting these programs. These are positions such as multicultural coordinator, directors of campus cultural centers, or assistant directors of inclusions programs. Generally, these employees do not have access within the organizational structure to make changes that would transform the way the campus engages around Difference. The programs affect individuals in the community primarily and may not necessarily change the campus in fundamental ways due to their limited focus and scope. Redefining multicultural initiatives by focusing on skill development to manage difference shifts actually expands the range and functionality of diversity efforts. It requires that all campus community members play a role in the process of deconstructing and reconstructing the environment. This requires that the institution embrace an ethos whereby each campus community learns the behaviors and dispositions of conscious scholar practitioners.

According to McClintock (2004), a scholar practitioner

> expresses an ideal of professional excellence grounded in theory and research, informed by experiential knowledge, and motivated by personal values, political commitments, and ethical conduct. Scholar practitioners are committed to the well-being of clients and colleagues, to learning new ways of being effective, and to conceptualizing their work in relation to broader organizational, community, political, and cultural contexts. Scholar practitioners explicitly reflect on and assess the impact of their work. Their professional activities and the knowledge they develop are collaborative and relational learning through active exchange within communities of practice and scholarship. (p. 393)

Many campus administrators, faculty, staff, and student affairs professionals consider themselves good stewards of their professions and apply these ideals within their discipline and/or in their work setting. Conscious scholar practitioners apply these principles not only to their profession, but also develop the skills to be good stewards of a campus community by doing critical examinations of the structural inequities as they do their day-to-day work. Conscious scholar practitioners intentionally seek to understand the structures within the realm of their work that limit the capacity for individuals to be more fully human as they learn at the institution. This requires that the institution support the exploration of the relationship between privilege and marginalization in ways that are productive. Critical consciousness about diversity develops when one's own privileged status is explored, often "through engaging in emotionally charged dialogue with others" (Watt, 2007, p. 116). In addition to balancing practice and knowledge from their discipline and/or work setting, conscious scholar practitioners need to commit to practices that will keep them awake as they assess their environment and work with others in the complex process of deconstruction and reconstruction.

McClintock (2004) identifies behaviors and dispositions of a scholar practitioner. Conscious scholar practitioners are committed to reflecting and assessing the impact of their work, grounding their work in research and theory, and engaging in active exchanges to learn within communities of practice and scholarship. Scholar practitioners situate their work in the broader context of organizations, communities, and political and cultural contexts. Scholar practitioners are collaborative and relational. In addition, they are conscious of their own personal values and political commitments. This

AAFES method helps any faculty, administrator, or student affairs professional develop the conscious scholar practitioner lens by exploring important elements of multicultural initiatives and identifying what leads to strengthening the effectiveness of campus efforts that dismantle systemic oppression. The next section exemplifies the qualities of process and the skills within the AAFES method. I share a specific example for how to practice the AAFES equipped with guiding questions.

Qualities of Process and Skills of the AAFES Method

Using the AAFES method will help conscious scholar practitioners develop multicultural initiatives that are transformative. In addition to the behaviors and dispositions identified by McClintock (2004) earlier, there are additional undertakings needed to work with others to transform a campus for intentional inclusion of Difference. Therefore, this method describes three qualities of process for transformative multicultural initiatives: (a) Authentic, (b) Action-Oriented, and (c) Framing for Environmental Shifts. Following you will find a description of the qualities of processes for transformational experiences, the skills related to that process element, and a set of reflective questions to use as a guide when designing a multicultural initiative that is process-oriented and focused on skill development. Additionally, I intermingle an example of the method applied inspired by problems arising from students with disabilities that involve mobility.

The qualities of process for being Authentic are when conscious scholar practitioners commit to practicing specific skills that aid in their ability to withstand the personal and relational turmoil that goes along with deconstructing and reconstructing environments for inclusion. These *practitioners commit to listen deeply/actively to multiple voices and competing views, to think critically about their own identities, beliefs, values and positionality, to participate authentically and intentionally in difficult dialogues, and to be open to personal development.* Being Authentic means that the focus of the multicultural initiative is on "you" and not "the Other." This process quality involves strategies to keep participants present in the dialogue by inviting them "to become critically reflective of the assumptions underlying intentions, values, beliefs, and feelings" (Mezirow, 1997, p. 6) that they hold. For example, a diverse group of participants explores their relationship to the social and political construct of disability/ableism. Collectively and individually, the participants explore the historical, social, and political experiences of ability/disability and ableism in this culture. The focus is on their personal relationship to disability/ableism (positive, negative, or indifferent). The group focuses on developing **the skills** of noticing (thoughts, information), nurturing (emotion, personal connections) and naming (meaning making) (Hare & LeBoutillier, 2014) the related social issues as the participants resituate themselves against this particular Difference. Samples of reflective questions to consider when creating an environment with the process-quality of being Authentic include:

1. Does the initiative invite a focus on personal learning and growth (not of the Other) in relation to understanding personal sense making of Difference in relation to the self?
2. Does the initiative create space for personal and collective explorations of the head (thoughts), heart (emotions), and hands (actions)?
3. Does the initiative ask participants to intentionally consider their particular positionality within the context of systemic oppression?
4. Is the initiative developing the participant's skills to live consciously reflecting on their values in relationship to the Difference or is it focused on dissecting the experience of the Other?

Action-Oriented is a process-quality that focuses on *creating a thoughtful balance between dialogue and action. An action-oriented process sets its sights on wrestling with meaningful questions and discovering innovative strategies to practice Diversity as a Value in ways that are constructive, generative, and central to the organization's identity* (Watt, 2011). In keeping with the example, a diverse group of participants deconstructs the structural inequities associated with disability at a societal level and their specific environment. The group focuses on developing **the skills** of mustering the stamina to sit with discomfort, engage in difficult dialogue, and continuously seek critical consciousness (Watt, 2007). The group balances dialogue with action as they carefully dissect this inequity at multiple levels and intentionally reconstruct an environment for inclusion. Reflective questions to assist in creating this quality within the environment are:

1. Does the initiative have stated goal and outcome alignment?
2. Does the initiative guide participants to deconstruct and reconstruct structural inequities that are within their particular environment?
3. How will the initiative prepare participants for the ensuing difficult dialogues?
4. What skills will they need?
5. Does the initiative guide the participants in a process that invites action on multiple levels (the individual, community, institutional and societal, policy, behavioral and attitudinal levels)?

Figure 2.1 Authentic, action-oriented, framing for environmental shifts (AAFES) method assumptions and related definitions.

The AAFES Method assumes:

1. Social oppression is a societal illness deeply rooted in our campus culture, history, tradition, and practices.
2. Communities need to be continually in a process of dialogue that deconstructs and reconstructs environments for inclusion.
3. Transformation occurs at the personal, institutional, community, or societal level when people in the environment balance their head (intellect/thought), heart (emotion/spirit), and hands (practical/real world application).
4. 4. Acts of inclusion are riveting processes for community members and the institution. Controversy has a greater potential to lead to a more just outcome, particularly for the marginalized and historically traumatized communities.
5. Change in the environment needs to occur rather than retrofitting individuals with non-centralized identities to fit within a pathological system.
6. Increasing the capacity of community members/citizens to engage Difference skillfully equips people with the skills to face cultural change that is ever-changing and nebulous. Ultimately, improving qualities of processes and developing skills equips communities with necessary features to create environments that are more just and inclusive.

Related Definitions:
Difference "is having dissimilar opinions, experiences, ideologies, epistemologies and/or constructions of reality about self, society, and/or identity" (Watt, 2013, p. 6).
A *multicultural initiative* "is any type of program and/or a set of strategies that promote skill development to better manage Difference on a personal, institutional, community, or societal level" (Watt, 2013, p. 7).
For the purposes of this book, a *third thing* is a process-oriented concept (Saussy, 2011; Smith, 2005). It refers to placing complex social constructs, such as race, gender, disability/ability, and sexual orientation, as subjects at the center of dialogue to examine them as shared experiences. Treating these social constructs as transcendent third things holds each community member accountable to the subject including as well as beyond their particular positionality. Traditionally, a third thing takes the form of text (poems, quotes, articles, etc.) and other experiences that open up dialogue (music, art, storytelling, etc.). This process increases the possibility that communities will examine social problems in a way that those with dominant and marginalized experiences will share the burden of creating solutions.

The *Framing for Environmental Shifts* quality focuses on deconstructing and reconstructing the environment for inclusion rather than creating strategies for communities to survive the dehumanization. This process-quality involves resituating social problems as "third things" (Saussy, 2011; Smith, 2005). For the purposes of this book, a *third thing* is a process-oriented concept. It refers to placing complex social constructs such as race, gender, disability/ability, and sexual orientation as subjects at the center of dialogue to examine it as shared experience. Treating these social constructs as transcendent third things holds each community member accountable to the subject including as well as beyond their particular positionality. Traditionally,

Figure 2.2   Authentic, action-oriented, framing for environmental shifts (AAFES) method qualities of process, questions, and skills.

Example inspired by problems arising from students with disabilities that involve mobility.

Qualities of Process for Transformational Experiences	Reflective Questions	Potential Practices
Authentic (**Process Quality**: Focus on You, not the Other) *Committing to listen deeply/actively to multiple voices and competing views; to think critically about their own identities, belief, values, and positionality; to participate authentically and intentionally in difficult dialogues; and to be open to personal development*	1. Does the initiative invite a focus on personal learning and growth (not of the "Other") in relation to understanding personal sense-making of Difference in relation to the self? 2. Does the initiative create space for personal and collective explorations of the head (thoughts), heart (emotions), and hands (actions)? 3. Does the initiative ask participants to intentionally consider their particular positionality within the context of systemic oppression? 4. Is the initiative developing the participants' skills to live consciously while reflecting on their values in relationship to the Difference? Or is it focused on dissecting the experience of the "Other"?	**Example**: Participants in a diverse group explore their relationship to the social and political construct of disability/ableism. Collectively and individually, the participants explore the historical, social, and political experiences. The focus is on their personal relationship to disability/ableism (positive, negative, or indifferent). The group focuses on developing **the skills** of noticing (thoughts, information), nurturing (emotion, personal connections), and naming (meaning making) (Hare & LeBouillier, 2014) the related social issues as the participants resituate themselves against this particular Difference.
Action-Oriented (**Process Quality**: Focus on thoughtful balance between dialogue and action) *Maintaining a balance between thoughtful dialogue and action; wrestling with meaningful questions and discovering innovative strategies to practice Diversity as a Value in ways that are constructive, generative, and central to the organization's identity*	1. Does the initiative have stated goal and outcome alignment? 2. Does the initiative guide participants to deconstruct and reconstruct structural inequities within their particular environment? 3. How will the initiative prepare participants for the ensuing difficult dialogues? What skills will they need? 4. Does the initiative guide the participants in a process that invites action on multiple levels (the individual, community, institutional and societal, policy, behavioral, and attitudinal levels)?	**Example**: A diverse group of participants deconstructs the structural inequities associated with disability at a societal level and their specific environment. The group focuses on developing **the skills** of mustering the stamina to sit with discomfort, engage in difficult dialogue, and continuously seek critical consciousness (Watt, 2007). The group balances dialogue with action as they carefully dissect this inequity at multiple levels and intentionally reconstruct an environment for inclusion.
Framing for Environmental Shifts (**Process Quality**: Focus on shifting the environment for inclusion not surviving dehumanization) *Engendering that traditional uses of power (i.e. patriarchy, coercion, extortion, intimidation, and patronization) for further gain are last-resort strategies; and yet, being keenly aware of the various uses of power and attempt to use power subversively or overtly to name injustices; taking the long view, recognize that social change happens through smaller movements, while simultaneously balancing deconstruction and reconstruction of structural inequities to attend to immediate needs; viewing social problems as third thing*	1. Does the initiative focus on the issue as a third thing? In other words, do the participants (stakeholders, community members, staff, administrators, etc.) have the opportunity to dialogue collectively about the issue using various mediums (artifacts, stories, poems, and images) related to the issue? Simultaneously, is the initiative primarily focused on individuals speaking from their positionality including some connection to collective empathy? 2. At the foundation, is the initiative shifting the environment to centralizing diversity, inclusion, and focusing on the lessons that Difference teaches? 3. Does the initiative ask participants to work together to locate and make meaning of the particular issue within larger societal and historical structures? 4. Does the initiative shift the focus toward how structural inequities limit the lives of those in the environment and away from how individuals can survive the dehumanization?	**Example**: Rather than focusing on making changes along the routes that a student travels to class, a diverse group of participants discusses the issue from the perspective of how the campus can use Universal Design for better access for all community members regardless of age, ability, or status in life (Higbee & Mitchell, 2009). Universal design is a broad-spectrum approach that focuses on building products and environments for multiuse (Higbee & Mitchell, 2009). The group focuses on developing **the skills** of keeping a flexible mind-set and a level of healthy skepticism about structures; viewing missteps as developmental rather than as fatal flaws; and holding the tension of paradoxes, which have competing and ambiguous conflicting notions in context (Johnson, 1996).

a third thing takes the form of texts (poems, quotes, articles, etc.) and other experiences that open up dialogue (music, art, storytelling, etc.). The process includes the recognition *that traditional uses of power (i.e., patriarchy, coercion, extortion, intimidation, and patronization) for further gain are last resort strategies; and yet, being keenly aware of the various uses of power and attempt to use power subversively or overtly to name injustices. Also, taking the long view, recognize that social change happens through smaller movements, while simultaneously, balancing deconstruction and reconstruction of structural inequities to attend to immediate needs.* This process increases the possibility that communities will examine social problems in a way that those with dominant and marginalized experiences will share the burden of creating solutions. To offer an example, rather than focusing on making changes along the routes that this student travels to class a diverse group of participants discuss the issue from the perspective of how the campus can shift its policies and practices toward inclusion by creating spaces where ease of mobility does not require special accommodations. This naturally invites the consideration of Universal Design for better access for all community members regardless of age, ability, or status in life. Universal design is a broad-spectrum approach that focuses on building products and environments for multi-use (Higbee & Mitchell, 2009). *The group focuses on developing **the skills** of keeping a flexible mindset, maintaining a level of healthy skepticism about structures; viewing missteps as developmental rather than as fatal flaws; holding the tension of paradoxes, which have competing and ambiguous conflicting notions in context* (Johnson, 1996). Questions for reflection on framing environmental shifts are:

1. Does the initiative focus on the issue as a third thing? In other words, do the participants (stakeholders, community members, staff, administrators, etc.) have the opportunity to dialogue collectively about the issue using the medium of artifacts, stories, poems, and images about the issue? Simultaneously, is the initiative primarily focused on individuals speaking from their positionality including some connection to collective empathy?

2. At the foundation, is the initiative shifting the environment to centralizing diversity, inclusion, and lessons that Difference teaches?

3. Does the initiative ask participants to work together to locate and to make meaning of the particular issue within larger societal and historical structures?

4. Does the initiative shift the focus toward how structural inequities limit the lives of those in the environment and away from how individuals can survive the dehumanization?

To summarize, the AAFES method includes three important environmental qualities for transformational multicultural initiatives. The method identifies skills for each process-quality.

Conclusion

The AAFES method identifies qualities of process that higher education institutions can use to improve their approach to managing cultural change. This method aligns with the principles of education as a practice of freedom. In other words, it suggests a process for how communities can engage in deconstructing and reconstructing environments for inclusion. Rather than creating programs to survive the dehumanization, this method focuses on constructing environments to be more fully human. This method embraces process-oriented action as a deeply civic, political, and moral act and connects to the principles of transformational learning theory (Giroux, 2010; Mezirow, 1997). The roots of the method locate transformation at the nexus between thoughts, feelings, and actions.

This method includes three qualities of process for transformative multicultural initiatives: (a) Authentic, (b) Action-Oriented, and (c) Framing for Environmental Shifts. It supports other approaches to diversity and inclusion efforts such as The Equity Scorecard (Bensimon & Malcom, 2012) and Facilitating Intergroup Dialogue (Maxwell, Nagda, & Thompson, 2011) by providing some details that support the quality of process. Currently, many diversity and inclusion initiatives are foundationally about Diversity as a Good. In other words, they aim to teach participants about "the Other" and aim to raise personal awareness. Diversity-as-a-Good inclusion efforts are useful approaches when beginning dialogue on a campus regarding Difference. Even though the AAFES method is foundationally about process and deconstructing systems, it can assist in strengthening the quality of dialogue within those efforts as well. The AAFES approach describes qualities needed to create environments for transformational learning.

References

Barker, R. L. (2003). *The social work dictionary* (5th ed.). Baltimore, MD: NASW Press.

Bensimon, E. M., & Malcom, L. (Eds.). (2012). *Confronting equity issues on campus: Implementing the equity scorecard in theory and practice.* Sterling, VA: Stylus.

Blumenfeld, W. J. (2010). How comprehensive is multicultural education?: A case for LGBT inclusion. *Journal of Multiculturalism in Education, 5*(2), 1–20.

Broom, D. M. (2006). Behaviour and welfare in relation to pathology. *Applied Animal Behaviour Science, 97*(1), 73–83.

Brown, L. I. (2004). Diversity: The challenge for higher education. *Race Ethnicity and Education, 7*(1), 21–34.

Cranton, P. (1994). *Understanding and promoting transformative learning: A guide for educators of adults.* San Francisco: Jossey-Bass.

Cranton, P. (1996). *Professional development as transformative learning: New perspectives for teachers of adults.* San Francisco: Jossey-Bass.

Du Bois, W. E. B. (1903). *The souls of black folk.* New York: Oxford University Press.

Elias, D. (1997). It's time to change our minds. *Revision, 20*(1), 2–6.

Freire, P. (1970). *Pedagogy of the oppressed.* New York: Continuum.

Giroux, H. (2010, October 17). Lessons from Paulo Freire. *Chronicle of Higher Education.* Retrieved from http://chronicle.com/article/Lessons-From-Paulo-Freire/124910/

Hardiman, R., Jackson, B., & Griffin, P. (2007). Conceptual foundations for social justice. In M. Adams, L. Bell, & P. Griffin (Eds.), *Teaching diversity for social justice* (2nd ed.; pp. 35–66). New York: Routledge.

Hare, S. Z., & LeBoutillier, M. (2014). *Let the beauty we love be what we do: Stories of living divided no more.* Pawleys Island, SC: Prose Press.

Higbee, J. L., & Mitchell, A. A. (Eds.). (2009). *Making good on the promise: Student affairs professionals with disabilities.* Lanham, MD: University Press of America.

hooks, b. (1994). *Teaching to transgress.* New York: Routledge.

Hutchinson, S. R., & Hyer, P. B. (2000). *The campus climate for diversity: Student perceptions.* Office of the Senior Vice President and Provost, Virginia Polytechnic Institute and State University. Retrieved from http://www.provost.vt.edu/archives/student_perceptions.pdf

Johnson, B. (1996). *Polarity management: Identifying and managing unsolvable problems.* Amherst, MA: HRD Press.

Kaleem, J. (2012). Buddhist "People of Color Sanghas," diversity efforts address conflicts about race among meditators. Retrieved from http://www.huffingtonpost.com/2012/11/18/buddhism-race-mediators-people-of-color-sangha_n_2144559.html

Maxwell, K. E., Nagda, B., & Thompson, M. C. (2011). *Facilitating intergroup dialogues: Bridging differences, catalyzing change.* Sterling, VA: Stylus.

McClintock, C. (2004). The scholar–practitioner model. In A. DiStefano, K. Rudestam, & R. Silverman (Eds.), *Encyclopedia of distributed learning* (pp. 393–397). Thousand Oaks, CA: Sage.

Mezirow, J. (1991). *Transformative dimensions of adult learning.* San Francisco: Jossey-Bass.

Mezirow, J. (1994). Understanding transformation theory. *Adult Education Quarterly, 44*(4), 222–244.

Mezirow, J. (1995). Transformative theory of adult learning. In M. Welton (Ed.), *In defense of the lifeworld* (pp. 39–70). Albany: State University of New York Press.

Mezirow, J. (1997). Transformative learning: Theory to practice. *New Directions for Adult and Continuing Education, 1997*(74), 5–12.

Milem, J. F. (2003). The educational benefits of diversity: Evidence from multiple sectors. In M. J. Chang, D. Witt, J. Jones, & K. Hakuta (Eds.), *Compelling interest: Examining the evidence on racial dynamics in higher education* (pp. 126–169). Stanford, CA: Stanford University Press.

Saussy, H. (2011). Comparison, world literature, and the common denominator. In A. Behad & D. Thomas (Eds)., *A companion to comparative literature*, (pp. 60–64). Malden, MA: Wiley-Blackwell Publishing, Ltd.

Sleeter, C. E., & Grant, C. A. (2009). *Making choices for multicultural education: Five approaches to race, class, and gender.* Danvers, MA: John Wiley & Sons.

Smith, M. K. (2005). Parker J. Palmer: Community, knowing and spirituality in education. In *The encyclopaedia of informal education.* Retrieved from http://infed .org/mobi/parker-j-palmer-community-knowing-and-spirituality-ineducation/

Stevens-Long, J., Schapiro, S., & McClintock, C. (2012). Passionate scholars: Transformative learning in doctoral education. *Adult Education Quarterly, 62*(2), 180–198.

Sveinunggaard, K. (1993). Transformative learning in adulthood: A socio-contextual perspective. In D. Flannery (Ed.), *35th Annual Adult Education Research Conference Proceedings* (pp. 275–280). University Park, PA: Pennsylvania State University.

Taylor, E.W. (2010). Transformative learning theory: A neurobiological perspective of the role of emotions and unconscious ways of knowing. *International Journal of Lifelong Education, 20*(3), 218–236. DOI: 10.1080/02601370110036064

Verbrugge, L. M., & Jette, A. M. (1994). The disablement process. *Social Science & Medicine, 38*(1), 1–14.

Watt, S. K. (2007). Difficult dialogues, privilege and social justice: Uses of the privileged identity exploration (PIE) model in student affairs practice. *College Student Affairs Journal, 26*(2), 114–126.

Watt, S. K. (2011). Moving beyond the talk: From difficult dialogues to action. In J. Arminio & V. Torres (Eds.), *Why aren't we there yet? Taking personal responsibility for creating an inclusive campus* (pp. 131–144). Sterling, VA: Stylus.

Watt, S. K. (2013). Designing and implementing multicultural initiatives: Guiding principles. In S. K. Watt, & J. Linley (Eds.), *Creating successful multicultural initiatives in higher education and student affairs* (pp. 5–15). San Francisco: Jossey-Bass.

Witt, D., Chang M., & Hakuta K. (2003). Introduction. In M. J. Chang, D. Witt, J. Jones, & K. Hakuta (Eds.), *Compelling interest: Examining the evidence on racial dynamics in higher education* (pp. 1–21). Stanford, CA: Stanford University Press.

Wood, P. (2003). *Diversity: The invention of a concept.* San Francisco, CA: Encounter Books.

Young, I. M. (2000). Five faces of oppression. In M. Adams, W. J. Blumenfeld, C. Castaneda, H. W. Hackman, M. L. Peters, & X. Zuniga (Eds.), *Readings for diversity and social justice*, (2nd ed., pp. 35–44). New York: Routledge.

3

PRIVILEGED IDENTITY EXPLORATION (PIE) MODEL REVISITED

Strengthening Skills for Engaging Difference

Sherry K. Watt

*P*rivilege is a social and political construct that references how individuals with dominant culture identities (i.e., White, male, cisgender, opposite-sex marriage) experience fewer obstacles and more benefits because their identity has social value within a culture (McIntosh, 1988). Having privilege means that those with dominant identities have more access to societal rights and resources available to them due to their social group membership. Peggy McIntosh's (1989) classic essay illuminated privilege by identifying the ways that being a White male, in particular, but also a White female has advantages in U.S. society such as seeing their race and gender combination widely represented in the media. McIntosh's examination of White privilege and others' calls for justice and equity through deconstructing systemic oppression (i.e., Berlack & Moyenda, 2001; Freire, 1970) began a more direct turn toward questioning the agency of dominant group members in social and political problems (i.e., Watt, 2007; Watt et al., 2009).

Researchers began to study the process of becoming a social justice ally and devising strategies for dominant group members to confront privilege (Broido, 2000; Edwards, 2006; Howard, 2011; Watt, 2007; Watt et al., 2009). Social justice allies are dominant group members who examine their privilege, power, and prejudices while taking positive action to change the system (Reason & Davis, 2005). Researching the role of social justice allies is an important step in deconstructing how privilege manifests. Scholars are evaluating how those with power experience resituating their identity as a power holder in an oppressive system. This shift is a subtle and important turn in the scholarship that informs multicultural initiatives that deconstruct systemic oppression and that call out the complications with conferred dominance (McIntosh, 1988). The primary purpose of this research is to highlight how those with privileged identities come to terms with the negative effects of social oppression and how others extend that awareness into becoming advocates. A secondary value of this research is that it also elucidates some of the benefits and consequences of living in an oppressive system for dominant group members. There are benefits to having privilege including greater tax credits, higher lifetime incomes, and possessing positive self-esteem as compared to those with social group memberships with marginal identities (Young, 2000). There are also consequences of having privilege such as limited contact with Difference. Difference is "having dissimilar opinions, experiences, ideologies, epistemologies and/or constructions of reality about self, society, and/or identity" (Watt, 2013, p. 6). Additional consequences include an uncalibrated sense of centrality, overwhelming feelings of guilt, and lack of self-awareness (Black & Stone, 2005; Howard, 2011). Yet, very few experience the world through only the lens of privilege or marginalization. This presents a paradox. Effective inclusion efforts create space for the paradoxical reality that some combinations of marginalized and privileged identities shape the worldview of many people. Wrestling with this paradox involves a push and pull between various facets of a person's sense of self, which creates complex feelings about the process.

Cornell West (1999) and others describe intellectual vertigo as "a shudder that unhinges us from our moorings or yanks us from our anchors" (p. xvii). This unhinging happens when individuals are required to consider their "location and learn to listen to those speaking from other places" (Hennessy, 2010, p. 47). Participating in dialogues to deconstruct and reconstruct environments can disrupt what individuals have always known to be true and take them on a journey whereby they instinctively need to make sense of this dissonance introduced into their reality. Killinger (1966) describes this as "they now experience a kind of ontological dizziness, a sense of remoteness from reality, as though nothing were sure or real anymore" (p. 221). Part of the process of making sense of this new reality is to locate the self within the deconstruction and reconstruction process. Inclusion programs that deconstruct systemic oppression and the role of dominant ideology generally involve confronting privilege and the complexities of intersecting identities in ways that bring about "intellectual vertigo" and "ontological dizziness." This sense of disequilibrium comes from having to reconceive the self in relation to others in ways that are counter to one's understanding of one's social and political position in society. *How does a person strengthen the skills to stay present in difficult dialogues? How does a conscious scholar practitioner engage fellow community members in meaningful experiences with Difference? How does one develop the skills to take action? How do people develop the awareness and skill to hold oneself accountable when dissonance arises? How do people avoid common pitfalls that derail multicultural initiatives? How does a conscious scholar practitioner work through the upheaval naturally associated with change?*

In this chapter, I rearticulate the privileged identity exploration (PIE) model (Watt, 2007). The PIE model (Watt, 2007) identifies eight defenses often displayed when individuals explore their privileged identities. Knowing the various ways individuals display these defenses can help manage reactions that potentially derail productive dialogue necessary for social change efforts. Finally, I describe a process to strengthen the skill of recognizing defensive reactions that will help conscious scholar practitioners maneuver through intellectual vertigo and muster the stamina to stay engaged in deep social change.

Privileged Identity Exploration (PIE) Model Revisited

The privileged identity exploration (PIE) model (Watt, 2007; Watt et al., 2009) is a tool that individuals can use to identify defenses that arise as observed in self or others when introduced to a dissonance-provoking stimulus (DPS). Privileged identity is social and political identity linked advantages in U.S. society. Privileged identities include, for example, racial (White), sexual (heterosexual), and ability (able-bodied) identity (Watt, 2007; Watt et al., 2009). The model explains the various defenses that arise as individuals recognize, contemplate, and address a DPS. The original research identifies eight defensive reactions for Recognizing Privileged Identity (denial, deflection, and rationalization), Contemplating Privileged Identity (intellectualization, principium, false envy), and Addressing Privileged Identity (benevolence and minimization) (Watt, 2007; Watt et al., 2009).

The qualitative research that informs this theory includes a data set of 75 students who each wrote three reaction papers, totaling 225 reaction papers. A particular section of this research, which analyzed the data by looking at 25 students or 75 reaction papers, informed the original PIE model (Watt et al., 2009). In these reaction papers, students responded to classroom dialogues in a multiculturalism course where they explored Difference. The research team examined their reactions using consensual qualitative research (CQR) methods. Another research team analyzed another section of the larger data set recently (Watt et al., under review). Currently, a research team is extending upon this research by creating an instrument to measure defensive reactions. Providing faculty, administrators, student affairs professionals, and policymakers with a tool that helps them to identify these defensive reactions can improve the effectiveness of their facilitation of dialogue about important social issues. Developing such a measure will further research on the phenomenon of privileged identity exploration as well as help facilitators (faculty, administrators, and policymakers) to better manage difficult dialogues. A PIE instrument could also benefit research that examines racial identity attitudes such as the White privilege attitudes (Pinterits, Poteat, & Spanierman, 2009). Identifying these reactions in a systematic way can help leaders more efficiently devise a plan to manage these normal defensive reactions in self and others with care and that can lead to overall improvement of the challenging conversations that are inherent but necessary in order to address social inequities in society.

This update to the PIE model rearticulates the order of the defenses and more clearly distinguishes the defenses. Additionally, this depiction of the model further develops the theory of how the defenses might manifest as individuals work to make sense of a DPS. The revised articulation of the PIE model provides descriptive detail about these defensive reactions that may appear as one integrates a new awareness about self or the other into one's sense of self and moves toward taking social action. In addition to sharing the revised order in the next section, I also discuss the underlying assumptions to the model and the theoretical framework.

Assumptions of the PIE Model Rearticulation

There are four underlying assumptions to the model. First, the model assumes that the exploration of privileged identity (i.e., White, heterosexual, and male) is an ongoing socialization process. In other words, *there is no ultimate level of consciousness*. Privilege is a social and political construct that constantly evolves as our society changes. Therefore, the exploration of privilege reveals new opportunities for deeper understanding of the construct as people develop and engage with others as well as aim to make changes to the societal structure that has historically advantaged some groups and disadvantaged others. The PIE model assumes that it is impossible to reach finite and/or advanced level understanding around evolving social and political problems. Second, this research assumes that to truly explore their privileged identities, people need to engage in self-awakening difficult dialogues about social oppression (i.e., racism, sexism/heterosexism, homophobia, and ableism).

A *difficult dialogue* "is a verbal or written exchange of ideas or opinions between citizens within a community that centers on an awakening of potentially conflicting views of beliefs or values about social justice issues (such as racism, sexism, ableism, heterosexism/homophobia)" (Watt, 2007, p. 116). The PIE model assumes that people must engage in dialogue about Difference to unravel how their socialization shapes their worldview and ultimately their actions. Third, the PIE model assumes that **defense modes are innate and normal human reactions** when introduced to a DPS. People use defenses when they are attempting to make sense of the location of the DPS in relation to the self. An introduction of a DPS can cause ontological dizziness or a disruption in how people view themselves (values, beliefs, etc.) in relation to the DPS. In response, it is normal to shield oneself with defenses while processing this new and dislocating information. Finally, the PIE model **assumes that there is an intersection of privileged and marginalized identities within each person**. *Intersectionality* is "the relationships among multiple dimensions and modalities of social relationships and subject formations" (McCall, 2005, p. 1). To be more specific, this model identifies reactions individuals might have when responding to dialogues about diversity from their worldview. Both their marginalized and privileged identities (i.e., being a female, White, and heterosexual) are likely to shape how they engage in difficult dialogues about social change. In summary, this model assumes that engaging in self-awakening dialogue about Difference is necessary and involves locating the self (privileged and marginalized identities) in relation to the DPS. This type of dialogue brings about a natural response from people to defend themselves.

The PIE Model Theoretical Framework

The PIE model is a process-oriented framework. In other words, this model identifies behavior people exhibit when they are engaged in self-awakening dialogue that explores their privileged identity. This theoretical framework supports the work of research that examines identity attitudes and development such as the White privilege attitudes (Pinterits et al., 2009), social justice ally development (Broido, 2000; Edwards, 2006; Howard, 2011), and Black and White racial identity development (Cross, 1991; Helms, 1995; Helms & Cook, 1999). The PIE model illuminates the defensive reactions individuals may display as they move through the development process of understanding their identity and provides a fuller explanation of their behavior as they work toward embracing a deeper understanding of themselves and their social and political positioning. Understanding the defensive reactions can help facilitators more effectively guide difficult dialogues. As importantly, identifying these defensive reactions within the self is an essential key to self-monitoring and a skill that bolsters self-awareness that can lead to individuals mustering the stamina to continue difficult dialogues that can result in deep social change.

When individuals confront a Difference ("dissimilar opinions, experiences, ideologies, epistemologies, and/or constructions of reality about self, society, and/or identity," [Watt, 2013, p. 6]), dissonance occurs. Cognitive dissonance is a state of being where people question their thoughts, beliefs, or ways of being in the world. The dissonance is animated by fear (afraid to go deeper to explore the dissonance) or entitlement (should not have to go deeper to explore the dissonance), which creates disequilibrium. This range of reactions manifests in specific defenses. People do not want to be in a state of disequilibrium so they innately want to change to resolve that inner conflict (Festinger, 1957, 1962). The rearticulation of the model explains eight defensive reactions that people often display when they experience a DPS and as they are in the process of managing that disequilibrium. As my research team began to develop the PIE instrument, we examined the original definitions and set out to operationalize each one. The instrument development process prompted this rearticulation of the model. The key revisions to the model include: (a) the illumination of the concept of the location of self in relation to the DPS; and (b) a revised order to the defenses that appears as people recognize, contemplate, and address their privileged identity.

Anna Freud's (1979) structural model informs the theoretical foundation of the PIE model. Freud suggests that the psyche has three structural elements whereby the ego (true self) mediates between the id (impulsive instincts) and the superego (moral and social conscience) (1979). The ego uses defense mechanisms to reduce the anxiety that arises as new stimuli move from the unconscious to the preconscious and ultimately into the conscious. The PIE model texturizes defense mechanisms that aid in reducing the anxiety associated with the dissonance that arises when individuals have to locate themselves in relation to Difference. It is key to note that the defenses rise as a protection while individuals work to locate the self in relation to the DPS. Leon Festinger's *Theory of Cognitive Dissonance* (1957) states that individuals strive to find balance and reduce the anxiety that causes psychological discomfort. The defenses regulate the distance between the self and the DPS while processing the discomfort. As an African American woman who is cisgender and heterosexual, I experience dissonance at the intersections of my privileged and marginalized identities. My marginalized status as a racial being is prominent to my sense of self. Simultaneously, I am not fully conscious of the centrality I enjoy as a heterosexual and as a cisgender female. Becoming aware of my privilege in these two particular areas requires me to relocate my conception of gender and sexual orientation outside of the dominant socialized norms. It also requires that I resituate my conception of my marginalized identity as a racial being because my sense of self as both Black and female is fundamental to my worldview. I will likely use defenses to help me to mediate the pace as I integrate this new awareness and attempt to make sense of myself in relation to redefined gender and sexual identity norms (DPS). The PIE model describes how individuals use defenses as they locate the self in relation to this new reality. The eight defense modes of the PIE model describe strategies people use to protect themselves as they redefine the self in relation to a DPS.

The revised articulation of the PIE model places the defenses in order and distinguishes them from one another. This revised order illuminates the distinctive qualities of each defense relative to the others. The order also reveals a pattern to the different response people have to the awareness of a DPS and how they move as Freud (1979) identified from unconscious to preconscious to conscious. The PIE model identifies what happens while people work to resolve internal inconsistency to regain balance (Festinger, 1957, 1962). In addition, the revised order makes a clearer distinction between the extent to which emotion and thought animate the reaction.

At the introduction of a DPS, individuals are in the process of *Recognizing Privileged Identity*. The DPS can be information that is new and completely unfamiliar, or not new but understood differently. This phase of the model points to the initial movement of the DPS from the **unconscious to the preconscious** (Freud, 1979). Individuals actively deny or displace the information away from their sense of self. To protect themselves from this DPS, people may use the *Denial and Deflection* defensive reactions. Denial is a defensive reaction that rejects or fails to recognize the existence of the DPS. This reaction denies the severity, the existence, or even the possibility of the DPS. Deflection is a defensive reaction that shifts the focus of the DPS toward another source. Deflection shields people while they are processing this new and unfamiliar information and distances the self by shifting the blame for the DPS onto another source to absorb. In the process of recognizing privileged identity, people are **not conscious of their emotion or thought processes**. As people begin to make more sense of DPS, **their emotion and thought begin to awaken,** as they are *Contemplating Privileged Identity*. At this phase in the process, people are taking a step toward a **preconscious understanding** of the DPS. While emotions are coming to the foreground, **thought processes** guide the reactions in this phase. To defend against the DPS, people may express *Minimization, Rationalization, and Intellectualization*. Minimization is a defensive reaction that downplays the emotional impact of the issues surrounding DPS. Minimization reduces the severity of the DPS without much thought and keeps it at a distance emotionally. Rationalization is a defensive reaction that generates tolerable alternative explanations to justify the DPS. Individuals defend themselves using this defense by providing context and bearable alternative theories that justify their position in relation to the DPS. Even though there is some emotion when rationalizing, thought processes override. Intellectualization is a defensive reaction that attempts to explain the DPS with scientific evidence. Thought processes supersede any emotion. Ironically, the defense emerges as individuals begin to feel conscious emotion. Therefore, people escalate the factual or theoretical evidence to support the justification to denounce the DPS. As people move from the preconscious to the conscious understanding of the DPS, emotion and intellect emerge together as they dissect their beliefs and values in relation to the stimulus. The *Addressing Privileged Identity* phase includes the defensive reactions of *False Envy, Principium, and Benevolence*. False Envy is a defensive reaction that compliments or expresses affection toward a person or a feature of a person that represents the DPS. Once people are conscious of the DPS, they may become uncomfortable with the power and position that they have in relation to those representing the DPS. This dissonance may cause them to attempt to equalize their position by martyrizing the DPS to manage the conscious emotional and intellectual awareness of the discomfort of the DPS in relation to the self. Principium is a defensive reaction that invokes a principle based on a personal value or belief to argue against the DPS. Principium involves emotional and intellectual investment. People present a principle that sets their beliefs and values as a valid reason to avoid closer examination of DPS. Benevolence is a defensive reaction that uses an act of charity or service to cloak the DPS. There is a higher level of both emotional and intellectual awareness within this defensive reaction. People use a magnanimous gesture as a buffer, such as donating time to serve or money to a related cause to temper their conflicting feelings of the relationship between self and the DPS. The PIE model (Figure 3.1) describes the various ways people might defend themselves as they process a DPS.

Whereas there is an arc to the defenses in relation to each other, this does not mean that all people move through each defense when responding to a DPS. The model distinguishes various types of reactions that become increasingly more complex as thought and emotion move from the preconscious to the conscious in response to a DPS. The PIE model does not describe developmental processes for a person's privileged identity. Yet, there is a progression to the defensive reactions in the PIE model from less complex (little or no emotion and cognitive processing) to more complex (more emotion and cognitive processing). People may display these defense reactions in any order and they may or may not display all of these reactions in response to a particular DPS. The model intends to describe the increasingly sophisticated

Figure 3.1   The privileged identity exploration (PIE) model.

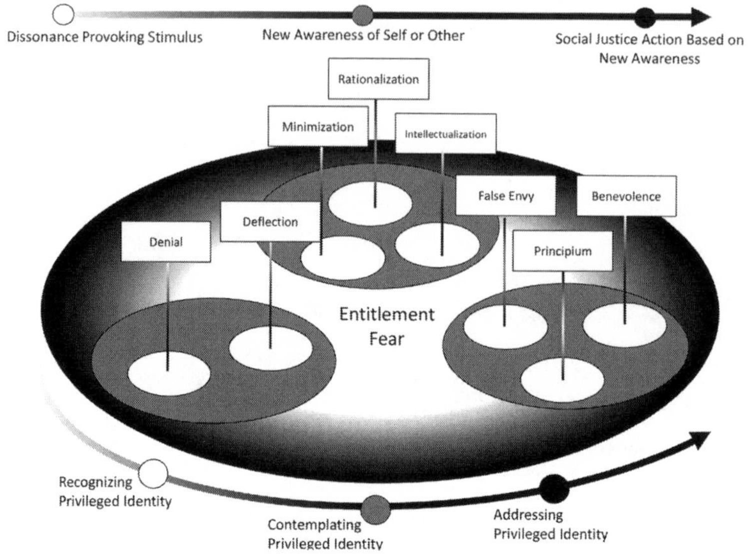

ways one might respond to a DPS and not to indicate a developmental process for resolving cognitive dissonance. Additionally, it is highly likely that particular individuals react in a similar way to DPS regardless of the scenario. In other words, people may have a *home-base defense* or *defense pattern* that emerges from their personality, experiences, and/or upbringing. A home-base defense is the one people retreat to first and likely is in response to any DPS regardless of the situation. For instance, people who grew up serving "the less fortunate" in their community may understand that social oppression exists but upon being introduced to a DPS that illuminates the deeper complexities of social class privilege, they may display defenses as they attempt to make sense of the relationship between those conditions and the self. Their home-base defense or defense pattern may initially minimize (Minimization) and then justify their acts of charity (Benevolence) in response. They may follow their pattern due to the personal experience of working with people in the community, because of their own personality type, and/or possibly due to their family value of service. It is important to note that likely people with these same experiences, and in the same situation, may have a different home-base defense pattern. The point here is that an individual may respond with any of these defense reactions at a given time and to any situation. Although, many people may retreat to a preferred response pattern when confronted with the disequilibrium brought about by a DPS. Understanding the various ways people respond to DPSs can help individuals maneuver conflicts as they work together to deconstruct and reconstruct environments. How well one manages conflict related to Difference is an essential skill set for living in diverse societies. Managing conflict includes identifying defensive reactions that inhibit progress toward resolution. These difficult dialogues often involve participants' strong emotional reactions grounded in long-held personal values and particular political viewpoints. The next section describes how people can strengthen the skill of recognizing defensive reactions by intentionally engaging Difference.

Strengthening the Skills for Engaging Difference

Teaching multiculturalism courses with a focus on raising awareness and examining social oppression presents many challenges for the instructor. Mio and Awakuni (2000) and Donaday (2002) point out how important it is for instructors to recognize and effectively manage the resistance that students display in classroom discussions. Donaday (2002) also explores the roots of resistance by suggesting that the course content uproots complex emotion about privilege and victimization. Students often feel very defensive and even fearful as they explore these concepts in an educational setting (Donaday, 2002). Mio and Awakuni (2000) suggest that the use of journal writing is a helpful tool that encourages the students to process the complex feelings that they have about course content. Among other strategies, Donaday (2002) suggests that instructors help students to wrestle with cognitive dissonance in hopes that they can learn and grow from it. Research on students suggests that wrestling with cognitive dissonance has benefits. Extending the knowledge from this research beyond students in the classroom and to all community members and their interactions is logical. In this section, I will share a process of how students, as well as administrators, faculty, student affairs professionals, and staff, can strengthen their skills to engage cognitive dissonance constructively. This process examines the self as one intentionally invites explorations of the difference of another into one's life as a learner. Further, I will explain how to use the PIE model to support the development of the skills to productively face and learn from one's own reactions to DPSs.

Encountering the Self in Relation to the "Other": Uses of the PIE Model in Practice

Research suggests moving to critical consciousness includes sustained involvement in self-awareness, engagement in social justice action and coalition building, and establishment of significant intergroup relationships (Landre-man, Rasmussen, King, & Jiang, 2007). Coursework is most effective in achieving these social justice outcomes when: course content incorporates examination of systemic oppression and individuals' perpetuation of inequal-ity, there is meaningful discussion and reflection about diversity, and there are diverse peer interactions that engage one in a process that encourages development (Mayhew & Fernández, 2007). Encountered situations are a strategy to create disequilibrium in the college classroom. Lechuga, Clerc, and Howell (2009) explain that encountered situations are an effective learn-ing activity that promotes social justice awareness in students. According to Lechuga, Clerc, and Howell (2009), such activity "elicits or alters the thought processes and/or behaviors of an individual or group" (p. 234). Encountered situations occur by means of students engaging in dialogue based on personal experience to explore issues of social equity and justice, and "can be used as a type of experiential learning tool to address differing levels of students' social justice awareness" (Lechuga et al., 2009, p. 234). Once a student engages in encountered situations and becomes self-aware, self-reflection becomes essential for students to make meaning of new information about equity and social justice, and to move toward new realization (Landreman et al., 2007). This research highlights the utility of experiences that bring about awareness that helps people to explore their own reactions to Difference rather than analyzing the "Other."

Research on new professional socialization indicates practicing compe-tently in the field of higher education and student affairs not only depends upon nurturing professional skills (ability to identify problems, use inquiry, ask useful questions), but also continuing to cultivate the development of a professional identity beyond graduate school preparation programs (Lid-dell, Wilson, Pasquesi, Hirschy, & Boyle, 2014). Liddell and others (2014) suggest that experiential opportunities outside of the classroom were most influential for new higher education and student affairs practitioners in the development of their identity as professionals in the field. This suggests that as individuals extend their opportunity to practice and test knowledge that they become more confident in their professional identity. For both new as well as seasoned professionals working in the field, organizations must continue to create opportunities for individuals to hone their skills to prac-tice as conscious scholar practitioners. Our campuses are fluid and evolv-ing as microcosms of the larger society. Finding ways that higher education administrators, faculty, staff, and student affairs professionals can continue to develop skills to manage Difference constructively is important. *How does one develop the stamina to manage the cognitive dissonance that arises as they test out their knowledge? What is a process campus community members can use to constructively engage difference? How do people go about strengthening the skills for engaging Difference?*

Currently, I am a faculty member. In my role, I primarily design multicultural initiatives for classroom settings. However, my broader mission as an educator is to guide individuals and communities through the dynamic process of moving toward personal and social liberation. I intend for my students to take with them practices that go beyond the classroom and skills that they can use in their professional as well as their personal lives. In light of that, I teach students to use a three-phase process for times when Difference enters into their life and they face resituating themselves in relation to a DPS. Any campus community member can use this process to strengthen their skills for positive interactions with Difference. I suggest that campus leaders embrace a lifelong learning ethos at their institutions whereby not only students but also their faculty, staff, administrators, and student affairs professionals intentionally explore Difference when dissonances arises through a structured process like the one described later.

The AAFES method (as described in Chapter 2) frames this experience. Therefore, the process includes a focus on the self (authentic) and not the other, a thoughtful balance of dialogue and action (action-oriented), and purposeful interaction with the other to resituate self in relation to the Difference (framing for environmental shift). Throughout this process, individuals reflect on their identity and explore the self in relation to a DPS. The three phases are (a) observation (initial self-awareness), (b) investigation (deepening by educating self about the "Other"), and (c) personal dialogue with the "Other" (deeper self-exploration while facing the "Other"). In each phase, people face the Difference that creates dissonance for them in increasingly complex ways.

In the Observation phase, people set out to educate themselves about the Difference through reliable sources in the public domain. People might attend a lecture that focuses on this groups' issue or concern, watch a movie that focuses on this group's experience, attend a church service or other activity, read a book related to this specific group, make a tour of this group's community to observe the homes, recreational facilities, pharmacies, etc. The task is to explore one's own reactions to the DPS and to educate oneself without taxing a person living the experience that causes one dissonance. Earlier, I shared that I am in the process of resituating my conception of gender. An example of an activity for this phase is choosing to read the book *Redefining Realness: My Path to Womanhood, Identity, Love & So Much More* by Janet Mock (2014). This book is a memoir of Mock's journey as a transwoman. Reading this memoir is a way to learn about this Difference in a less threatening way and to start finding out basic information about this stimulus that creates dissonance for me. I noticed that I commented on the beauty of Janet Mock to my friends. Even though it is true that Mock is beautiful, I recognized this as a defensive reaction to overcompensate for my feelings of dissonance regarding gender and transition (False Envy Defense). People may decide to do more than one Observation activity to learn to educate themselves. Observation activities require thought and emotion, but in indirect and less intense ways. Educating myself as well as noticing the defenses that arose in me helped me to move further into my exploration of this DPS.

After completing one or more Observation activities, people build on their basic education by exploring more in depth this Difference and conduct an Investigation. Investigation activities require slightly more direct, deeper levels of emotional and intellectual engagement. Examples of investigation activities might include arranging to meet community leaders (ministers, politicians, teachers, etc.) from this community to listen to their perceptions of the needs and concerns of the group. People might choose to visit a college or university campus to hear a lecture about the needs and critical issues facing this Difference. Some people might choose to talk with their parents about their attitudes toward this group and explore how they developed their attitudes. I chose two investigation activities to explore my dissonance with gender. I discussed my feelings about resituating my conception of gender with a number of close family members and friends. I also attended a presentation at my national conference focused on the topic and reviewed research on gender identity development. As I became more aware, I began to identify defenses such as denying (Denial Defense) the need to verbalize my preferred pronouns was a relevant concern. Both the Observation and Investigation phases take people gradually closer to the Difference that creates their dissonance. Each of these phases prepares people to interact responsibly with a person who represents that Difference. Being aware of the defenses that arise helps people to deepen their self-awareness.

The third phase is inviting a person who lives with the Difference into a Personal Dialogue. The purpose of this dialogue is twofold. Primarily, it helps people directly examine both their thought and their emotional reactions to a Difference that creates dissonance for them. Secondarily, it helps people to learn about another person with a different lived experience. The drawback of the personal dialogue is that people often confuse it with an interview. This interaction is different from an interview. In an interview, one person gathers information from another. The personal dialogue is different because it is an exchange between two individuals. Both people in the dialogue are not only learning about the other, but also sharing about themselves. Most importantly, the people who feel the dissonance from the Difference are resituating their relationship with that Difference by being in dialogue with some who is different. This is a shift because people are focusing on learning more about how they respond and why rather than continuing to "other" that Difference. To examine more directly my reactions to resituating myself in relation to gender norms, I invited a colleague, who is transgender, into dialogue with me. I hope to have a series of dialogues with this person and others to share with them how I am wrestling with resituating myself as it relates to gender. In our first dialogue, I started to think through with the person how I might infuse gender inclusion practices into my classroom teaching. I talked about what makes it difficult for me by sharing more about my background. I rationalized (Rationalization Defense) whether or not to integrate using gender inclusive pronouns in my communications. I expect to continue being in dialogue with friends and colleagues as I reconstruct my understanding of gender. I directly examined the emotion and thoughts that construct my perception of gender and what the use of pronouns means to me.

After people have worked through each phase, they can pause and reflect on what they learned about the self in relation to the DPS. Below are some questions to guide people's reflections as they complete this three-phase process:

1. What did you learn about yourself, *not* what you learned from or about your dialogue partner?
2. What did you hear in the experience of your dialogue partner that connects to an advantage or disadvantage in your life? How has the disadvantage or advantage played out in your life?
3. What are the historical social and political issues/assumptions that are relevant to things you discussed with your dialogue partner? How have you interacted around those (or not) issues/assumptions in your life?
4. How did the process of learning about "the Other" demonstrate how you might apply this process in other experiences in your life? What do you need to do to continue your own learning and build relationships with those who are different from yourself?
5. How has this three-phase process helped you to make sense of your life? How then shall you live?

This three-phase process develops the skills to manage better Difference. People are learning how to observe, investigate, and engage in dialogue about differences that cause dissonance for them. This process focuses on individuals finding constructive ways to examine issues that incite reactions of fear and entitlement in them. Examining the dissonance by recognizing the ways that individuals are reacting to the Difference strengthens people's ability to deconstruct social issues entangled in power, privilege, and oppression.

It is helpful for people to be aware of the defense modes described in the PIE model as they walk through each phase of this process. Being aware of the possible defenses that might emerge is a step in skill development. Once aware of the possible defenses, people can learn how to identify those defenses and how they appear to oneself and others. Identifying what emerges for people as they reflect on the self in relation to the DPS strengthens an essential skill when seeking to create inclusive communities. Many multicultural initiatives derail because people are unaware and/or unable to manage the defensive reactions that interrupt dialogue about power, privilege, and oppression. Being able to identify defensive reactions is an essential skill because the awareness that comes from being able to recognize defenses can help a community stay on track during difficult dialogues that are necessary when deconstructing and reconstructing environments for inclusion. This three-phase process hones that skill as individuals face and reflect on the self in relation to this Difference that they fear or have not explored. Practicing using this skill of becoming aware and identifying defensive reactions helps individuals to understand better the fear and entitlement that goes along with privilege.

There are benefits to exploring this DPS along with others. Those include, but are not limited to support with confronting emotion and help with managing defenses. This type of exploration brings about feelings of powerlessness, fear, and other unexpected emotions. Individuals learn from others strategies for how to maneuver the uncomfortable feelings associated with confronting a fear or an unknown. Sharing it with others does not make the emotional exploration easier, but knowing that others are supporting you while they are also experiencing this difficult task helps. When done as a shared experience, individuals can process the emotions and thoughts that arise with others. Listening to and/or talking with others can help individuals to manage the defenses that emerge in a more constructive way. People are generally more open to hearing others in the group point out their blind spots. Knowing that others are experiencing this along with you creates a trusting bond that helps you work through learning about the self in relation to this DPS.

This section describes a process people can use in their personal and professional lives to explore a DPS.

Conclusion

Privileged identity exploration theory (Watt, 2007) adds to the scholarship in the field of higher education and student affairs by providing information to scholars, administrators, and practitioners about what happens as individuals engage in dialogues that deconstruct the influence of dominant identities within a societal structure. This model identifies normal reactions that people often display as they attempt to incorporate ideas that challenge the very structure of their beliefs and values. Being able to identify defensive reaction is a skill that leads to greater self-awareness. Raising self-awareness through intentionally seeking to learn about one's own reaction difference rather than dissecting the "Other" from a position of privilege is valuable. Self-awareness strengthens the capacity of people to stay in the difficult dialogues that are necessary for reconstructing environments that are more inclusive. Developing the skills to identify these defensive reactions can help people to incorporate the new knowledge and grow (Stewart, 2012). Being able to identify defensive reactions that arise in others and ourselves is an essential skill.

References

Berlack, A., & Moyenda, S. (2001). *Taking it personally.* Philadelphia: Temple University Press.

Black, L. L., & Stone, D. (2005). Expanding the definition of privilege: The concept of social privilege. *Journal of Multicultural Counseling and Development, 33*(4), 243–255.

Broido, E. M. (2000). The development of social justice allies during college: A phenomenological investigation. *Journal of College Student Development, 41,* 3–17.

Cross Jr., W. E. (1991). *Shades of black: Diversity in African-American identity.* Philadelphia: Temple University Press.

Donaday, A. (2002). Negotiating tensions: Teaching about race issues in graduate feminist classrooms. *NWSA Journal, 14*(1), 82–102.

Edwards, K. E. (2006). Aspiring social justice ally identity development: A conceptual model. *NASPA Journal, 43*(4), 39–60.

Festinger, L. (1957). *A theory of cognitive dissonance.* Palo Alto, CA: Stanford University Press.

Festinger, L. (1962). Cognitive dissonance. *Scientific American, 207*(4), 93–107.

Freire, P. (1970). *Pedagogy of the oppressed.* New York, NY: Continuum.

Freud, A. (1979). *The ego and the mechanisms of defense.* New York: International Universities Press.

Helms, J. E. (1995). An update of Helms's White and people of color racial identity models. In J. G. Ponterotto, J. M. Casas, L. A. Suzuki, & C. M. Alexander (Eds.), *Handbook of multicultural counseling* (pp. 181–198). Thousand Oaks, CA: SAGE.

Helms, J. E., & Cook, D. A. (1999). *Using race and culture in counseling and psychotherapy: Theory and process.* Needham Heights, MA: Allyn & Bacon.

Hennessy, C. M. (2010). *Raiding the inarticulate: Postmodernisms, feminist theory and black female creativity* (Unpublished doctoral dissertation). University of Massachusetts-Amherst, Amherst, MA.

Howard, A. (2011). Privileged pursuits of social justice: Exploring privileged college students' motivation for engaging in social justice. *Journal of College and Character, 12*(2), 1–14.

Killinger, J. (1966). Jean Genet and scapegoat drama. *Comparative Literature Studies, 3*(2), 207–221.

Landreman, L. M., Rasmussen, C. J., King, P. M., & Jiang, C. X. (2007). A phenomenological study of the development of university educators' critical consciousness. *Journal of College Student Development, 48*(3), 275–296.

Lechuga, V. M., Clerc, L. N., & Howell, A. K. (2009). Power, privilege, and learning: Facilitating encountered situations to promote social justice. *Journal of College Student Development, 50*(20), 229–244.

Liddell, D., Wilson, M., Pasquesi, K., Hirschy, A., & Boyle, K. (2014). Development of professional identity through socialization in graduate school. *Journal of Student Affairs Research and Practice, 51*(1), 69–84.

Mayhew, M. J., & Fernández, S. D. (2007). Pedagogical practices that contribute to social justice outcomes. *The Review of Higher Education, 31*(1), 55–80.

McCall, L. (2005). The complexity of intersectionality. *Journal of Women in Culture and Society, 30*, 1771–1800. Retrieved from http://www.journals.uchicago.edu/doi/pdf/10.1086/426800

McIntosh, P. (1988). *A personal account of coming to see correspondences through work in women's studies.* Working Paper 189, Center for Research on Women, Wellesley College, Wellesley, Massachusetts.

McIntosh, P. (1989, July/August). White privilege: Unpacking the invisible knapsack. *Peace and Freedom*, 10–12.

Mio, J. S., & Awakuni, G. I. (2000). *Resistance to multiculturalism: Issues and interventions.* Philadelphia: Brunner/Mazel

Mock, J. (2014). *Redefining realness: My path to womanhood, identity, love & so much more.* New York: Simon & Schuster, Inc.

Pinterits, E. J., Poteat, V. P., & Spanierman, L. B. (2009). The White Privilege Attitudes Scale (WPAS): Development and initial validation. *Journal of Counseling Psychology, 56,* 417–429.

Reason, R. D., & Davis, T. L. (2005). Antecedents, precursors, and concurrent concepts in the development of social justice attitudes and actions. In R. D. Reason, E. M. Broido, T. L. Davis, & N. J. Evans (Eds.), *Developing social justice allies* (pp. 5–15). San Francisco: Jossey-Bass.

Stewart, D. L. (2012). Promoting moral growth through pluralism and social justice education. New Directions for Student Services, 2012(139), 63–71.

Watt, S. K. (2007). Difficult dialogues, privilege and social justice: Uses of the privileged identity exploration (PIE) model in student affairs practice. *College Student Affairs Journal, 26*(2), 114–126.

Watt, S. K. (2013). Designing and implementing multicultural initiatives: Guiding principles. In S. K. Watt & J. Linley (Eds.), *Creating successful multicultural initiatives in higher education and student affairs* (pp. 5–15). San Francisco: Jossey-Bass.

Watt, S. K., Curtiss, G., Drummond, J., Kellogg, A., Lozano, A., Tagliapietra, N. G., & Rosas, M. (2009). Privileged identity exploration: Examining White female counselor trainees' reactions to difficult dialogue in the classroom. *Counselor Education & Supervision, 49,* 86–105.

Watt S. K., Harmon, N., Mindrup, K., Goodman, K. M., Linley, J., Stinson, R., ... Parker III, E. (Under Review). *Exploring privilege: Student affairs graduate student reactions to difficult dialogue on racism, heterosexism, and ableism.* Manuscript submitted for publication.

West, C. (1999). *The Cornel West reader.* New York: Basic Books.

Young, I. M. (2000). Five faces of oppression. In M. Adams, W. J. Blumenfeld, C. Castaneda, H. W. Hackman, M. L. Peters, & X. Zuniga (Eds.), *Readings for diversity and social justice* (2nd ed., pp. 35–44). New York: Routledge.

PART TWO

DESIGNING MULTICULTURAL INITIATIVES: EFFECTIVE STRATEGIES

What techniques do conscious scholar practitioners use to develop a multicultural initiative that will lead to a successful outcome?

4

MULTICULTURAL INITIATIVES AS BRIDGES

Structures Necessary for Successful Facilitation

Cindy Ann Kilgo and Richard Barajas

The philosophical framework within a multicultural initiative is analogous in several ways to the structure, support, and features of a bridge. A bridge will not hold strong for cars or people to pass without solid structure and planning during construction. The same is true for multicultural initiatives. Multicultural initiatives need structural and support features to allow them to stand "strong" within a practical setting. The following example provides a basis to begin our discussion on the structure and support necessary for facilitation of successful multicultural initiatives.

You are a private consultant specifically hired by a college of nursing to help them develop their new strategic plan. The administration has told you that they want the college to be at the forefront of issues regarding culturally responsive care and make sure that is evident in the new strategic plan. Although you have worked with other health professional schools before, this is the first time that you have specifically worked with a college of nursing. The first thing you do is examine various accreditation standards present in nursing and research exemplar programs at other colleges. Additionally, you have meetings with faculty and staff in the college to see how culturally responsive care is being addressed currently and what they would like to see in the future.

Support Structures: Necessities for a Secure Bridge

In order to develop and facilitate a successful multicultural initiative, a few tasks are essential from the start. These tasks include defining the problem, reviewing relevant literature, clarifying a rationale, and setting goals and learning objectives. These basic tasks serve as the necessary components of multicultural initiatives, similar to support structures on bridges.

In the previous example, it is evident that before a multicultural initiative can be developed and facilitated, several "support" features need to fall into place. First, you need to define the problem you want the initiative to address. You meet with others to describe the problem in very specific details. You need to meet with appropriate constituents to gain an understanding of the current strategic plan, as well as examine assessment documents that allow you to gauge the current state within the college. Developing and facilitating a multicultural initiative warrants this process, and it is essential if you are new to a position as outlined in the previous example.

The second essential task involves reviewing relevant literature. Talking to campus constituents and reviewing prior assessment reports allows you to gain an understanding of the problem; however, it is only step one in preparing your multicultural initiative for success. The relevant literature is an essential next step. When reviewing relevant literature, be sure to include a broad search that goes beyond a specific discipline or functional area. This allows you to gain varying perspectives on the subject of interest to you. For the example provided earlier, the literature search could include nursing specific journals or references, as well as sources from other health-related fields.

The review of literature allows you to move into the third support structure: clarifying the rationale for your multicultural initiative. The rationale for your initiative is a critical foundation that provides you with strong footing and support in reaching your desired outcomes. The rationale is similar to the strong support structure on a bridge. Without a clear and grounded rationale for your multicultural initiative, your initiative will not have the support necessary to hold strong—or in the bridge analogy, the bridge will not stand tall.

The next essential "support" structure needed for creating and facilitating a multicultural initiative is to set goals and create learning objectives. The rationale for your initiative should lead you toward the process of setting goals for your initiative. In the previous example, you might convene meetings in which you determine other constituents of the nursing program's aims for the updated strategic plan. You also have reviewed literature on the topic and can gauge what others have used as goals for culturally responsive healthcare within their strategic plans.

One important consideration for creating goals and learning objectives is to distinguish the differences between these. Although people use these two terms interchangeably, Harden (2002) argues that there are distinct differences between outcomes or goals and objectives. Harden (2002) asserts that there are five areas of distinction. Specifically, Harden (2002) lists "1) the detail of specification; 2) the level of specification where the emphasis is placed; 3) the classification adopted and interrelationships; 4) the intent or observable result; 5) the ownership of the outcomes" (p. 151) as the differences between goals/outcomes and objectives. These differences are important to consider when creating broad goals and specific learning objectives for your multicultural initiative.

Beyond Support Structures: The "How" and "Why" a Bridge Is Built a Specific Way

The structure and support features, however, are not enough alone to allow a multicultural initiative to thrive. The values and aims of the facilitator are needed. Engineers and construction managers make decisions pertaining to bridge creation based on their individual values of "how" a bridge is constructed. This "how" shapes the practical function of the bridge. For example, is the bridge for pedestrians or cars? How many car lanes will the bridge contain? Will the bridge be a one-way traffic bridge? Practitioners should make decisions about multicultural initiatives based on their values and aims in similar ways that these engineers and construction managers decide how to create bridges. In particular, practitioners should examine the "how" of the multicultural initiative when planning for its facilitation. What personal assumptions do I hold as a facilitator for the purpose of the multicultural initiative? How will my values be included in the creation of my multicultural initiative? What are the goals for the multicultural initiative?

Strong Suspension Beams: Individuality Within Bridge Design

This "how" is the philosophical framework for creating and facilitating multicultural initiatives. The philosophical frame is an essential component in creating and facilitating multicultural initiatives, as it allows the facilitator to align his or her values with the intent in the initiative. This chapter will now outline several philosophical frames that practitioners can use to create multicultural initiatives. We will provide practical examples of multicultural initiatives using each of the philosophical frames highlighted in this chapter. We will also provide context for each of the frames, the aims associated with using each of the frames, and pros and cons of using each of the frames.

To make our framework more manageable, we created a figure that includes all of the components we feel are necessary for the successful facilitation of multicultural initiatives. These components include the ones already discussed, as well as the philosophical frameworks that are covered later within the chapter.

Single Group Studies

Your college is in an area with a relatively large concentration of Native American/American Indian students. You have noticed that many of them do not attend your institution. Additionally, regarding their academic and social experiences, those that do attend seem to struggle and do not engage with the campus community. This observation seems to be extremely prevalent for the Native American/American Indian students majoring in engineering degree programs. You are a member of a task force at your university charged specifically with creating a multicultural initiative aimed at attending to these observations. You and the other task force members have decided to integrate engineering curriculum that affects Native American/American Indian communities into the engineering first-year seminar that all engineering majors take during their first semester. This course typically provides examples of engineering projects, and you and the task force decide to focus solely on engineering project examples from within Native American/American Indian communities.

Figure 4.1 Components essential for the successful facilitation of multicultural initiatives.

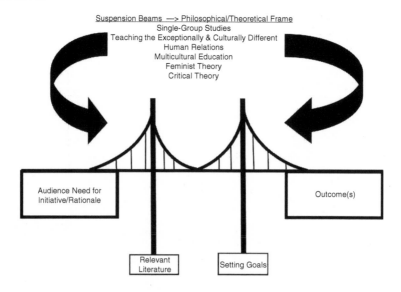

This example illustrates a need for the Native American/American Indian student subpopulation at this institution. The focus specifically on engineering students makes this a small subpopulation. The practitioner decided to integrate curricula focused specifically on this subpopulation's ethnic identity. This example is a multicultural initiative that is using a single-group study philosophical frame. Sleeter and Grant (2009) state the aim of single-group studies is to "empower oppressed groups and develop allies" (p. 123). This is evident by the multicultural initiative focusing exclusively on one population, in this case Native American/American Indians in the context of engineering.

Using the single-group study philosophical frame allows practitioners to hone in on one specific identity group and work toward empowerment. Single-group studies are appropriate within course-settings or within programmatic efforts. The main context, however, for single-group studies is that they do not delineate from the identity group of focus. Although they provide a perfect arena in which to delve deep into one specific identity group, they do not allow for much discussion or depth into intersecting identities or within-group differences.

Teaching the Exceptionally and Culturally Different

You are the coordinator of your campus's McNair program. Every year you have a group of 20 minoritized students who are graduating and preparing to submit applications to various graduate programs.[1] Through your experience and research, you know that on average these students perform lower than White counterparts on the various standardized tests used for graduate entry, such as the Graduate Record Examinations (GREs). To address this inequity, you have decided to devote effort throughout the year to prepare these students, such as teaching workshops on the test question strategies these tests employ as well as effective test time management and subject areas specifically for minoritized student subpopulations.

This example highlights a research finding that suggests that White students perform at higher levels on standardized testing. Of course, this comes as no surprise to the practitioner, as historically these tests served as a mechanism of oppression toward multiple non-White subpopulations. The practitioner decides to focus on the possible "deficit" of "difference" by attempting to make up for the gap in test scores typically observed. This example uses the philosophical frame, teaching the exceptionally and culturally different. The goal of this initiative is vastly different from the previous example using single-group studies frame. Sleeter and Grant (2009) state that the aim of teaching the exceptionally and culturally different is changing how the material is taught to "enable them [minoritized students] to achieve in school and better meet the traditional demands of U.S. life" (p. 43).

This frame puts the emphasis on both the teacher, or facilitator, and the students, but in two distinct ways. The emphasis on the facilitator is that the facilitation may vary based on the subpopulation of interest. In this case, the practitioner is deviating from typical coordinator duties and responsibilities to focus on teaching a specific perceived need for one subpopulation of students. Conversely, the emphasis placed on the students more often sparks criticism. This emphasis is that the students have an inherent "deficit" or "difference" that needs a specific approach or remedy. These emphases do align, however, with the aim of assimilating these students into mainstream or majority demands of life.

Human Relations

You oversee the introductory practice experiences of students at a college of pharmacy. You know that these students will have a large amount of patient interaction both as students and as future practitioners. These patients come with a variety of lived experiences, identities, and backgrounds. In order to ensure that your students are prepared to engage with all future patients, you have included throughout their schooling educational activities to teach them about different populations. These educational activities include both historical and modern reasons why certain subpopulations might hold certain beliefs and values about healthcare and healthcare providers. You particularly focused these educational activities to incorporate building listening and oral communication skills.

This example focuses on the relationships necessary for future healthcare providers working in pharmacies. This initiative focuses not only on the "why" but also the "how" in that it centers on providing students with context for why certain subpopulations might hold certain beliefs or values and allowing students to build communication skills necessary to sustain relationships within the field of pharmacy. The "why" and "how" as illustrated in this example is associated with the human relationships philosophical frame. The "why" and "how" is illustrated by Sleeter and Grant (2009) in their aim for human relations as, "creat[ing] positive feelings among students and reduc[ing] stereotyping, thus promoting unity and tolerance in a society composed of different people" (p. 85). Stereotype reduction is the "why"— as theoretically when students understand why certain subpopulations hold certain values and beliefs it leads to reduced stereotypes. The "how" is the positive feelings and the unity aspects of the aim of human relations.

In terms of pharmacy students honing the skill sets necessary to sustain relationships with future patients and colleagues of varying backgrounds, the human relations philosophical frame allows for growth to success. The limitation, however, is that it promotes a baseline of tolerance that does not affect or influence the overlaying power structures that are present.

Multicultural Education

You are the coordinator of the pre-medicine undergraduate program at your college. In the current curriculum, there is an introductory course to introduce pre-medicine students to the healthcare system. You have decided to interweave throughout the semester-long course, discussions on various equity issues in the health sciences. The topics that you plan to include are the varying degrees of access to medical care for differing subpopulations, health disparities, the importance of providing culturally relevant care, and the intersection of epigenetics. These topics were largely absent from this course when it was offered in previous semesters.

This example has a focus on pluralism and the "melting pot" idea of having many diverse perspectives at the table. This initiative focuses on the fact that topics of diversity were largely absent from prior years, and attempts to incorporate a diverse array of perspectives into the curriculum. Sleeter and Grant (2009) describe the center of the multicultural education philosophical frame being to promote both "structural equality and cultural pluralism" (p. 164). These aims are evident in the previous initiative, as the new content both provides some level of equity (or is reaching toward equity) in content presented as well as providing multiple viewpoints or perspectives that were previously ignored by society in general.

Using this frame allows practitioners to cover varying content and perspectives, in attempts to promote more structural equality in content. It also allows one to see multiple perspectives in one movement, similar to the "melting pot" analogy. The negatives to using this approach are that it typically halts at content. For example, it does not go beyond just attempting to promote structural equality by acting on the views or thoughts.

Multicultural Social Justice Education

You are the same coordinator as in the earlier example about multicultural education. You have decided that your course does not address social justice aims in healthcare education. In addition to introducing the previously mentioned topics, you have now also added reflections for students to think about why these inequities exist. As part of the final project for the class, students have to prepare and present ways to reduce these inequities currently and how they can aid in this once they become health practitioners.

This example illustrates a step beyond the previous frame of multicultural education. In this example, the practitioner does not halt at structural equality, but instead moves toward action. This action is the social justice aspect of the multicultural social justice philosophical frame. This practitioner has students considering action plans for actually reducing the inequities they learn about through the course content. The key in multicultural social justice education is that it links content to action. Sleeter and Grant (2009) portray multicultural social justice education as "individuals need[ing] to learn to organize and work collectively in order to bring about social changes that are larger than individuals" (p. 201).

Multicultural social justice education allows students to incorporate and involve action into their lives. This is a positive of this frame, but can be a negative. The negative view would be that this frame could potentially take longer to facilitate given the action component. Further, this frame relies on students wanting to enact change, which may come with resistance by some. Overall, however, this frame is the closest in actually getting at the structural inequities present within the system of oppression.

Feminist Theory

On your campus, you have decided to start a WISE (Women in Science and Engineering) program. Currently, women are underrepresented in the total population of science, technology, engineering, and mathematics (STEM) majors. You know this is not from lack of ability, but instead hypothesize that a larger hostile climate issue is at play for this subpopulation. Studies have suggested that an environment of all women can boost confidence in science achievement and this is what you hope to engender with the new WISE program. This will provide a built-in support network for these students as they navigate their STEM education. This program will also provide allies once students graduate and enter their careers.

In this example, the focus is specifically on the subpopulation of science and engineering students who identify as female. The aim of this multicultural initiative is to empower students who have been historically and are currently largely absent in their academic fields. This practitioner has framed the initiative within the feminist theory philosophical frame. Sleeter and Grant (2009) state, "women find themselves seeking space and autonomy in a context that defines these as contrary to nature" (p. 140). This relates to the earlier example in that women have been historically absent from these fields of study.

Feminist theory allows one to empower a subpopulation, women. A negative, however, exists in that as we move toward acceptance and understanding of gender as fluid and not set on a binary, feminist theory suddenly becomes more complicated. Essentially, practitioners should be careful when employing feminist theory—to ensure that they do not omit individuals from empowerment based on gender identity and expression beyond the binary.

Critical Theory

You are an upper administrator in the College of Liberal Arts and Sciences. You have noticed that in certain departments in your college that minoritized students seem to struggle. Additionally, the graduate students that these same departments admit tend to be from majority populations. In discussions with these departments, department chairs express that minoritized students lack academic preparation or engagement at both the undergraduate- and graduate-level. You have expressed to them that this may be part of the cause, but you additionally want each department to submit a report of how minoritized students are engaged in the classroom and possible strategies that can be put in place to address this gap in graduate admissions. Further, you request that these reports of engagement consist entirely of minoritized student experiences from the students' point of view.

Sleeter and Grant (2009) state that "critical theories examine how groups struggle with each other for control over resources and ideas" (p. 201). In the earlier example, the practitioner is going to examine the perspectives of minoritized students in these departments through the lens of these students. By using this approach, the administration can glean how power differentials are at play with regard to engagement within the college and departments.

Critical theories are relatively recent concepts, yet acknowledge underrepresented voices in a way that is sometimes ignored in other philosophical frameworks. Even if other frames have the best of intentions, the potential for voices to remain unheard exists—yet critical theory aims to get at this very aspect. There are several critical theories, focused on race, gender, and sexuality, among other identity groups.

Concluding Thoughts

As shown, developing a successful multicultural initiative involves many factors. The surrounding climate is important and influences the type of initiative designed. Foundationally solid multicultural initiatives can fail by ignoring climate. Outside factors include the overall campus climate, the makeup of the student population, the amount of institutional support, and faculty and staff resources, among others. Considering and thinking about these outside factors before an initiative is implemented can help avoid burn out and frustration that can sometimes arise.

It is also vastly important for faculty and staff who implement multicultural initiatives to recharge in order to keep pushing forward. This work is often hard and may take a lot of both professional and personal energy to move from the planning stages to actual facilitation. There is the chance that negative feedback will arise, but it is essential to remember that small incremental changes can often lead to significant changes. This is especially the case when talking about larger institutionally ingrained systems of oppression. A good idea to think about is that of planting seeds. Initially one waters newly planted seeds but no visible results appear. It is only after considerable time and with continued care that a plant starts to germinate and eventually produce fruit.

With that said, it also may take multiple attempts to facilitate the initiative with ease. Trials and reformatting are likely to occur. As with bridge construction, engineers and construction managers spend much time and energy on the initial stages of development—but the construction itself also takes time, energy, and effort. This process is intricate and meticulous, as bridges need to hold to be safe. The development of a multicultural initiative should also be developed and facilitated with care. As this chapter outlines, support structures and design (philosophical frame) are essential components. Perhaps more essential, however, is the facilitator. You are in a position of control with the initiative you are facilitating. We hope that you realize the magnitude of your control in this setting. It can be overwhelming, feel like a failure at times, and expend much of your energy. If you keep your eyes forward toward your goals, however, and build your initiative with ample support structures and anchored with a philosophical framework, you can create much change.

Note

1. We have chosen to use the term *minoritized* throughout our chapter instead of other terms such as *minority* or *underrepresented*. This term is used in solidarity with a number of scholars and critical race theorists in reference to the societal construction of subordination of certain racial/ethnic groups in global social institutions (Bensimon & Bishop, 2012; Harper, 2012).

References

Bensimon, E. M., & Bishop, R. (2012). Introduction: Why "Critical"? The need for new ways of knowing. *The Review of Higher Education, 36*(1), 1–7.
Harden, R. M. (2002). Learning outcomes and instructional objectives: Is there a difference? *Medical Teacher, 24*(2), 151–155.
Harper, S. R. (2012). Race without racism: How higher education rsearchers minimize racist institutional norms. *The Review of Higher Education, 36*(1), 9–29.
Sleeter, C. E., & Grant, C. A. (2009). *Making choices for multicultural education: Five approaches to race, class, and gender* (6th ed.). San Francisco: Jossey-Bass.

Additional Sources for Further Reading

Adams, M., Bell, L. A., & Griffin, P. (2007). *Teaching for diversity and social justice* (2nd ed.). New York: Routledge.

Awé, C., & Bauman, J. (2010). Theoretical and conceptual framework for a high school pathways to pharmacy program. *American Journal of Pharmaceutical Education, 74*(8), 1–11.

Capomacchia, A. C., & Garner, S. T. (2004). Challenges of recruiting American minority graduate students: The coach model. *American Journal of Pharmaceutical Education: 68*(4), 4–6

Cooper, K. J. (2012). Besting the Ivies. *Diverse Issues in Higher Education, 29*(9), 13–14.

Gahagan, J., Dingfelder, J., & Pie, K. (2010). *A faculty and staff guide to creating learning outcomes.* Columbia, SC: National Resource Center for The First-Year Experience and Students in Transition and the University of South Carolina Office of Student Engagement.

hooks, b. (1994). *Teaching to transgress: Education as a practice of freedom.* New York: Routledge.

Landerman, L. M. (2013). *The art of effective facilitation: Reflections from social justice educators.* Sterling, VA: Stylus.

Lundy-Wagner, V. C. (2013). Is it really a man's world? Black men in science, technology, engineering, and mathematics at historically Black colleges and universities. *The Journal of Negro Education, 82*(2), 157–168.

Murray-Garcia, J. L., & Garcia, J. A. (2008). The institutional context of multicultural education: What is your institutional curriculum? *Academic Medicine, 83*(7), 646–652.

Palmer, R. T., Davis, R. J., & Thompson, T. (2010). Theory meets practice: HBCU initiatives that promote academic success among African Americans in STEM. *Journal of College Student Development, 51*(4), 440–443.

Rackley, B. P., Wheat, J. R., Moore, C. E., Garner, R. G., & Harrell, B. W. (2003). The southern rural access program and Alabama's rural health leaders' pipeline: A partnership to develop needed minority health care professionals. *The Journal of Rural Health, 19*, 354–360.

Taylor, E., Gillbor, D., & Ladson-Billings, G. (2009). *Foundations of critical race theory in education.* New York: Routledge.

Toney, M. (2012). The long, winding road: One university's quest for minority health care professionals and services. *Academic Medicine: Journal of the Association of American Medical Colleges, 87*(11), 1556–1561.

Wear, D. (2003). Insurgent multiculturalism: Rethinking how and why we teach culture in medical education. *Academic Medicine, 78*(6), 549–554.

Wear, D., Kumagai, A. K., Varley, J., & Zarconi, J. (2012). Cultural competency 2.0: Exploring the concept of "difference" in engagement with other. *Academic Medicine, 87*(6), 752–758.

5

IN PURSUIT OF A STRONG, CLEAR VISION

Initiating and Sustaining Multicultural Change in Higher Education Organizations

Lacretia Johnson Flash

How does an organization that has struggled with recruiting and retaining students, faculty, or staff from diverse and underrepresented backgrounds shift this pattern? How can a higher education organization create a culture in which all of its members understand and feel compelled to confront racial bias, homophobia, ableism, sexism, and the myriad of other –isms that curtail the full potential of those who work, learn, and interact with the organization? What compels those in senior leadership positions as well as the institution's faculty, staff, and students to recognize barriers to success and seek meaningful changes to policies, practices, and programs to make them more accessible and inclusive?

The answers and solutions to these and related questions are often elusive and complex, but the starting place is often a desire and a strong clear vision to initiate and sustain multicultural organizational change. With multicultural organizational change, the organization's values, systems, practices, policies, and norms are examined and altered to be more inclusive, accessible, and socially just. To be successful, these changes must occur broadly and deeply within the systems and practices of the organization and often involve sustained effort over many years.

This chapter introduces characteristics of a multiculturally competent organization as measured by the multicultural competence in student affairs organizations (MCSAO) model (Flash, 2010). The MCSAO builds on the scholarship of Grieger (1996) and Pope, Reynolds, and Mueller (2004). The commitment, knowledge, and experiences of individuals are valuable for any multicultural change efforts. However, the MCSAO model focuses on the characteristics and collective behaviors of organizations that are key to initiating and sustaining multicultural organizational change. In this chapter, I describe characteristics of the organizational context and the conditions that should be present or cultivated in order to sustain multicultural change in higher education organizations. The term *higher education organization* refers to a wide range of organizational units, including institutions (e.g., universities), divisions (e.g., student affairs, human resources), academic units (e.g., departments, colleges, and centers), other administrative units (e.g., business services) with processes and products (e.g., programs, services, courses, initiatives) that need to be well-coordinated and sustained.

I recognize that individual practitioners, administrators, faculty, staff, students, and other constituents of the organization have an important role to play, but I believe that deep multicultural change cannot occur if only a few individuals are involved. Multicultural organizational change requires a close examination and modification of the organization's systems, not just changes in the attitudes, knowledge, and skills of a few individuals. This approach to higher education organizational level change builds from the classic multicultural organizational development (MCOD) models like those of Jackson and Hardiman (1994) and the frameworks of Grieger (1996) and Pope, Reynolds, and Mueller (2004).

To close the chapter, I offer strategies and insights needed to initiate and sustain multicultural organizational change within higher education contexts. These insights are based on the MCSAO and are gleaned from many years of experiences, successes, and missteps in a wide range of higher educational programs, initiatives, and collaborations at all levels (e.g., student programming, departmental initiatives, curricular and co-curricular institutional projects) and across organizational cultures (e.g., student affairs, academic affairs, multicultural affairs, human resources, legal, and facilities).

Characteristics of the Multiculturally Competent Higher Education Organization

Many higher education institutions want to become a multicultural organization, yet find it difficult to achieve and even more challenging to sustain this goal. Some may have a vague notion that the organization (e.g., institution, division, and department) needs to do something different or better in order to attract and retain students and others from diverse backgrounds. Others think that they need to improve access to and the quality of their services and programs, in order to fulfill other critical organizational goals. When it comes to multicultural change, it is often challenging to define the problem and even more difficult to develop a comprehensive and effective strategy for achieving the strategic goals and objectives related to diversity, multiculturalism, and social justice. This section provides a framework for understanding the organizational characteristics and behaviors that are often present in institutions, divisions, and departments that are striving to become more multiculturally competent. These characteristics and behaviors extend beyond what one or a few individuals may choose to do to make their organizations more inclusive and affirming, but address the work that must occur throughout the organizational system.

The seven components in the MCSAO model emerged from research conducted to operationalize and test the conceptualization of organizational multicultural competence in the student affairs context through the MCSAO questionnaire. This questionnaire assesses multicultural competency at the organizational level, rather than the individual level. Grieger (1996) developed the *Multicultural Organizational Development Checklist for Student Affairs* and Pope et al. (2004) adapted the *Student Affairs Multicultural Organizational Development Template.* Although these tools were not psychometrically tested, they serve as a useful starting point in thinking about the practices and apparatuses needed for higher education organizations to be multiculturally competent. In this chapter, *multiculturally competent organizations* are defined as organizations that are able to effectively educate, serve, and work with constituencies from a wide range of diverse backgrounds (e.g., race, ethnicity, gender, ability, class, nationality).

The research that informed the creation of the MCSAO assessment tool came from a desire to operationalize and test the constructs outlined by Grieger and Pope, Reynolds, and Mueller. The researcher tested the MCSAO questionnaire at various institutions across the United States. Out of this research a reconceptualization of the constructs that define multicultural competence in student affairs organizations emerged. The MCSAO model takes the earlier 10 constructs and reconfigures these concepts into seven components (Table 5.1).

Although the MCSAO model targets organizational units in student affairs, many of the characteristics described in this model are present across organizational cultures within various higher education institutional contexts. The section describes each of the seven components of the MCSAO model (Table 5.1) and provides examples of how to apply these components across organizational cultures.

TABLE 5.1.

Summary of the Seven Components of the Multicultural Competence in Student Affairs Organizations (MCSAO) Model

MCSAO Component	Characteristics
1. Organizational Culture of Commitment, Encouragement, and Support for Multicultural Engagement	• Multiple ways and forums in which diversity and multicultural learning and conversations are supported and encouraged within the organization • Leaders modeling multicultural engagement
2. Peer/Colleague Influence, Behaviors, and Expectations for Multicultural Engagement	• Demonstrated commitment to diversity and multicultural engagement by members of the organization • Taking responsibility for developing multicultural competence is valued and practiced by employees
3. Clear and Coherent Multicultural Organizational Mission	• Presence of multicultural values in the mission of the organization • Multicultural values are communicated across multiple forums and through multiple modes
4. Provision of Multiculturally Inclusive Services	• Services are developed to be inclusive for people from a wide range of underrepresented backgrounds
5. Support for and Creation of Diversity/Multicultural Programming and Events	• Presence of and support given to diversity and multicultural programs and events
6. Incorporation of Multiculturalism in Strategic and Formal Organizational Practice	• Multicultural lens is incorporated into organizational practices (e.g., policy creation, assessment, and goal setting) • Support is provided to employees from underrepresented backgrounds
7. Multicultural Recruitment Practices	• Organization demonstrates a commitment to multicultural values in the recruitment process (e.g., effort made to generate a diverse candidate pool and attract candidates with a demonstrated commitment to diversity)

Component 1: Organizational Culture of Commitment, Encouragement, and Support for Multicultural Engagement

Taking active steps to foster a culture of commitment, encouragement, and support for multicultural engagement is a critical starting place for any higher education organization that seeks to initiate and sustain multicultural change. Not surprisingly, this emerged as the strongest component of the MCSAO. Creating a culture of engagement requires that organizations provide many opportunities for those in the organization to engage in conversions about diversity. Also critical to this component is that the organization's leaders model a commitment to multicultural engagement.

As institutions across the United States engage in efforts to create more diverse and inclusive organizational climates, the role of organizational leaders are instrumental in creating significant changes in organizational culture and improving an organization's ability to serve diverse constituents (Haro, 1993; Smith, 1997). This perspective, on the importance of leadership, is mirrored by Sims and Dennehy (1993), who stated that "multiculturalism will not occur, in fact cannot occur, without creative leadership. . . . We have learned that the mere affirmation of the desire for diversity, or even apparent success in obtaining diverse representation, is insufficient to activate the result of multiculturalism" (p. 36).

Hope and good intentions to create a diverse, affirming, and multiculturally competent organization are admirable, but good intentions alone will not fulfill this goal. It is critical that leaders have an understanding of how diversity, multiculturalism, and social justice fit into the organization's mission, construct a vision for how to realize these goals, and have the will to take steps to implement the vision. Leaders must also be willing to widely communicate this multicultural vision, allocate resources to support the vision, and ensure accountability of the members in the organization to work toward the vision.

Examples of leader and organizational behavior include:

- participating in diversity-related professional development opportunities;
- placing diversity-related topics on meeting agendas;
- effectively addressing incidents of bias that occur within the department or are reported by students to the department; and
- providing the space and opportunities for members of the organization to raise and grapple with questions about diversity, multiculturalism, and social justice (e.g., staff and department meetings, unit or departmental retreats, supervision meetings, informal conversations with one's colleagues).

For example, faculty, staff, or administrators may discuss the presence of racial, gender, religious, or other dynamics (e.g., discrimination, ableism, and homophobia) in a recently published article or book. They may further explore whether and how the dynamics or circumstances around these events are present in their department or at their institution. In some cases, these conversations may serve as the impetus for changes in an individual's awareness, attitudes, and behavior, or for changes in the practices of the department or division.

Creating the space for sharing observations, thoughts, and insights about diversity is just one part of this component. Perhaps even more important is whether individuals within the organization believe they have a voice in helping to shape the focus of their organization's diversity initiatives and collective multicultural learning. Conversations by themselves about diversity topics, without other strategic actions, will not create sustained multicultural change, but in the collegial culture of higher education, conversations, deliberation, and discourse are the vehicles that can help spark multicultural engagement. Without providing the space for conversations about diversity, multiculturalism, and social justice, it is improbable that any other actions (short of a legal threat or public crisis) will be enough to propel and sustain change.

Creating this space for multicultural engagement and discussions about diversity within the organization is a challenging yet important aspect of multicultural organizational behavior. It is particularly challenging given the dynamics of power and hierarchy that exist within higher education organization. Some employees may be fearful to engage in these conversations due to their status in the organization. Positional leaders may be fearful of appearing multiculturally incompetent in front of their colleagues or those who report to them. Likewise, employees may fear saying something that would be offensive to their peers or supervisors.

Despite the risk and vulnerability of engagement, organizations should provide employees with multiple opportunities to discuss how organizational goals align with the employees' experiences, knowledge, skills, and behaviors. Without the ability or opportunity to engage in these conversations there is little possibility that enough support, expertise, or collective understanding will be generated to inform and enact more substantial multicultural change initiatives.

Component 2: Peer/Colleague Influence, Behaviors, and Expectations Regarding Multicultural Engagement

The second component in the MCSAO model focuses on the attitudes, expectations, and conduct of peers and colleagues within the organization. For an organization to sustain cultural change, the organization's members must actively practice multicultural engagement and demonstrate a commitment to diversity and multicultural goals. This is not solely the work of the leaders of the organization, but is a responsibility that resides with all members in the organization. Peer engagement matters, and the attitudes and behaviors of other staff, faculty, and administrators can either help propel or inhibit organizational multicultural change.

Engagement manifests through observable actions, such as:

- incorporating relevant multicultural material in course materials and assignments, and discussing the successes and challenges of incorporating multicultural content with their peers;
- participating in or leading committees or initiatives that seek to improve the inclusiveness of the department's or institution's services for those from underrepresented or marginalized backgrounds;
- speaking up when one recognizes an act of bias or a microaggression occurring during a meeting (e.g., naming when an idea that comes from a member of a marginalized group is ignored, but embraced when that same idea is offered by a person with more dominant group memberships); and
- using commonly understood diversity terminology with others in the organization to reinforce the values and intention of being inclusive and respectful.

Institutions of higher education are places where ideas are explored, knowledge is created, and development occurs. For the health of the organization, employees must not stagnate, but continue to grow through professional development opportunities such as "formal programs, individual mentoring, performance appraisals, and self-directed learning" (Mills, 2000, p. 143). Members of the organization need to continuously develop the multicultural awareness, knowledge, and skills to interact effectively with those from diverse backgrounds and to help create a more inclusive and affirming organization. In this component, the members of the organization understand that multicultural learning and engagement is not just in the domain of organizational leaders, but is the work of all.

Component 3: Clear and Coherent Multicultural Organization Mission

The mission of an organization reflects its deep sense of purpose and core values. The mission also functions to help guide the planning and daily practices of the organization, define its long-term purpose, and describe the constituencies served by the organization (Barr, 2000). Mission serves as a light that guides the direction and focus of an organization so that it can effectively direct its human and fiscal resources toward a well-understood and broadly articulated purpose.

There is an inextricable link between mission and values and they serve as foundational guides for what the organization deems as important and worthy. Values influence our work, shape our choices, and guide how we navigate through dilemmas (Rhatigan, 2000). For higher education organizations, ideals such as justice, service, equality, and fairness may function as the foundation of the organization's core values. Reflecting these ideals, the institutional mission may include language such as *preparing students to become leaders in a global community.*

Without clarity and alignment of organizational activities with the values and mission of an organization, the organization's efforts will be unfocused and flounder. Expressing a strong clear organizational mission of why and how diversity and multicultural values are relevant is necessary to ensure that any multicultural programs, curricular objectives, and other initiatives are tied to the central mission of the organization, and not experienced as a superfluous activity. These diversity and multicultural values can be communicated in the central mission statement of the organization, spoken publicly, or appear in other materials that are developed and used by the organization. For example, at the institutional level the mission foci could be *preparing students to work and live in a diverse and complex world.* At the divisional or departmental levels, the organization may express a desire to ensure that its curricula and educational opportunities, programs, and other activities meet the needs of a diverse world and evolving student body.

Beyond a formal written mission statement, there are many avenues to express a multicultural mission. For example:

- admissions staff perform outreach to recruit a diverse body of students;
- the college president or dean speaks of the values and mission of the institution during convocation or other events welcoming new students to the campus community;
- faculty members explain why they incorporate the exploration of the dynamics of power and privilege as a part of their courses; and
- staff train student leaders to be multiculturally aware resident assistants, orientation leaders, or peer educators.

Component 4: Provision of Multiculturally Inclusive Services

In addition to their educational mission, colleges and universities offer a wide array of services to students, faculty, staff, community members, and other constituencies to facilitate learning and development, provide support, and address other needs. These services may include healthcare and counseling; tutoring and academic support; employment and human resource services (e.g., benefits, classification, and compensation); support in resolving grievances, conflicts, and allegations of bias or misconduct; and social support.

In addition to services that are generally available, higher education organizations may also provide services for specific populations of underrepresented or underserved groups to facilitate more equitable academic and social participation within the institution. Targeted services can be in the form of affinity or counseling groups, tutoring and other academic support, academic programs that provide a pipeline to groups who are traditionally underrepresented in certain fields of study, or mentoring to support junior faculty members or entry-level staff.

Organizations that choose to provide services for those from underrepresented groups generally do so based on characteristics such as: race/ethnicity, gender, gender identity and expression, religion, class, sexual orientation, and nationality. Although services based on disability were not specifically named in this component, disability-related services appeared elsewhere in the MCSAO model (i.e., strategic and formal organizational practice), which can perhaps be attributed to the formal compliance obligations with the Americans With Disabilities Act.

Multiculturally competent organizations tend to incorporate what they learn into the services they offer. For example, a student affairs division may offer a series of professional development workshops for the staff on experiences commonly faced by international students (e.g., culture shock, language and communication barriers, and insensitivity to cultural differences). Staff who attend these workshops may determine that important meetings with students should be followed with written communication outlining the action steps. This written communication minimizes confusion and miscommunication due to language barriers. In addition to students for whom English is not their first language, potentially all students would benefit from having follow-up written communication. In the academic context, a faculty member interested in making his/her/hir course more accessible to individuals who process information differently due to cognitive differences may seek out services to incorporate Universal Design for Learning principles into the course.

Component 5: Support for and Creation of Diversity/Multicultural Programming and Events

Programs and events with a diversity or multicultural focus provide a rich avenue for students, faculty, staff, and community members to gain and

deepen multicultural awareness, knowledge, skills, and ⌐
differences. Developing and providing programs are not
that are valuable. Professional service that promotes dive
tural goals may include serving on committees and task fc
with others to develop new programs and services, and contributing through
professional activities and associations at the state, regional, and national
levels (Scott, 2000).

Beyond developing a program or coordinating an event, this component
also reflects the support an organization gives for diversity programs and
efforts beyond one's specific department, college, or division. For example, a
department may:

- support diversity and multicultural programming by serving on planning committees, providing financial assistance, displaying information and announcements about these programs in the unit's public
  spaces, and attending these programs and events; and
- be an active and visible supporter of multicultural programs organized
  by other units (e.g., department or division).

Component 6: Incorporation of a Multicultural Lens in Strategic and Formal Organizational Practice

Organizations that link their multicultural goals to strategic and formal
processes are better positioned to sustain and institutionalize multicultural
change. The organizational activities in this component refer to the strategic and formal practices within an organization that are linked to ensuring accountability with multicultural goals, providing support to employees
from underrepresented backgrounds, as well as minimizing legal risk and
liability. Assessment, evaluation, and the review of policies and procedures
also fall within this component.

Policies, procedures, and practices reflect the rules and formal operations
of an organization and influence how constituents formally interact with the
organization. This component includes activities and tasks such as applying
for a job or academic admission, requesting information or a service provided
by the organization, or appealing a decision made by the organization.

It is imperative that institutions who want to become a more multicultural organization "illuminate and eradicate inequities in education[al]
practice, structures, and resources to make educational environments more
inclusive" (Jenkins & Walton, 2008, p. 88). This is partially achieved by
acknowledging the "significant subsystems in an organization (e.g., mission, policies, procedures, training, and evaluation)" and developing new,
as well as reviewing and updating current policies and procedures so they

are more inclusive of diverse populations (Pope et al., 2004, p. 64). In addition to the review of the organization's policies, procedures, and practices through the lens of diversity, multiculturalism, and social justice, assessment refers to:

- the effort made to collect, analyze, and interpret data, which can then be used to help inform organizational practice, improve organizational effectiveness, and guide policy development, strategic planning, and the allocation of resources;
- whether an organization evaluates how well programs serve students and other users from diverse backgrounds; and
- whether the organization has mechanisms to assess the multicultural competence (e.g., awareness, knowledge, and skills) of its staff.

Pope et al. (2004) describe applying assessment to organizational multicultural change by determining who is being served by the organization; the satisfaction with the services, programs, and courses being offered; the strengths and weaknesses of an organization; and the multicultural competence of the employees. In their article, Pope, Mueller, and Reynolds (2009) discuss diversity research in student affairs, and lament the many challenges that inhibit practitioners from conducting diversity-related research. Institutional multicultural organizational assessment is one of the most challenging activities within higher education organizations due in large part to the lack of psychometrically valid tools with which to assess complex constructs such as organizational multicultural competence.

Component 7: Multicultural Recruitment Practices

The final component of the MCSAO model is multicultural recruitment practices. This component reflects the importance an organization places on having a diverse workforce by taking steps to generate a diverse candidate pool and recruit members from underrepresented backgrounds, as well as seeking applicants with a demonstrated commitment to diversity and multicultural goals.

For many organizations, diversity-related recruitment and retention goals are focused on having a compositionally diverse organization. Pope et al. (2004) wrote that "[t]o have a truly multicultural department/division, it is essential that the staff be culturally diverse. Without diversity [of] voices, life experiences, and cultural backgrounds, staff may be limited in their ability to meet the needs of some students" (p. 66).

The recruitment facet of this component reflects the value placed on having a diverse and multiculturally competent workforce and the strategies used to recruit these potential employees. Recruitment strategies can include:

- making personal contact with diverse and/or multiculturally competent individuals who have the potential to be strong candidates for the open position;
- utilizing networks to identify potential candidates; and
- advertising positions in venues that focus on the interests of underrepresented groups (Taylor & von Destinon, 2000).

Organizations may incorporate a demonstrated commitment to diversity, multicultural goals, inclusion, and social justice in job postings, and take active steps to network with potential applicants from underrepresented groups before and during the search process. Although this effort may seem costly, higher education institutions that embrace multicultural change will aim to advance the organization by attracting and retaining high quality, diverse, and culturally competent faculty and staff, which can result in a strong return on investment. This requires that organizational leaders pay special attention to the attrition rates of employees and examine whether marginalized faculty and staff are leaving the institution due to the climate or negative experiences at the institution. If an organization does not address these concerns, its reputation will prevent it from being able to recruit and hire diverse and talented community members, as well as those who value interactions with difference in its environment.

Initiating and Sustaining the Journey: Insights and Strategies for Multicultural Change in Higher Education Organizations

The previous sections outline the qualities, characteristics, and behaviors of multiculturally competent higher education organizations as identified by the MCSAO. Even for organizations that have taken all of these steps, the journey is never fully completed. For organizations that are on the multicultural change journey, complacency is the greatest risk. For organizations that are new to the journey, overcoming inertia is often the biggest challenge. This chapter ends with four insights and strategies on how to initiate and sustain the journey of multicultural organizational change in the higher education setting.

Create a Compelling Vision

Vision serves as the potential of what could be. It is within reach (but barely), and reflects aspirations and possibilities. It requires the imagination of someone like an artist, who is not afraid to take paint to a blank canvas and offer a picture where none had existed before. It takes imagination to conjure a vision, and courage to name it and expose the vision to critique and even hostility. Sometimes the desire for multicultural organizational change is a public or political crisis. Other times, it is the more subtle sense that the organization is not living up to its fullest potential. Leaders and others in the organization, who want the organization to be successful must ask probing questions, and come up with creative solutions.

Some steps those in the organization can take to create a compelling vision are to:

1. Examine the core institutional, disciplinary, and professional values that are connected to diversity, multiculturalism, and social justice and explore how these values could be more fully executed within the organization;
2. Engage those within the organization and other key constituent groups in conversations about what the organization can look like, be, or do better, if it more fully integrated diversity, multicultural, and social justice goals into its vision, core functions, and practices; and
3. Engage respected allies and champions to help shape and communicate this vision to those within and beyond the organization including why having a more multicultural organization is important and meaningful.

There may be those in the organization who will fear or resist multicultural change. They may be comfortable with the way things are and want to maintain the status quo. At best, they will lack enthusiasm and at worst, they may actively resist or try to sabotage multicultural efforts. If clear and open communication does not work, leaders may need to develop a strategy for minimizing the damage caused by those who are ambivalent to change. In some cases, leaders will need the courage and clarity to either work with those who are hostile to change or help them transition out of the organization.

Take an Honest Look

Often there is a gap between the aspiration and the reality. For organizations that wish to engage in a multicultural change process, they must be willing to take a hard and honest look at the place from which they are starting. Assessment is an important part of the process of multicultural change, but for organizations that are fearful of potentially difficult feedback, they may prefer to avoid asking the hard questions about how the organization functions. As a precursor to any assessment process, it is important to remember the vision and mission that the organization is working toward and to seek data that will help inform the creation or modification of systems, initiatives, and practices that will bring the organization closer to its multicultural goals.

Some actions that organizations may want to take are to:

1. Create a multicultural change team composed of individuals throughout the organization, including representation at different levels within the organization's hierarchy, who can provide important insights and perspectives about the current multicultural state of the organization;
2. Collect a range of data and artifacts including quantitative data (e.g., disaggregated recruitment/admission and retention statistics for those from underrepresented groups, number of multicultural programs or course offerings), qualitative data (e.g., focus groups with members from diverse backgrounds to learn about their experiences of interacting with the organization), artifacts (e.g., brochures and written materials), and environmental surveys (e.g., accessibility or universal design of spaces, or in public areas); and
3. Have a plan for sharing the data and applying it to create change in the organization.

Resist Stagnation to Break Through Plateaus

When organizations take clear steps to become more diverse, inclusive, and socially just in their practices, functions, and systems, there will eventually come a time when they meet their initial multicultural goals. Perhaps the initial resistance or fear around the multicultural vision has faded after 1, 3, 5, or even 10 years of multicultural change work. At this point some may believe that they completed the hard work and it is now time to take a break and focus on something else.

Rather than take a break from multicultural change work, organizations should capitalize on the foundation laid. Now is the time to take the organization's multicultural work to the next level and the plateau can serve as the platform on which the organization can strive to greater heights. Organizations that have experienced successes in their multicultural change work can continue to grow if they:

1. Revisit their original multicultural vision and goals, to examine what work remains undone;
2. Note the opportunities and challenges that are occurring in broader institutional and social contexts (e.g., legal challenges to affirmative action, immigration reform, social justice movements), which may have an impact on their multicultural and diversity efforts;

3. Consider issues and identities that were not on the organization's radar when the organization began its multicultural change work, but should now be explored so that the organization can be proactive with its interventions;

4. Reflect on whether there have been any significant shifts within the organization (e.g., changes to senior leadership, new strategic goals within the institution, and emerging economic and political opportunities and threats), which create new opportunities for multicultural engagement or challenges that must be addressed; and

5. Consider sharing the lessons learned and the wisdom gained from their multicultural change process with others through professional scholarly activities, such as workshops, presentations, and professional writing.

Recognize, Acknowledge, and Celebrate Success

There is always more that an organization can do. Even when there has been significant progress, it is common for a staff or faculty member, administrator, or even the students to name the problems and challenges that remain unaddressed. It is certainly important for organizations to hear these critiques. Yet, it is also equally important to recognize, acknowledge, and celebrate successes.

Sometimes these successes will be significant and measurable. For example, increases in the admission and retention of students from certain underrepresented identities may increase after several years of implementing a strategic multicultural retention initiative. The organization may be recognized institutionally, regionally, or nationally for its multicultural change work. The leaders in the organization should recognize and celebrate the successes that resulted from the vision, courage, and significant work.

It is also important to recognize the less dramatic and obvious successes. For example, there may be an increase in the reporting of incidents of bias or discrimination because the organization has created procedures that make it easier and psychologically safer to report such incidents. Members of the organization who hold less positional power may participate more actively in diversity professional development sessions than in previous years because the organization has created a culture in which all voices are listened to, not just the voices of the positional leaders. These seemingly small successes indicate powerful cultural shifts within an organization that is striving to be more inclusive and affirming of all.

Conclusion

Pursuing a strong, clear vision of multicultural change is a long-term pursuit. The work does not end with one successful initiative or one substantial failure. It may take an organization a decade or more before it accomplishes a vision of becoming a multicultural organization. Qualities such as discipline, commitment, courage, vulnerability, and tenacity must be present in the leaders and critical scholar practitioners charged with helping to advance a multicultural vision. A multicultural organization is not one whose work is completed—it is the organization that continues to strive.

References

Barr, M. J. (2000). The importance of the institutional mission. In M. J. Barr & M. K. Desler (Eds.), *The handbook of student affairs administration* (pp. 25–36). San Francisco: Jossey-Bass.

Flash, L. J. (2010). *Developing a measure of multicultural competence in student affairs organizations* (Unpublished doctoral dissertation). University of Vermont, Burlington.

Grieger, I. (1996). A multicultural organizational development checklist for student affairs. *Journal of College Student Development, 37*(5), 561–573.

Haro, R. P. (1993). Leadership and diversity: Organizational strategies for success. In R. R. Sims & R. F. Dennehy (Eds.), *Diversity and differences in organization: An agenda for answers and questions* (pp. 47–62). Westport, CT: Quorum.

Jackson, B. W., & Hardiman, R. (1994). Multicultural organizational development. In E. Y. Cross, J. H. Katz, F. A. Miller, & E. W. Seashore (Eds.), *The promise of diversity: Over 40 voices discuss strategies for eliminating discrimination in organizations* (pp. 231–239). Burr Ridge, IL: Irwin.

Jenkins, T. S., & Walton, C. L. (2008). Student affairs and cultural practice: A framework for implementing culture outside the classroom. In S. R. Harper (Ed.), *Creating inclusive campus environments for cross-cultural learning and student engagement* (pp. 87–101). Washington DC: NASPA.

Mills, D. B. (2000). The role of the middle manager. In M. J. Barr & M. K. Desler (Eds.), *The handbook of student affairs administration* (pp. 135–153). San Francisco: Jossey-Bass.

Pope, R. L., Mueller, J. A., & Reynolds, A. L. (2009). Looking back and moving forward: Future directions for diversity research in student affairs. *Journal of College Student Development, 50*(6), 640–658.

Pope, R. L., Reynolds, A. L., & Mueller, J. A. (2004). *Multicultural competence in student affairs*. San Francisco: Jossey-Bass.

Rhatigan, J. J. (2000). The history and philosophy of student affairs. In M. J. Barr & M. K. Desler (Eds.), *The handbook of student affairs administration* (pp. 3–24). San Francisco: Jossey-Bass.

Scott, J. E. (2000). Creating effective staff development programs. In M. J. Barr & M. K. Desler (Eds.), *The handbook of student affairs administration* (pp. 477–491). San Francisco: Jossey-Bass.

Sims, R. R., & Dennehy, R. F. (Eds.). (1993). *Diversity and differences in organizations: An agenda for answers and questions.* Westport, CT: Quorum.

Smith, D. G. (1997). Institutional transformation: Findings on comprehensive campus commitments to diversity. In D. G. Smith (Ed.), *Diversity works: The emerging picture of how students benefit* (pp. 39–45). Washington DC: Association of American Colleges and Universities.

Taylor, S. L., & von Destinon, M. (2000). Selecting, training, supervising, and evaluating staff. In M. J. Barr & M. K. Desler (Eds.), *The handbook of student affairs administration* (pp. 154–177). San Francisco: Jossey-Bass.

6

SHARING POWER AND PRIVILEGE THROUGH THE SCHOLARLY PRACTICE OF ASSESSMENT

Wayne Jacobson

This chapter discusses what is at stake in our decisions about designing the assessment of multicultural initiatives, and considers the risks we take when we fail to apply the lens of the critical scholar practitioner to the examination of our efforts. This chapter also provides a rationale for distinguishing assessment and research as each relates to deepening our understanding of these types of initiatives. The goal of this chapter is to provide practitioners with entry points for examining the quality of their work to facilitate social change and identifying the extent to which their initiatives can be considered successful.

Reasons for Assessing, or Not Assessing, Multicultural Initiatives

Values that shape assessment are deeply ingrained in initiatives that develop skills for engaging with difference. Assessment highly values decision-making based on evidence of change, rather than on the singular perspective of one's own incidental observations of an initiative. A thorough, systematic examination of an initiative and its effects allows practitioners to have a more confident, inclusive understanding of the impact of their work.

Through assessment, we prioritize shared understandings and collaborative practice as we work with colleagues, participants, and stakeholders to interpret evidence we have collected. Without systematically collected evidence, we may end up trying to make sense of multiple competing recollections of an experience, each shaped by unique vantage points and priorities of different stakeholders or participants. Assessment may still leave us with varying ideas about implications, next steps, and further questions raised by the data, but it gives our dialogue a common reference point outside of each person's particular experience with the initiative.

Assessment can be designed to express commitments to learning and change. We can easily think of an initiative in terms of what it is intended to teach about engaging with difference; however, the value of an initiative is best assessed not in terms of what ideas are presented to participants, but what they learned or how they changed as a result. Through assessment we can look beyond facilitator intentions by purposefully gathering evidence to show the extent of change in behavior, knowledge, attitudes, or values among participants.

Assessment honors transparency and accountability, making it possible to recognize and replicate successful practices. Shulman (2007) reminds us that accountability is, in essence, "being able to render an account"—a narrative act that may take many forms. Its guiding principle is not that something is being hidden and must be uncovered, but that there's a fuller story to tell. Assessment lets us better tell our story; and frankly, if we don't tell the stories of our own initiatives, who will tell them for us? That's not a rhetorical question. Part of leading an initiative is being able to give an account of it; Shulman writes, "Our responsibility is to take control of the narrative" (2007, p. 35).

These values are widely shared among multicultural scholar practitioners. And yet, systematic, scholarly assessment is not always standard practice, and it is sometimes seen as something we can afford to think about later, or not worry about if we don't get to it—because, after all, we are committed to our programs and we can see what goes well or doesn't.

First of all, assessment can be costly and time-consuming, and we all have a lot of other things to do. When resources are limited, any time taken for assessment feels like less time for the initiative. But even before that, designing and conducting meaningful assessment takes time from practitioners who are usually managing many other demands on their resources already.

Multicultural initiatives often engage with complex constructs—culture, identity, power, and privilege—with multidimensional systems of cause and effect, in many cases at the intersection of individual agency and community engagement. We can get paralyzed by complexity and the array of potential things to focus on, knowing that any attempt to assess the initiative is bound to leave something out.

Knowing that, we are wary of over-simplifying complexity or impos-
ing values by defining criteria for the success of the initiative, treating participants as objects of study, or asking people to give us data to serve our
purposes. Or, facing the complexity, we are tempted to look for shortcuts,
perhaps using standard instruments that weren't necessarily designed for the
purposes of the initiative, or superficial low-cost options that are easy to
administer, such as participation rates and satisfaction surveys.

All of these challenges are genuine, and pose real obstacles to effective,
credible assessment. But none is sufficient to justify the risk of inattention to
assessment. Carelessness about assessment presumes a high degree of trust in
decision-makers to accurately perceive intended and unintended outcomes
of an initiative, adequately account for varying perspectives and experiences
of diverse participants and stakeholders, and know what decisions will be in
the best interests of all involved. Because there's no avoiding the fact that I
will be called on to make decisions about initiatives I create, and I'll be faced
with making them based on the evidence I have—even if my best available
evidence is my own informal observation within the realm of my immediate
experience.

Without assessment, decisions become a matter of who has the power
and interest to prevent or enforce change. More than anything else, assessment is about sharing the privilege held by decision-makers to determine
what is to be valued and how to value it. The only people empowered by
lack of assessment are the ones who get to make decisions without systematically assuring that they have responsibly accounted for the perspectives and
experiences of participants and stakeholders in the initiative.

For scholarly practitioners of multicultural initiatives, assessment is
imperative: If we want to give due consideration to diverse voices and perspectives of participants, stakeholders, and communities with which we're
engaged, then we need to go beyond our good intentions and incidental
observations of what we think is happening through our initiatives. If we
want to be able to improve upon and advocate for the initiatives we create,
we need intellectually rigorous, critical examination of our practices and their
effects so that we can credibly demonstrate the value of what we accomplish
and identify needs for further change. As practitioners who are also scholars,
we need to design the assessment of multicultural initiatives with full awareness of the challenges and with respect for the complexity of the questions
we are taking on, bringing all the commitments, tools, and frameworks for
inquiry that scholars bring to difficult questions.

This chapter offers a framework for bringing the same level of scholarly
rigor and integrity to assessment that we bring to other forms of scholarly

work, and provides entry points for engaging in the complexity of assessing multicultural initiatives.

Scholarly Rigor and Integrity of Assessment

In the academic world, we quickly see parallels between the work of assessment and the work of research, and we often draw on similar techniques for each (surveys, participant observation, discourse analysis, etc.). However, thinking of assessment as a form of research can also become an obstacle: We rarely have the same control over an educational initiative that researchers hope to exercise over a phenomenon they are studying, and so we can find ourselves trying to impose conditions of research that might be incompatible with an initiative (such as random assignment to experimental and control groups), or we can conclude that in the absence of those conditions, it's not possible to draw meaningful conclusions about its effects.

Rather than seeing assessment as a form of research, we need to recognize both as forms of inquiry, with distinct purposes and operating assumptions. The goal of research is discovery: Researchers want to examine a phenomenon closely, and draw conclusions about it in ways that let them make claims which hold across conditions and contexts. Though researchers may see their work as contributing to social change, their primary audience is the community of fellow researchers, who will build on their work and continue adding to the body of knowledge about the phenomenon being studied. Research may be applied, but by practitioners in the field that is represented by the phenomenon, not by practitioners of research. The extent to which it is applicable is not necessarily considered a reflection on the quality of the research.

Assessment is also a form of inquiry: We have questions about the effects of an initiative, and seek to systematically examine it in ways that let us know what our observations represent and what questions still remain. It is highly contextualized, and its primary audiences will consist of stakeholders directly affected by an initiative and practitioners who make decisions about its future implementation. Assessment is designed to be applied, and its value is determined by its direct applicability and relevance to the local initiative, not by whether it provides a basis for broader claims about similar initiatives implemented elsewhere.

To put it another way, research is putting something under a microscope; it might lead to discoveries based on what we see, but not necessarily with the goal of changing the particular item on the slide currently being magnified. The tool for assessment is not a microscope, but a mirror: We look at it to make a fuller image apparent, so that we have a more complete basis for deciding what to change about the very thing we are looking at, and what can remain as is.

Distinctions like these are not always clear-cut, and each works best in light of the other. Assessment is best when informed by research that is relevant to the program; more extensive research may grow out of assessment findings. Putting something under a microscope might yield important discoveries that lead to significant change; holding up a mirror might lead to an informed decision to act no further until more evidence is available. The important differences are the assumptions on which they are based and the questions they are designed to answer.

Consider, for example, a residential early immersion (REI) program designed to help recent graduates transition from high school to college. Research might examine effects of REI on student academic and social integration during the first year of college. It would attempt to identify and control for conditions such as participant selection criteria, program structure, and staffing, so that conclusions will reflect the REI experience rather than effects of open enrollment versus recruited cohorts, highly structured versus unstructured programming, or varying staff expertise (though accounting for those differences might be an important dimension of the research). The goal of the research will be to make claims about the effect of REI that will hold across a range of conditions and circumstances where REI programs are implemented.

However, assessment will be looking at a particular instance of a local program, asking what can be learned from this year's program that will help further develop or improve it in the future. It may be useful to know what others have learned about REI programs implemented elsewhere, but assessment is guided by local contexts and decisions that need to be made locally. If decision-makers are considering changes in participant recruiting, program structure, or staffing, they will find much in a contextualized, local assessment of a particular program that could not be learned from generalized findings of a cross-institutional research study. These distinctions are summarized in Table 6.1.

In these two cases, similar forms of data collection and analysis may be used, and people conducting the inquiry would benefit from similar areas of expertise. Conclusions are equally legitimate for the purposes of each study, and equally useful for their respective purposes. However, underlying purposes are distinct, and it would not make sense to judge the quality of research on how specifically it applies to next year's programming decisions at a particular institution, nor would it make sense to judge the quality of assessment at one institution on the basis of how effectively it characterizes similar initiatives at other institutions.

TABLE 6.1.
Distinctions Between Assessment and Research

	Research	*Assessment*
Key Verb	Discover	Identify
Key Noun	Knowledge	Outcome
Immediate Audience	Fellow researchers	Practitioners and stake-holders
Metaphorical Tool	A microscope	A mirror
Guiding Questions	How can we better understand this phenomenon?	What can we learn about this program that will help us further develop or improve it?
Example: Residential Early Immersion (REI) Programs	How does REI program participation affect student academic and social integration during the first year of college?	What can be learned from this year's REI program that will help us make next year's REI program more effective?

These distinctions are important because research and assessment differ not only in underlying assumptions and purposes, but in how they tend to be valued. Research has a great deal of currency in higher education, and the scholarly quality of someone's work is often valued in terms of how closely it resembles research. For assessment, this bias becomes an obstacle when, as noted earlier, it creates the impression that we must create optimal conditions for research in order to conduct meaningful assessment. Or, if that's not possible, we view assessment findings as a lesser form of knowledge because they weren't attained through something we recognize as research. Assessment practices (and more to the point, assessment practitioners) are then seen as less intellectually rigorous and less capable of producing value-able results.

In order to recognize assessment as a form of scholarly work, it is useful to consider what exactly makes something scholarly. In 1990, Ernest Boyer challenged the higher education community to reconsider the notion of scholarship, arguing that scholarliness is not simply a matter of attaining an advanced degree or publishing research, but a principle that can be extended across various types of work that scholars do. Boyer argues that it is not the form of the product that makes work scholarly, but the extent to which it is done in ways that are consistent with values and practices of scholars. Glassick, Huber, and Maeroff (1997) build on Boyer's foundation to articulate characteristics of work that make it scholarly, and their framework also provides a useful way of looking at assessment as a scholarly activity.

First, the scholar's work is characterized by clear goals. Scholars explicitly state the basic questions that motivate and guide their work. Within that context, they define realistic objectives that can be achieved within the scope of a specific project. For multicultural initiatives, do we clearly articulate not only a broader vision for change, but also the particular questions we hope to address through an initiative and the rationale for assessing it in the ways that we do?

Second, scholars have adequate expertise for the work they are undertaking. Scholars build on previous work in the field, and appreciate the knowledge and skills required for the work they are doing. Scholars also strategically bring added resources and expertise to a project in needed areas. For initiatives designed to develop skills for engaging with difference, do we have the social and cultural competence, understanding of theories of learning and change, and inquiry skills necessary to design, conduct, and assess the initiative? Do we seek out collaborators who can bring additional strengths and areas of expertise to the project when needed?

Third, scholars use appropriate methods, intentionally designing or adapting methods that are uniquely suited to the goals they are pursuing and the contexts in which they're working. They effectively implement their chosen methods and adapt procedures in response to changing circumstances or unexpected findings. For assessment of multicultural initiatives, are implementation and assessment congruent with stated goals for the project, participant characteristics, and types of information we need to collect?

Fourth, scholars are able to determine the significance of their results. Scholars can recognize how well they have achieved the goals they set for their work, and also when and why goals were not achieved as expected. How well do our initiatives achieve intended outcomes, and can we make a plausible case for our methods and our findings? Where things don't turn out as planned, do we have evidence that lets us develop reasonable explanations for why they didn't?

Next, scholars effectively disseminate their work. Scholars seek to advance their field by presenting their work with integrity and openness, communicating the methods, analyses, and rationale for their work in ways that fellow scholars can review and replicate. Do we represent the assessment of our initiatives in ways that let others trace our steps and follow our reasoning so that even those who don't fully agree with our conclusions can still see how we reached them?

Last of all, scholars demonstrate reflective critique of their own work. Scholars critically evaluate their own effectiveness, seek out substantive feedback from peers, and use the lessons learned from self-examination and peer review to contribute to the quality of future work. For multicultural initiatives, are we able to identify and own our role in the initiative's relative level of effectiveness? Are we engaged in critical dialogue about our work with fellow scholars? Can we identify next steps for advancing the quality or reach of future work?

Glassick, Huber, and Maeroff (1997) do not suggest that work done by scholars always meets all six of these criteria—only that, to the extent they do, they raise the scholarly quality of their work. Applied to other scholarly work such as teaching, this model does not suggest that all pedagogical innovators begin with a thorough review of other scholars who have attempted similar changes in their teaching—but when they do, they situate their work in an intellectual community of practice, and contribute further innovations for others to build on. Applied to the scholarly work of civic engagement, this model does not suggest that all community initiatives are documented for others to replicate—but when they are, they invite review, critique, and further work by fellow scholars with similar interests and commitments.

Applied to assessment, we can see work as scholarly to the extent that it is designed with clear goals and appropriate methods that are tailored to address the questions posed by the initiative. We can consider it scholarly to the extent that those carrying it out have acquired or collaborated to provide relevant expertise, and are able to situate their work in the tradition of others who have done similar work. We see it as scholarly to the extent that methods and findings are critically examined and effectively communicated to peers and colleagues, inviting scrutiny and also potentially contributing to their future work in the field.

To understand, improve, and advocate for the quality of multicultural initiatives, we need to assess them with scholarly rigor and integrity. But to state that assessment can be scholarly is not to suggest that it always is, just as not all research is accepted for publication in scholarly journals. Before an initiative is launched, plans need to be made for assessing it in ways that will adequately characterize the initiative and stand up to the scrutiny of scholarly examination.

Assessment Entry Points

The final section of this chapter will identify four entry points for conducting rigorous, scholarly assessment that will provide a credible basis for identifying the quality of initiatives to develop skills for engaging with difference. These entry points do not by themselves provide a full blueprint for carrying out an assessment. But they should help articulate assumptions, identify strategies, and prioritize among the many possible steps that need to be taken in planning, implementing, and assessing a multicultural initiative.

Entry Point #1: Articulate Intended Outcomes

As critical scholar practitioners, we are often motivated by a vision for change we hope to create through the initiatives we facilitate. Because we see the importance and complexity of the issues an initiative is designed to address, a narrow focus on its specific outcomes may feel artificial, or even that it diminishes the bigger goals we hope to achieve.

For this reason, outcomes statements are best seen as terms of success for identifying progress, not a full statement of commitments, values, or mission. If we do not state in specific terms what we hope to accomplish within the scope of time and resources available to us, we have little on which to base claims about the quality or reach of the initiative, and it leaves room for others to step in and judge the initiative's success in terms of their own. An initiative motivated by a vision for significant change—such as "increase social and economic justice in the community"—might, in practical terms, consist of three hours of direct interaction with participants over a six-week period. In that case, intended outcomes need to be expressed in terms of three hours' worth of progress toward achieving the larger vision. It would not make sense to define the quality of a three-hour initiative solely in terms of whether a need for increased justice still remained at the end of the third hour.

If intended outcomes are going to be useful for identifying progress, they need to be stated in observable terms. Not all outcomes can be easily, unambiguously measured, but they should be expressed in terms that will be recognizable to peers and colleagues who share the same expertise, values, and commitments. In short, if I ask colleagues what outcomes they see for my initiative, and they know what I am trying to accomplish and have the skills to recognize it, will they see the same things that I do?

Though they should be stated in terms that are observable, outcomes should also express meaningful change. Sometimes efforts to articulate observable outcomes can lead to an emphasis on visible expression of what happens without indicating its significance. For example, "increased attendance at community meetings" might be a directly observable outcome of an initiative, but presence at a meeting is probably not the social transformation we originally set out to create. The most powerful outcomes statements are those which manage the complexity of articulating desired changes in terms that are meaningful, observable, and achievable.

Entry Point #2: Identify Evidence That Will Demonstrate Progress Toward Outcomes

Many useful resources are available that provide strategies for collecting assessment data (see for example Angelo & Cross, 1993; Bresciani, Zelna, & Anderson, 2004; Suskie, 2009). Before selecting or devising strategies,

however, it is necessary to identify types of evidence that will help demonstrate progress toward achieving identified outcomes, and to select strategies
on the basis of the type of evidence that each yields.

Program outcomes related to acquisition of knowledge or skills are best
demonstrated through documentation of participant behaviors or artifacts
that directly show learning or change. In a traditional classroom setting,
teachers might examine student work produced for class projects or tests; in a
training setting, facilitators might review performance tasks that demonstrate
competency in a particular area of the training. Outcomes related to changes
in attitudes or values might require evidence from systematic observation
of participant behaviors, language used, or emotions expressed. Outcomes
related to changes in self-awareness or efficacy might require evidence from
interviews or surveys that directly address participant self-perceptions such as
confidence levels or likelihood of taking an action.

Some significant indicators of learning or change might emerge in the
dynamic setting of dialogue or in a participant's personal reflections, and
steps to capture these types of indicators can also be built into implementation of the initiative. For example:

- Have participants write down observations or conclusions that you
  can collect, rather than asking them only to reflect privately or discuss
  what they have learned with peers.
- Document themes of group discussion on a whiteboard and work
  with participants to confirm the extent to which the recorded themes
  represent group consensus.
- Create small group activities that allow you to interact directly with
  participants who appear to be less willing to express themselves in
  front of a larger group.

These are just a few examples of potentially rich evidence of learning or
change that can be gleaned from activities woven into interactions with participants.

A second type of evidence, distinct from these direct demonstrations
or observations, is self-reported learning or change. Learners are usually not
experts in judging the extent of their own learning, and self-report cannot
be taken as a direct or complete measure of change. However, participants
are experts on their own experience, and much can be discovered about an
initiative's effect on participants by directly asking them to articulate what
they learned from it, or how their understanding has changed from what it
was before participating in the initiative. Taking the additional step of asking
participants to reflect on their learning can provide further evidence of what

participants valued in a program as they write in response to questions such as, "What do you think is the most important thing you gained from this experience?" and "What questions do you think still need to be discussed?"

Participant feedback can also add to assessment if it is designed to elicit information that participants can be expected to have a basis for knowing, and which can be used for future planning. Participants may have little basis for directly judging facilitator expertise or program design, for example; finding out what participants liked or disliked may say very little about program effectiveness. (In fact, it's possible to imagine an initiative that participants distinctly disliked as they were successfully stretched beyond familiar comfort zones.) Rather, feedback is most useful for identifying, from the perspective of participants, what elements of the initiative helped most to bring about change, what could have been more helpful, and why.

This set of examples is not a complete inventory of all types of evidence that can be used for assessment, but it illustrates ways that different forms of evidence lead to different types of findings: Finding out what participants learned requires different evidence from finding out what they valued, both of which require different evidence from finding out what helped them learn.

Entry Point #3: Raise the Trustworthiness of Your Findings

Assessment should be designed to provide a confident basis for acting on its findings. As a scholar practitioner, my goal is to structure assessment so that I can be sure I'm not simply seeing what I want to see or confirming my biases by attending only to data that puts my initiative in the best light. In all cases, trust in the quality of data can be raised by explicitly demonstrating that assessment has been systematically designed, transparently conducted, and genuinely participatory—reaching out to participants and stakeholders to seek input on design, implementation, and processes for collecting and interpreting data.

Because nearly all forms of data on learning and change are limited and partial, drawing on more than one type of evidence can increase confidence in findings drawn from each, and provide a more credible assessment of the program overall. To assess a program designed to train teachers to interact differently with students, for example, teacher self-reports of changes in classroom behavior would be useful, but more credible if viewed alongside additional evidence gained through peer observations of their teaching. But observations would be most useful for showing the extent to which teachers carried out the changes, and would not be as helpful for identifying why some of them did not. The program could be assessed with greater confidence if evidence from self-reports and observations could be supplemented with teachers' reflective writing about what helped or hindered their ability to apply what they learned in the program.

Findings also become more trustworthy when more than one perspective is represented in the evidence. Teacher self-report, peer observation of teaching, and reflective writing by teachers are three distinct types of evidence, but all represent the perspective of teachers. It would further increase confidence in an assessment of teacher change to include other perspectives such as those of students or parents.

A third option for increasing credibility is to utilize evidence from more than one point in time. Assessment of participants' prior knowledge or skills adds perspective to information collected during or at the end of an initiative; longer term follow-up will greatly strengthen confidence in an immediate assessment conducted at the close of a workshop.

Across all these options, critically evaluating and communicating the rationale for our own analyses will also contribute to increasing trust in our findings. We don't do ourselves any favors when we try to argue for the certainty of conclusions on the basis of partial, contingent evidence. Rather, we need to make a plausible case based on the evidence we have, demonstrating awareness of both what it can tell us and what it cannot, inviting constructive critical input on both the evidence and our conclusions. We need to make it clear that we're not uncritically accepting findings or merely seeing what we want to see.

Assessment can only be simple when we assess simple things—and in the scholarly practice of multicultural initiatives, we don't often do simple things. As a result, to be confident (and give others confidence) in conclusions we draw, we seek to create an appropriately complex composite assessment by working with multiple sources and forms of evidence, neither overlooking nor overstating what we learn from each, and using each to inform the other.

Entry Point #4: Plan to Take Action on Assessment Findings

Few people have the luxury of enough time to gather data that no one intends to use. An important entry point for planning assessment is to identify in advance the eventual courses of action or decisions that assessment findings will be used to support.

A common course of action is to use assessment to identify what to do differently next time. Most multicultural initiatives involve multiple moving parts and numerous variables not fully under our control, and it would be unrealistic to assume that there are no lessons to be learned that might help improve future implementation of an initiative.

Though we don't expect assessments to lead to generalizable outcomes that apply in all contexts, another possible course of action is to articulate lessons learned that might benefit others in similar programs. No one wants to re-invent the wheel; just as we can benefit from lessons learned by others, so too we can plan on contributing to their future work.

Because all assessment will be limited in some way, another potential course of action is to determine needs for further assessment in future iterations. For instance, having learned what we can from short-term assessment of immediate outcomes, we can identify ways to gather data that will reflect longer-term outcomes; having learned what we can from participant self-report and demonstration of learning at the end of training, we might start looking for ways to observe participants applying their learning in other more diverse settings.

One often-overlooked course of action is to make successes visible. It is easy to think of assessment as looking for problems to solve. In fact, assessment often uncovers outcomes we should be celebrating and making more widely known. Even participants who directly experience an initiative might not fully realize its effects, or may assume their perceptions are representative of everyone else's. When we make successes visible, both participants and stakeholders benefit from seeing a fuller portrayal of the initiative and its effects.

These potential courses of action should be identified as part of the assessment plan, which should itself be in place before an initiative is launched. Obviously, prior to the initiative, it won't be possible to know what lessons will be learned or what successes should be made visible, but potential uses for findings play a significant role in shaping the assessment: If one desired course of action is to show that a program develops participant skills for engaging with difference, for example, then the assessment plan needs to include collecting evidence that participants genuinely acquired the skills, not only indirect evidence of their self-reported change or satisfaction with the training. Similarly, if a desired course of action is to demonstrate program successes from the perspective of participants, then the assessment plan should include systematic efforts to capture participant voices, or else we risk hearing only from those who go out of their way to express their views to us on their own initiative, and we will have no way of knowing if those perceptions also represent less vocal participants. Anticipating intended uses of assessment findings, even at the early stages of planning the assessment, can contribute significantly to decisions about the type, amount, and timing of data collection for assessment.

Conclusion

These are entry points for making assessment scholarly, rigorous, and credible. They won't necessarily make it easier or provide shortcuts, but they offer pathways through complexity that promise to make assessment more constructive, meaningful, and worth the effort. Most importantly, these entry points set the stage for redistributing power and challenging those of us with the privilege of making decisions to take responsibility for making them in light of systematically collected, critically examined evidence of our practices and their effects.

References

Angelo, T. A., & Cross, K. P. (1993). *Classroom assessment techniques.* San Francisco: Jossey-Bass.

Boyer, E. L. (1990). *Scholarship reconsidered: Priorities of the professoriate.* San Francisco: Jossey-Bass.

Bresciani, M., Zelna, C., & Anderson, J. (2004). *Assessing student learning and development: A handbook for practitioners.* Washington DC: NASPA.

Glassick, C. E., Huber, M. T., & Maeroff, G. I. (1997). *Scholarship assessed: Evaluation of the professoriate.* San Francisco: Jossey-Bass.

Shulman, L. S. (2007). Counting and recounting: Assessment and the quest for accountability. *Change, 39*(1), 28–35.

Suskie, L. (2009). *Assessing student learning: A common sense guide.* San Francisco: Jossey-Bass.

PART THREE

SCHOLARLY EXAMPLES OF MULTICULTURAL INITIATIVES IN TEACHING, HIGHER EDUCATION ADMINISTRATION, AND STUDENT AFFAIRS PRACTICE

What are examples of the varying types of multicultural initiatives in higher education and student affairs?

7

TEACHING CONTEMPORARY LEADERSHIP

Advancing Students' Capacities to Engage With Difference

John P. Dugan and Daviree Velázquez

"People do not learn by staring in the mirror, they learn by engaging differences with others and with themselves" (Heifetz, 2010, p. 27). In stating this simple truth, leadership scholar Ronald Heifetz situates leadership development as inherently grounded in the work of transformative multiculturalism. He argues that the leadership most needed to address complex social issues necessitates the ability to create holding environments that engage with and can sustain difficult dialogues. This type of leadership is grounded in social responsibility with *leadership* defined as "a purposeful, collaborative, values-based process that results in positive social change" (Komives, Wagner, & Associates, 2009, p. xii). The work of leadership education on college campuses, then, is concerned with the pedagogical practices that cultivate individual, group, and organizational capacities to work collaboratively in pursuit of shared goals (Allen & Roberts, 2011).

Empirical research supports the centrality of difficult dialogues to leadership development indicating that the degree to which individuals engage in interactions about and across Difference is associated with gains in socially responsible leadership capacity (Dugan, Kodama, & Gebhardt, 2012; Dugan & Komives, 2010). These dialogues require groups to explore deeply at the individual, institutional, and systems levels contradictions between espoused and actualized values simultaneously working toward the dismantling of systems of oppression. This interplay of theory and research supports the critical and reinforcing role of transformative multiculturalism in leadership development.

The scholarship on leadership aligns with not only transformative multiculturalism, but also supports the positioning of diversity as a social value focused on "embracing strategies to disrupt systemic oppression on a deeper level" (Watt, this volume, p. 18). Many contemporary leadership theories integrate social justice as a critical outcome and scholars increasingly advance critical perspectives that examine issues of power and normativity (Dugan, 2013; Higher Education Research Institute, 1996; Ospina & Foldy, 2009; Ospina & Su, 2008; Preskill & Brookfield, 2009). Thus, a scan of contemporary literature reveals a clear recognition that developing leadership that contributes to social change begins with cultivating individuals' skill sets to engage with Difference. At this point, one might begin to wonder whether this conceptualization of leadership positions it as identical to transformative multicultural education. Are there legitimate distinctions between the two when defined in these ways? A philosophical response might be: "Should they not be the same if the goals are building human capacity and contributing to social transformation?" A more pragmatic response might suggest that the areas overlap and leadership education ought to be in service of transformative multiculturalism, but often falls short.

In truth, the practice of leadership education has struggled significantly with the integration and implementation of multicultural initiatives that target students' abilities to engage with and across Difference (Dugan, 2013; Dugan, Kodama, Correia, & Associates, 2013). The delivery of leadership education frequently reproduces and perpetuates a dominant narrative with an over-simplified approach to engaging with differences and a content-base that rarely examines issues of privilege and oppression in complex ways (Dugan, 2013; Munin & Dugan, 2011; Ospina & Foldy, 2009; Preskill & Brookfield, 2009). In fact, the content and delivery of early leadership education initiatives (e.g., courses, workshops, and certificate programs) as well as leadership research often reflected a focus on individual achievement, command and control approaches to influencing, and a willful blindness to issues of social stratification. All of these are antithetical to contemporary understandings of the concept.

Advancing diversity as a social value requires the transformation of leadership education. The purpose of this chapter is to provide practical advice educators can use to bring leadership education's espoused and actualized values related to social justice into greater alignment. This centralizes the concept of diversity as a social value and emphasizes the cultivation of skills associated with engaging with difference as a precursor to the work of leadership for social change. The chapter focuses on considerations specific to the design and delivery of credit-bearing leadership courses, but the concepts presented are transferable to the co-curricular arena as well through highlighted activities and advice for practical application.

Integration of Transformative Multiculturalism Into Leadership Education

At the heart of a transformative multicultural approach in leadership education is the cultivation of the knowledge and skills necessary to engage with issues of Difference. This skill set facilitates the ability to consider and eventually disrupt systemic oppression operating at the individual, institutional, and systems levels. It also aids students in recognizing and responding to the ways in which leadership as a social construct reflects broader social systems thus differentially privileging and marginalizing those who assume leadership roles and/or engage in the process of leadership.

This chapter offers techniques for infusing transformative multicultural approaches into a leadership course, but there are transferable themes for working with co-curricular leadership education as well. Similarly, the proposed approaches are not specific to graduate or undergraduate education, but are worthy of consideration regardless of educational level. Although the quantity of leadership education initiatives continues to grow exponentially (Komives, 2011), most fail to incorporate complex approaches associated with transformative multiculturalism and every opportunity for leadership learning should be grounded in these considerations.

In designing a leadership course, three principles emerge that target the cultivation of students' competence for engaging with Difference. First, socio-cultural conversations between and among peers should reflect developmental appropriateness and be infused throughout the curriculum. Second, designers should diversify the content of leadership education, including material that extends beyond and challenges the traditional and dominant narrative. Third, there must be an intentional cultivation of students' capacities for critical perspectives and critical self-reflection, preparing them to serve as conscious scholars and practitioners in their fields. This aligns with Watt's assertion in Chapter 1 of this book that we need a greater population of educators who view their role as that of conscious scholar practitioners ready to address social inequity. The sections that follow introduce each principle, connect its importance explicitly to the work of leadership education, and offer examples of how leadership courses can practically address the principle.

Infusion and Developmental Sequencing of Socio-Cultural Conversations

Socio-cultural conversations are opportunities for students to engage about or across Difference with peers. This may happen formally or informally as part of a structured course or outside the classroom. Socio-cultural conversations include a wide range of topical areas from personal and political values to identity differences (Dugan et al., 2013). This definition aligns with the framing of interactions across Difference present in the broader higher education literature.

Empirical evidence indicates that socio-cultural conversations are the single greatest predictor of leadership development in the college environment (Dugan et al., 2012; Dugan & Komives, 2010; Kodama & Dugan, 2013). Scholars suggest engagement in these types of conversations stimulate more complex cognitive reasoning as well as enhance empathy, perspective-taking skills, and the ability to engage in effective group processes. This, of course, is predicated on the assumption that students' experiences with socio-cultural conversations are positive ones. Ensuring socio-cultural conversations have a beneficial influence involves sequencing them in developmentally appropriate ways. This means accurately gauging students' psychological and intellectual preparedness and then structuring socio-cultural conversations that reflect students' starting points while pushing for a compounding of complexity in both content and process (Dugan et al., 2013; Hannah & Avolio, 2010).

An example of developmentally sequencing socio-cultural conversations involves beginning with opportunities to cultivate dialogue skills rather than assuming students already possess them. Educators should focus on differentiating discussion from dialogue, building students' abilities to recognize and respond to process (e.g., who is speaking, who is not speaking, how individuals respond to one another) as well as content, and centering conversations around less complex and/or polemic topics so students are more willing to take risks as they learn skills. As skills build students may demonstrate readiness to engage in socio-cultural conversations around more complex topics such as social stratification and its effects on leadership. This is a prime opportunity for students to explore leadership experiences through lenses of privilege (e.g., unequal access to leadership training and positional opportunities) and oppression (e.g., navigating stereotype threat, double binds when serving in positional roles). To avoid compounding complexity too rapidly an intermediate step might involve within-group conversations that facilitate empathy, solidarity, and social perspective-taking. Creating room for affinity group spaces for within-group dialogue may nurture greater vulnerability and willingness to challenge assumptions about leadership. Finally, a more advanced approach to socio-cultural conversations involves "fish bowl" structures that allow students to speak when they choose, yet require all participants to observe. Fish bowls may evolve from identity-based affinity spaces to intergroup dialogues.

The focus of any leadership course should be to stimulate socio-cultural conversations as a pervasive pedagogical tool in the delivery of curriculum. Consequently, this brings transformative multiculturalism and leadership development into direct alignment. This approach means that students are often learning about the skills and processes associated with dialogues across Difference while simultaneously engaging in them. Facilitating these types of dialogues effectively requires a high degree of comfort on the part of the instructor, which may require additional personal and professional development. Helpful resources include *Facilitating Intergroup Dialogues: Building Bridges, Catalyzing Change* (Maxwell, Nagada, Thompson, & Gurin, 2011); *Teaching for Diversity and Social Justice* (Adams, Bell, & Griffin, 2007); and *The Art of Effective Facilitation: Reflections From Social Justice Educators* (Landreman, 2013).

The actual integration of socio-cultural conversations into leadership education curriculum has been a point of struggle at times for leadership educators (Dugan et al., 2013). This struggle may be a function of the degree to which traditional approaches to leadership both reflect a dominant narrative leaving little room to challenge normative assumptions and an overemphasis on skill building for management instead of leadership grounded in social justice. The infusion of consistent socio-cultural conversations as a primary pedagogical tool requires a transformation of the leadership curriculum that creates opportunities for students to engage with one another as well as the literature, while simultaneously augmenting their skills associated with navigating Difference. The second and third principles provide concrete recommendations on how to do this.

Diversification of Content Beyond the Traditional and Dominant Narrative

Traditional and dominant narratives propagate a *singular* story typically reflecting the people, beliefs, and values of those with the societal power to frame reality. This obscures multiple perspectives and often entirely omits the lived experiences of those who do not reflect majority identities. Dominant narratives reflect someone's reality, but not the multiple realities that co-exist simultaneously, and they often serve to perpetuate systemic oppression.

The leadership literature is particularly guilty of perpetuating a dominant narrative that frequently goes unchallenged, and this narrative is proliferated in the design and delivery of leadership education interventions. This is evident in the pervasive Whiteness, masculinity, and Western-orientation of the broad leadership studies literature. For example, Western values associated with individualism often result in dominant narratives that highlight individual achievements of exemplary leaders (e.g., John F. Kennedy, Bill Gates, Abraham Lincoln), and do not equally honor the communities and people who worked alongside these leaders. Collective action and movements, however, focus on the gathering of a community that works together to create social change (e.g., the Arab Spring, Women's Suffrage Movement). Dominant narratives about leadership in the United States also typically omit the stories of women, people of color, and those from other traditionally marginalized communities. The occasional mentioning of Martin Luther King Jr. or Nelson Mandela often has a tokenizing effect; it suggests that infrequent representation is a function of the absence of impact rather than an issue of representation by those with the power to construct the narrative. The effect is a further reinforcement of the dominant narrative.

Scholars increasingly express concern with the ways in which the literature fails to center issues associated with social identity (Ayman & Korabik, 2010; Dugan, 2013; Eagly & Chin, 2010; Fassinger, Shullman, & Stevenson, 2010; Ospina & Foldy, 2009; Sanchez-Hucles & Davis, 2010), often focusing instead on international cultural differences. This is a convenient sidestep that avoids the need to deeply examine our own embeddedness in systems of oppression in the U.S. context.

The presence of a dominant narrative is also seen in the traditional presentation of leadership theory as comprising two distinct paradigms with the earlier representing industrial approaches (i.e., focus on management, productivity, and control) and the latter emerging at the end of the 1970s and representing a post-industrial approach (i.e., focus on relational processes, shared responsibility, and social change). In reality, this "paradigm shift" was largely one for socio-economically privileged White men as communities of color, women, LGBT communities, and the labor movement had long employed post-industrial approaches dismissed as either unsustainable or dangerous to the status quo. Scholars' framing of a paradigm shift in leadership theory not only reinforces the dominant narrative, but also is a form of cultural co-optation (Dugan & Komives, 2011).

The impact of the dominant narrative in leadership for many people is marginalization from leadership roles and distancing from the concept of leadership itself. Scholars particularly note women students' and students of color's reluctance to engage in leadership stemming from perceptions of *leadership* as a "dirty word" or something to which they cannot relate based on traditional definitions (Arminio et al., 2000; Balón, 2005; Boatwright & Egidio, 2003). The dominant narrative also carries with it negative consequences for those in the majority who must navigate the costs of perpetuating systemic oppression.

So, how does one begin to counter the dominant narrative present in so much of leadership education? First, and perhaps most obviously, leadership courses must move away from introducing content related to diversity and social identity as a single-week theme. Dugan et al. (2013) stress the importance of integrating content related to diversity both across the curriculum and in dedicated ways. What does this look like specifically in a course?

- We frame our course as inherently concerned with issues of social justice and grounded in diverse conceptualizations of leadership. Stating upfront that the course integrates multiculturalism-related content weekly breaks down preconceptions that diversity and leadership are separate bodies of knowledge.
- The course provides both consistent and dedicated attention to issues of diversity and justice. In our teaching of leadership, we explicitly prompt students to consider these issues through weekly reflection questions. Additionally, the course provides dedicated sessions addressing the intersections of topics such as justice, culture, gender, race, and socio-economic status with leadership. These sessions build upon one another leading to an intersectional understanding of the multiple influences of social identities on leadership.

Second, course content should include literature that purposely centers race, gender, sexual orientation, and culture. This includes diversity among authors presented in the course, the use of counter evidence that disrupts the dominant narrative, and multiple life narratives that illustrate a broad range of lived experiences that shape leadership. Note that it is critical that in restructuring course content instructors avoid using women and people of color as authors solely in sections on diversity but throughout course topics. Given many leadership educators receive little formal training for their roles (Owen, 2012), the construction of course content that can challenge the dominant narrative may feel like a challenging feat. The information that follows highlights both recommended readings and process points to consider.

- Inclusion of diverse authors in a leadership course requires instructors to understand a range of literature broader than just that belonging to the leadership development of college students. There are phenomenal scholars in public policy, gender studies, psychology, and other disciplines studying leadership in complex ways. Consider work by Grace Lee Boggs, Juana Bordas, Jean Lau Chin, Alice Eagly, Gil Hickman, Crystal Hoyt, Sonia Ospina, Janis Sanchez-Hucles, and Ronald Walters, just to name a few.

- Challenging the dominant narrative is essential. We do this in a variety of ways starting with the use of counter-evidence that is typically empirical in nature. This involves presenting a dominant narrative and coupling it with readings that provide evidence that it is flawed and/or does not adequately capture the full range of information. For example, students might read chapters from a traditional leadership text covering a range of theories. We would also have them read Ayman and Korabik's (2010) article that challenges the accuracy and applicability of the same theories when gender and culture are considered. Simultaneous use of counter-evidence complicates students' ability to accept the dominant narrative, as they do not hear one universal truth, but conflicting information. Additionally, because the work is empirical students are often less likely to dismiss it wholesale, as can happen with the use of life narratives too early in the process of disrupting normative assumptions.

- Socio-historic information can also disrupt the dominant narrative. For example, rather than beginning with a traditional timeline documenting the evolution of leadership theory based on dominant narratives, we often begin by asking students to provide historical examples of leadership focused on social change. This typically elicits responses ranging from the civil rights and women's suffrage movements to anti-war and labor movements. We then shift to a presentation of the traditional evolution of leadership and ask how that timeline aligns with students' historical examples. The exercise highlights the conflict between the dominant narrative of the emergence of post-industrial approaches to leadership and the actual history. It also calls into question why some forms of leadership possess academic "legitimacy" whereas others remain unacknowledged. This is rich fodder for disrupting students' perceptions of earned and unearned attribution as well as the ways in which systems authorize history in ways that might not reflect reality.

- We also use a diverse range of life narratives in class to draw comparisons between what the literature frames as valid and individual experiences. Life narratives provide a greater degree of representation of social identities than is typical in the dominant literature. An excellent source of narratives is *Identity and Leadership: Informing*

Our Lives, Informing Our Practice by Alicia Fedelina Chávez and Roni Sanlo (2013). Instructors may also choose to use biographies with significant themes related to leadership, although we urge caution to avoid reinforcing "great leader" perspectives grounded in personal achievement and positionality. The use of life narratives can provide a means to validate students' lived experiences with leadership and disrupt internalized messages regarding what is valued and what is not.

Diversification of the content of leadership classes serves two purposes in the pursuit of diversity as a social value. First, it provides critical content knowledge that can serve as a foundation for informed dialogues about and across Difference. Second, the content itself and the process of challenging dominant narratives is the very fodder of such discussions. Engaging purposefully with these issues undergirds the development of skills to engage with Difference.

Cultivate Students' Capacities for Critical Perspectives and Critical Self-Reflection

The third principle essential for integrating a transformative multicultural approach in leadership education involves cultivating students' capacities to adopt critical perspectives and engage in critical self-reflection (CSR). These concepts largely derive from critical social theory, which is a multidisciplinary framework focused on advancing the emancipatory role of knowledge through the examination of conflicts and contradictions associated with power, privilege, and oppression in social systems (Anyon, 2008). Preskill and Brookfield (2009) suggested the effective use of CSR involves the ability to examine "how power is distributed, how it moves around a community, organization, or movement, and the degree to which it is used responsibly or abused" (p. 42).

Any understanding of leadership requires the exploration of power and its unequal distribution in society, and critical perspectives provide a concrete way to tackle this problem (Kezar, Carducci, & Contreras-McGavin, 2006; Preskill & Brookfield, 2009). The use of a critical perspective also can counter the often aspirational and utopian character of approaches to leadership that permeate contemporary literature. These views situate leadership as inherently positive as well as value neutral. CSR also pushes individuals to consider their own positionality within systems, as well as how that position manifests itself within the context of leadership. As Preskill and Brookfield

(2009) note "without the ability to see how power and hegemony inscribe themselves in our daily actions and decisions—and to challenge how they suppress true democracy—we are at the mercy of seemingly random forces" (p. 44).

Advancing a critical approach to leadership education involves cultivating both students' meaning-making abilities and functional skills. We tackle this in a variety of ways attempting to move from skills that are more intellectual to personal considerations, and then to systems-based perspectives.

- From a more intellectual starting point, we ask students to examine various theories of leadership and deconstruct them using a critical perspective. Students are then introduced to the concept of implicit leadership theory, which suggests that there are socially constructed and culturally contingent prototypes for leadership that guide how people make meaning of the concept. These prototypes often reflect hegemonic norms associated with social identities. For example, in the United States the implicit leadership prototype typically finds grounding in strength, assertiveness, decisiveness, and other stereotypically masculine traits. What happens when a woman, for example, employs those same skills? Using prompt questions, students explore double-bind scenarios (i.e., lose if you do and lose if you do not) that emerge from the theories' inattention to these issues. A classic example of this is authentic leadership, which advocates for relational transparency (i.e., openness in relationships characterized by vulnerability, realness, and both positive and negative aspects of self). Students explore the degree to which individuals have unequal access to engaging in this and the role of systems of privilege and oppression in shaping considerably different implications for those who do. Depending on the skill level of students for interacting across Difference, the goal is to move from an intellectual conversation to one that is personalized and eventually explicitly linked to issues of systemic oppression in society.
- Beginning from a more personal lens, we attempt to build students' capacities for CSR through the exploration of group dynamics and positionality. The concept of CSR is introduced as a tool for examining group process about a quarter of the way into the semester giving enough time for patterns and norms to emerge in how the students are engaging with one another. Students silently work through a series of guided reflection questions that include (a) what patterns of communication have you observed in the class (standard reflection approach that does not take a critical perspective)?; (b) what dimensions of power and/or hegemony underlie these patterns

of communication (adding the critical component)?; (c) how does considering the critical dimension make you feel?; (d) how do the patterns you have identified make you feel (connecting to personal implications)?; and (e) what is important for you in terms of how we address these patterns moving forward? This progression provides useful comparative evidence to explore how and why students surfaced different communication patterns with or without the prompting of a critical perspective. It also provides an opportunity to dig deeply into issues of gender, race, and other social identity considerations that play out not just in terms of leadership content, but also influence the process of engaging with Difference in the classroom.

- Connecting the personal and systems lenses, we also examine the implications of oppression and privilege in shaping students' leadership efficacy (i.e., internal beliefs in one's ability to be successful engaging in leadership). This is an opportunity to explore the ways in which systemic oppression may cause students from targeted identities to internalize constraining beliefs as well as how systemic oppression may cause those from majority identities to develop unrealistic self-appraisals due to systemic privilege. The goal is to help students develop CSR as well as recognize that life circumstances are not the function of random forces. The exercise asks students to work individually through a series of questions reflecting on both positive and negative experiences from their lives that have had significant influence on their leadership efficacy. They then identify triggers that surface these empowering or constraining beliefs in their day-to-day lives even if the life experiences are ones for which they've largely come to resolution. Students are then placed in triads and asked to practice skills central to dialoguing about Difference (e.g., perspective-taking, empathy, active listening) as they share. The exercise concludes with a large group discussion of influences on leadership efficacy that reflect both individual experiences and complex systems that privilege and oppress based on social constructions along with ways individuals have built personal and collective agency.

Intentionally cultivating students' abilities to employ critical perspectives and practice CSR is essential in leadership education. Understanding the content of leadership requires the exploration of its deep embeddedness in both cultural prototypes and the distribution of power. Furthermore, critical approaches and the integration of CSR provide a platform to engage in dialogues around Difference while simultaneously sharpening students' skills to do so effectively.

Conclusion

When leadership educators are able to address the principles discussed previously in meaningful ways in a leadership curriculum, the natural result is a course predicated on and infused with socio-cultural conversations about and across Difference. The result is also a more direct alignment between the espoused and actualized values of social justice that undergird so much of contemporary leadership literature. Advancing this perspective requires that educators responsible for leadership initiatives see transformative multiculturalism as an essential dimension of their work.

References

Adams, M. J., Bell, L. A., & Griffin, P. (2007). *Teaching for diversity and social justice* (2nd ed.). New York: Routledge.

Allen, S. J., & Roberts, D. C. (2011). Our response to the question: Next steps in clarifying the language of leadership learning. *Journal of Leadership Studies, 5*(2), 63–69.

Anyon, J. (2008). *Theory and educational research: Toward critical social explanation.* New York: Routledge.

Arminio, J. L., Carter, S., Jones, S. E., Kruger, K., Lucas, N., Washington, J., . . . Scott, A. (2000). Leadership experiences of students of color. *NASPA Journal, 37,* 496–510.

Ayman, R., & Korabik, K. (2010). Why gender and culture matter. *American Psychologist, 65,* 157–170.

Balón, D. G. (2005). *Racial, ethnic, and gender differences among entering college student attitudes toward leadership, culture, and leader self-identification: A focus on Asian Pacific Americans* (Unpublished doctoral dissertation). University of Maryland. Retrieved from http://drum.lib.umd.edu/handle/1903/1776

Boatwright, K. J., & Egidio, R. K. (2003). Psychological predictors of college women's leadership aspirations. *Journal of College Student Development, 44,* 653–669.

Dugan, J. P. (2013). What is privileged in leadership texts: Differentiating between established works, popular press, and dominant narratives. *Concepts & Connections, 19*(2), 23–27.

Dugan, J. P., Kodama, C., Correia, B., & Associates. (2013). *Multi-institutional study of leadership insight report: Leadership program delivery.* College Park, MD: National Clearinghouse for Leadership Programs.

Dugan, J. P., Kodama, C. M., & Gebhardt, M. C. (2012). Race and leadership development among college students: The additive value of collective racial esteem. *Journal of Diversity in Higher Education, 5,* 174–189.

Dugan, J. P., & Komives, S. R. (2010). Influences on college students' capacity for socially responsible leadership. *Journal of College Student Development, 51,* 525–549.

Dugan, J., & Komives, S. R. (2011). Leadership theory. In S. R. Komives, J. P. Dugan, J. E. Owen, W. Wagner, C. Slack, & Associates (Eds.), *Handbook for student leadership development* (pp. 35–58). San Francisco: Jossey-Bass.

Eagly, A. H., & Chin, J. L. (2010). Diversity and leadership in a changing world. *American Psychologist, 65*, 216–224.

Fassinger, R. E., Shullman, S. L., & Stevenson, M. R. (2010). Toward an affirmative lesbian, gay, bisexual, and transgender leadership paradigm. *American Psychologist, 65*, 201–215.

Fedelina Chavez, A., & Sanlo, R. (2013). *Identity and leadership: Informing our lives, informing our practice.* Washington DC: NASPA.

Hannah, S. T., & Avolio, B. J. (2010). Ready or not: How do we accelerate the developmental readiness of leaders? *Journal of Organizational Behavior, 31*, 1181–1187.

Heifetz, R. (2010). Leadership and values. In R. A. Couto (Ed.), *Political and civic leadership: A reference handbook* (pp. 24–27). Thousand Oaks, CA: Sage.

Higher Education Research Institute. (1996). *A social change model of leadership development.* College Park, MD: National Clearinghouse for Leadership Programs.

Kezar, A. J., Carducci, R., & Contreras-McGavin, M. (2006). *Rethinking the "L" word in higher education: The revolution in research on leadership.* San Francisco: Jossey-Bass.

Kodama, C., & Dugan, J. P. (2013). Leveraging leadership efficacy in college students: Disaggregating data to examine unique predictors by race. *Equity & Excellence in Education, 46*, 184–201.

Komives, S. R. (2011). Advancing leadership education. In S. R. Komives, J. P. Dugan, J. E. Owen, W. Wagner, C. Slack, & Associates (Eds.), *Handbook for student leadership development* (pp. 1–34). San Francisco: Jossey-Bass.

Komives, S. R., Wagner, W., & Associates. (2009). *Leadership for a better world.* San Francisco: Jossey-Bass.

Landreman, L. (2013). *The art of effective facilitation: Reflections from social justice educators.* Sterling, VA: Stylus.

Maxwell, K. E., Nagada, B. R., Thompson, M. C., & Gurin, P. (2011). *Facilitating intergroup dialogues: Building bridges, catalyzing change.* Sterling, VA: Stylus.

Munin, A., & Dugan, J. P. (2011). Inclusive design in leadership program development. In S. R. Komives, J. P. Dugan, J. E. Owen, W. Wagner, C. Slack, & Associates (Eds.), *Handbook for student leadership development* (pp. 157–176). San Francisco: Jossey-Bass.

Ospina, S., & Foldy, E. (2009). A critical review of race and ethnicity in the leadership literature: Surfacing context, power and the collective dimensions of leadership. *Leadership Quarterly, 20*, 876–896.

Ospina, S., & Su, C. (2008). Weaving color lines: Race, ethnicity, and the work of leadership in social change organizations. *Leadership, 5*, 131–170.

Owen, J. E. (2012). *Findings from the multi-institutional study of leadership institutional survey.* College Park, MD: National Clearinghouse for Leadership Programs.

Preskill, S., & Brookfield, S. D. (2009). *Learning as a way of leading: Lessons from the struggle for social justice.* San Francisco: Jossey-Bass.

Sanchez-Hucles, J. V., & Davis, D. D. (2010). Women and women of color in leadership: Complexity, identity, and intersectionality. *American Psychologist, 65,* 171–181.

8

ALIGNING ACTIONS WITH CORE VALUES

Reflections of a Chief Diversity Officer and National Science Foundation ADVANCE Director on Advancing Faculty Diversity

Paulette Granberry Russell and Melissa McDaniels

> Rhetoric is not important. Actions are.
> —Nelson Mandela

I have often thought about the last fifteen years of my career as a chief diversity officer (CDO) at a large, public, research intensive university where I have the great fortune of doing work that I care passionately about—I literally wake up in the morning thinking about what lies ahead and I often go to sleep thinking about it as well. Perhaps not the best thing to do as an African American woman, with two teenagers, and a family history of high blood pressure, but, admittedly it is, who I am. I am an "advocate" and practitioner of what is often referred to as diversity work. When I was approached to consider writing this chapter, I was intrigued by the editor's goal to produce a book that was not only theoretical and research focused, but practically focused as well; I wanted on board. I have wanted to create the space and time to be reflective on the research, daily experiences, individuals, partners, allies, and organizational units that contribute to advancing diversity within the academy. This work cannot be done alone. As good as one may think she is, it takes support from those who are just as committed to move beyond rhetoric. Six years ago an opportunity to work on a National Science Foundation ADVANCE grant occurred and with that a new journey of discovery with Melissa, the program director and ally began.

—Paulette Granberry Russell, JD

Engaging in social activism around issues of equity and inclusion run in my blood. As a third generation PhD, White queer woman from a middle-class background, I had the good fortune of being witness to my grandfather—a White engineer from Pennsylvania with a PhD—engage in activism on issues of peace and justice, racial and gender equality, and fair labor practices up until he died at 91 years old. In the late '80s I had the privilege of meeting, collaborating, and studying with Dr. Taylor Cox, a leading scholar and thinker about creating inclusive workplaces. In the early 1990s I developed and taught the first course on diversity in the workplace at Boston College. I continued to be involved in training others to do this work in my many roles—faculty member, academic administrator—over the past two decades. More importantly (to me), I invest a lot in understanding my own privilege and marginalities, and how my own positionality impacts how I behave and how my behavior impacts others. When I accepted the job as director of Michigan State University's ADVANCE grant in 2008, I was thrilled for the first time to have a full-time job supporting an institution to diversify its workforce. My relationship with my colleague and ally Paulette is one of the most important outcomes of my 4½ years with ADVANCE. It is a privilege to have the opportunity to reflect upon on our work in this way.

—Melissa McDaniels, PhD

Introduction

"This grant is about women," asserted one of the grant leadership team members. "Women are not monolithic," responded Paulette. This interchange occurred at an early ADVANCE leadership meeting at Michigan State. We did not know each other well at this moment—we were friendly but our relationship was not built on the firm foundation of trust that it is today. After these statements were made, tension filled the room. Melissa, ADVANCE director and convener of the meeting, thinking Paulette made a terrific point, jumped in and said, "I think what Paulette was trying to say was . . . ." Melissa thought what she needed to do was to "help" and re-emphasize what Paulette said—maybe it was, she thought to herself, a case of people around the table just not hearing or listening. Much to Melissa's surprise, Paulette responded, "I don't need White women speaking for me."

The work we both do is not just *work*, it is our *life's work*. Our own identities—our subjectivities—permeate our professional commitments to diversity and inclusion. As such, we chose to open this chapter with our individual voices as well as a description of a pivotal moment that we both believe changed the course of Michigan State's ADVANCE grant, as well as marked the beginning of a trusting and powerful partnership that is built upon our differences as much as our similarities.

The purpose of this chapter is to share a journey through the eyes of a chief diversity officer (CDO) and a strategic partner and program director of a five-year National Science Foundation (NSF) project to advance faculty diversity using strategies, tactics, legal constructs, social capital, evolving research, and promising practices that are designed to not only "level the playing field" but create a *new* playing field. We begin with the role of affirmative action in setting the stage for workplace equality broadly, and early attempts to foster change with some success. We introduce an organizational change model that served as a foundation for the NSF ADVANCE institutional transformation grant at Michigan State University (MSU), led by the Provost of the University (Principal Investigator) and strategic administrators and faculty on the project's leadership team. Our project utilized a strategic human resource management framework and focused on aligning academic human resource policies and practices with the core values of our institution. We share lessons learned along the way, along with advice for leaders or those who desire to actively engage in advancing faculty diversity.

Historical Legal Context of Affirmative Action

It would be impossible to write about higher education's valuing of diversity and faculty excellence without acknowledging the role of affirmative action in advancing these values. Affirmative action is one of the tools necessary to achieve racial, ethnic, and gender diversity within narrowly prescribed strategies. As federal contractors, we are required to have employment affirmative action programs.

After the 1954 Supreme Court's *Brown v. Board of Education* decision, efforts to make access, equality, and full citizenship a reality for minorities were undertaken. Black students were not graduating from high school in any significant numbers, and in 1940, less than 2% had a college degree. Without adequate education and skills, access to higher-paying occupations was limited to very few Blacks (Bowen & Bok, 1998). After years of struggle to create laws to protect the civil rights of U.S. Blacks and other minorities, President Lyndon B. Johnson signed the Civil Rights Act of 1964, which prohibited discrimination against persons on the basis of their race, color, religion, sex, or national origin. Employment discrimination was prohibited under Title VII of the 1964 Civil Rights Act. Deliberate equal opportunity and affirmative action efforts in employment, contracting of services, and education were being implemented and guided by federal and state regulations.

Signed by President Johnson in 1965, Executive Order 11246 prescribed the steps federal contractors, including colleges and universities, needed to take to ensure not only nondiscrimination in employment, but "take affirmative action to ensure that applicants are employed, and that employees are treated during employment without regard to their race, creed, color, or national origin. Such action shall include . . . employment, upgrading, demotion, or transfer; recruitment or recruitment advertising; layoff or termination; rates of pay or other forms of compensation."

Eliminating the effects of past discrimination in employment and education began in earnest because of the Civil Rights movement of the 1950s and after the passage of the 1964 Civil Rights Act. However, the challenges to such efforts have been just as vigorous. As case law evolved interpreting Title VII and the Fourteenth Amendment's Equal Protection Clause, the circumstances for using race as a consideration in employment and admissions decisions withstood the most rigorous of scrutiny by the judiciary. This became particularly apparent as the Supreme Court addressed the use of race in undergraduate and law school admissions (*Regents of the Univ. of Cal. v. Bakke*, 1978; *Gratz v. Bollinger*, 2003; *Fisher v. Univ. of Texas at Austin*, 2013; *Grutter v. Bollinger*, 2003).

Resultantly, current challenges to diversity efforts within the United States include long-standing tensions between both racial minorities and Whites as well as amongst men and women. The changing societal values regarding the role of religion in society, sexual orientation and gender identity, and other domestic and international debates are on the minds and in the hearts of students, faculty, and staff in our institutions.

Justifications for continuing affirmative action and other programs to achieve diversity in higher education include the need to correct the effects of past discrimination, prevent future discrimination (both intentional acts and acts that have a discriminatory effect), and the belief that organizations benefit from inclusion and diversity (Edley, 1996). Proponents point to the success of affirmative action and research findings that a racially and ethnically diverse student body has significant benefits for all students. For example, researchers have found that students in diverse environments benefit from improved critical thinking skills, and that such settings alter the persistence of racial separation in American society (Gurin, 1999). Research also supports that students benefit from racial and ethnic diversity of peers, but also in the faculty and staff (antonio, 2003).

Opponents of affirmative action argue that it is itself a form of unlawful discrimination and that it stigmatizes all members of the benefited minority group and women, and therefore, perpetuates stereotypes that minorities are not as capable as Whites, or women are not as competent as men. Finally, opponents argue that continued emphasis on race-conscious efforts in the United States does not allow our society to move beyond racial differences.

This difference in position on affirmative action led to a number of legal challenges and resulted in a closer examination of the benefits of diversity (Connerly, 2006 ; *Gratz v. Bollinger*, 2003; *Ricci v. DeStefano*, 2009).

Advancing diversity in higher education requires an understanding of the legal constraints to such efforts, whether it is the continued use of affirmative action in employment, or diversifying the student body, and the need to collaborate with various stakeholders within the college or university (Russell et al., 2013). Institutions that are successful in diversifying their campuses have approached diversity initiatives in a comprehensive manner.

Why choose to focus on the faculty? As the readers of this chapter likely understand, the work of the faculty (and quality thereof) directly affects the ability of institutions to serve their primary stakeholder (students), remain financially stable, and contribute to the local, regional, national, and international communities within which these institutions reside. Faculty members provide quality teaching and mentoring to undergraduate and graduate students, pursue and receive research funding for scholarly research, participate in faculty governance and other institutional service activity, and contribute to the well-being of communities through community-based research and outreach activity. This broad-sweeping impact of the faculty role helps us understand why an institution's ability to retain and nurture a diverse faculty will have strategic importance for the institution. The faculty role is regarded as a help or hindrance in diversifying our campuses and our actions must begin to speak more loudly than our words. Institutions must understand the need for campus climates that support diverse faculty, staff, and students and assess the campus climate to understand better how the campus community perceives the institution to hold the leadership accountable. These efforts have led to significant gains in the participation of minorities, women, and other underrepresented groups in higher education. Yet, significant challenges remain.

Given the persistent underrepresentation of women faculty and faculty of color on our campuses, it is reasonable to ask, why, after almost 50 years of federally required efforts, have we seen so little progress? The opposite question may be just as appropriate: Would we have seen greater progress without these laws and policies? There is no way of knowing the answer to this question, however, because discrimination and both conscious and unconscious bias still exist (Dasgupta, 2012). Systems of inequality operate over time to advantage some individuals and disadvantage others (Shuford, 2009). Affirmative action is intended to dismantle persistent structural inequalities in recruiting, hiring, advancement, and retention of diverse faculty. What is clear is that we either miscalculated the resistance to the tool, or underestimated how deeply embedded and reinforced the structural inequalities had become over time and misjudged the benign or overt tactics that would aid in their maintenance.

Organizational Change Model and the CDO as a Catalyst for Change

Too often, the work of many CDOs is reactive, with little time (and resources) available to think strategically about achieving the institutions' desired outcomes related to diversity and inclusion, including increasing the representation of women faculty and faculty of color. Perhaps this is a result of defining the work in the earlier years as increasing the numbers of underrepresented groups on our campuses, and ignoring the need also to understand the complexities associated with recruiting, hiring, advancing, and retaining a diverse workforce. CDOs are required to attend to challenges such as responding to individual faculty (staff and student) needs and concerns, providing support to administrators who need counsel, monitoring and assessing institutional goals, and attending to internal and external constituencies. Strategic diversity leadership in this context requires more. One cannot simply assume that just increasing minority hires will solve the "problem." If it were that simple, the academy could have erased not only the underrepresentation of women faculty and faculty of color throughout higher education, but the other associated issues that are a part of the daily work of CDOs as well. Those associated issues include challenges facing women faculty and faculty of color such as undervaluing their research interests, questioning their credentials and intellect in the classroom, maneuvering tenure and promotion all while combatting feelings of isolation and marginalization. The fact is while we have made progress over the last 50 years, the barriers to increasing faculty diversity are entrenched, complex, and considerable.

The challenges of a CDO involving workforce diversity include hiring, retaining, and advancing a diverse faculty while simultaneously shifting the institutional culture from representational diversity by the numbers to structural change. The entire institution must move beyond the rhetoric of diversity and inclusion toward it being a fundamental value. Using new tools and strategies, institutions must dismantle barriers to inclusion, and articulate as well as reinforce accountability measures.

At the 2002 University of Minnesota Symposium entitled *Keeping Our Faculties: Addressing the Recruitment and Retention of Faculty of Color*, there was a session with a presentation that focused on the work that had begun in earnest within our office to identify and implement new strategies to diversify the faculty. The session, *Creating Greater Diversity in the Halls of Ivy*, outlined proactive, evidence-based strategies developed between 1999 and 2002 to assist academic units in the recruitment of faculty of color and women. In early 1999 we began to recalibrate the work of the office from a regulatory, "affirmative action compliance" role to an office that was regarded as a resource in support of unit efforts to hire for faculty excellence and diversity through aggressive, creative recruitment and providing the provost and deans with data that reflects the outcomes of expanded unit efforts. We developed a searchable web-based resource containing links to online resources for recruiting and advertising faculty and academic staff positions that were discipline specific and targeted diverse candidates by discipline. Staff within the office began working one-on-one with search committees on their recruitment strategies. We developed a "practical tips and resources" guide building on the literature regarding diversifying the faculty that included information on ways to enlarge and diversify applicant pools, screening for diversity, conducting an objective interview process, and communications with candidates during and after the interview process (Knowles & Harelston, 1997; Smith, Wolf, Busenberg & Associates, 1996). Our goal, at that time, was to bring life to the research that addressed the issues of faculty diversity and demonstrate how the work to recruit new faculty using structured hiring processes that recognized the value of diversity as an institutional priority could yield positive outcomes. We were able to demonstrate, through the assessment of the various identified approaches, that using evidence-based strategies produced expanded recruitment efforts determining an increased diversity in the applicant and candidate interview pools and in the number of women and minorities hired during a three-year period. During that same period, the institution saw declines in the overall number of faculty hired.

Then, as now, diversifying the faculty requires institutions to look closely at the effectiveness of the hiring processes, as well as the efficiency of the various offices, including academic units and the work of search committees to advance diversity. Institutions must also make it a regular practice to define metrics and use data to begin holding faculty and leadership accountable for getting the work done. In 2008, an article in the *Journal of Diversity in Higher Education*, entitled "Faculty of Color in Academe: What 20 Years of Literature Tells Us," presented a literature review and synthesis of 252 publications addressing the status and experience of faculty of color who continue to be seriously underrepresented as full-time faculty in the academy (Turner, Gonzalez, & Wood, 2008). Similar observations have been made about women, particularly the abysmal representation of women in the sciences, technology, engineering, and mathematics (STEM) (National Research Council,

2007). As noted by Turner, Gonzalez, and Wood, we must have faculty (and staff) who are active in preparing all students for a diverse society (antonio, 2002; Stanley, 2006; Umbach, 2006); and having a diverse faculty has been shown to contribute to student success (Hagedorn, Chi, Cepeda, & McLain, 2007). As the literature indicates, advancing faculty diversity is confounded by numerous, complex factors, and the work of a university CDO is one of advocating change at the institutional level—that must by necessity occur based on data, evolving research, and an understanding of organizational design and change management.

The role of the CDO in higher education has evolved significantly since being defined by D.A. Williams and Wade-Golden (2006) as "the 'face' of diversity efforts [that] carry formal administrative titles like vice provost, vice chancellor, associate provost, vice president, assistant provost, dean, or special assistant to the president for multicultural, international, equity, diversity, and inclusion" (p. 1). CDOs in higher education are also regarded as change agents within their respective institutions, who take on the challenging task of creating a diverse and inclusive work and learning environment for faculty, staff, and students (Williams & Wade-Golden, 2007). The work of the CDO is not a role for the faint of heart, nor a role that can simply be played and cast off when the work becomes frustrating because of the lack of progress or because of the inevitable resistance to change. The CDO function is a senior executive function that includes committed individuals and scholars in related fields (e.g., multicultural affairs, gender or ethnic studies). However, if they are not seasoned practitioners in the field of diversity leadership, or have not previously held administrative positions, they will struggle to manage the varied and complex tasks and responsibilities. Failure to recognize the changing nature of the role is an injustice to "the work" and only frustrates the ultimate goal of creating structural and systemic change.

Academic units must engage differently if the academy is to see sustainable change in faculty demographics and achieve work environments that are welcoming and supportive of diverse faculty. The CDO, in partnership with senior academic leadership and other strategic partners, can influence diversity efforts through evidence-based research. In this partnership, they can make change by providing support services (e.g., faculty development on recruiting for faculty excellence and diversity; facilitate understanding on the impact of bias in evaluation of faculty in hiring, promotion, and tenure; and mini-grants for faculty diversity initiatives); monitoring and reporting on unit progress in achieving identified goals; and troubleshooting problems and conflicts.

It is also critically important to recognize that while the CDO may be centrally responsible for diversity and inclusion efforts the CDO is not solely responsible for this critical work (Williams & Wade-Golden, 2013). Many want to do the work out of a sense of commitment and passion for social justice, but increasingly senior executive CDOs must also possess the ability to influence the broader strategic interests. This includes conveying the vision and plans of their institutions; engaging senior administrative staff; possessing organizational leadership skills; utilizing data and metrics to establish goals and track progress; and understanding public relations and possessing effective communication skills. In the absence of such skills, talents, and professional experience, the daily frustrations and snail-like pace of change will disillusion many. The role of the CDO in higher education is gaining greater acceptance during a time when the United States is experiencing a downturn in the national economy, resulting in defunding at the state and national level of higher education. It is important to find ways to show how the role is increasingly important for institutions to retrench and to find new sources of funding even amidst intervening lawsuits and other state-level initiatives challenging race- and gender-conscious strategies to diversify post-secondary education. The work to influence structural change and align workplace equality with institutional values of diversity and inclusion has become even more complex.

A New Organizational Change Model: One CDO's Influence on the Broader Strategic Interests of a University and the Beginning of Our Collaboration

Eliminating barriers and bias that impact the representation of women in STEM requires intentionality and strategic efforts by higher education (National Research Council, 2007). In support of higher education efforts to increase the participation of women in STEM, the ADVANCE program was established by the NSF in 2001. In 2008, the NSF's ADVANCE program awarded Michigan State University a $3.98 million grant to assist us in our efforts to recruit, retain, and advance women and underrepresented minorities in the STEM fields. With these funds, Michigan State University launched the ADAPP Initiative—Advancing Diversity through the Alignment of Policy and Practices (principal investigators [PIs]: Kim Wilcox, Terry Curry, Estelle McGroarty, Mark Roehling, Tamara Reid Bush, and Clare Luz). This project was designed to test a unique conceptual model (Arthur & Doverspike, 2005; Dyer & Ericksen, 2005; Evans, Pucik, & Barsoux, 2002; Gratton & Truss, 2003) addressing how increased structure of supportive employment practices and their alignment with the institutional values of diversity and inclusion will lead to an increasingly diverse and high quality faculty workforce.

Melissa was hired as director of this initiative charged with convening key stakeholders (PIs, CDO, others) needed to achieve grant goals, overseeing the budget, and leading grant strategic planning efforts. Melissa was not involved in writing the grant and was not a Co-PI. As CDO, Paulette was involved in the reviewing of the various drafts of the grant, but was not a Co-PI, nor initially a member of the grant management team. Based on the role of the CDO's office in the institutional transformation process expected under the grant, the CDO was subsequently added to the grant management team.

What did we learn about our progress? We realized early that the initiative needed to place an emphasis on data-driven changes and decision-making. As such, in Years 1 and 2 of the project, our evaluation team collected data from both individual faculty and department chairs to get their *perceptions* of the objectivity, transparency, and consistent implementation of faculty search, annual review, and reappointment, promotion, and tenure. We also reviewed retention, promotion, and tenure (RP&T) policies and practices (this was done through a work-environment survey), as well as a baseline of actual faculty search, annual review, and RP&T practices (as reported by department chairs in a set of policy and practice inventories). We discovered inconsistent implementation (across MSU colleges) of existing policies and practices, as well as varying reports of perceived transparency of these policies and practices. From Paulette's perspective as CDO, there were no surprises in these initial findings. However, having the weight and resources of the NSF behind the effort gave immediate credibility to the findings and allowed the grant management team to leverage the data to advocate for policy and procedural changes.

Not surprisingly, any differences between majority and minority faculty (in the work-environment survey) were impossible to ascertain (statistically) due to small sample sizes. In Years 3, 4, and 5, an in-depth qualitative study, led by our CDO and a tenured faculty member, was initiated to more deeply understand the department climates at MSU, from the perspective of underrepresented faculty of color at the institution. In seeking to identify factors that impact tenure and promotion, grant team members, including the CDO, also studied how external funding patterns influenced the relationship between research and RP&T, gender differences in grant activity, and gender differences in retention and promotion (McGroarty et al., 2014).

As a result of this data collected during the early years of the grant, and existing institutional data analytics of the faculty workforce, we created an agreed-upon set of metrics to be used by the provost to assess the progress of each college (not just STEM colleges) on diversity goals. Thus, part of the impact that the ADVANCE grant had at MSU was to help the institution's leadership move closer to an agreed-upon set of metrics and ongoing data collection protocols to help MSU institutionalize an ongoing process of evaluation and review of our progress recruiting, retaining, and advancing women and underrepresented faculty.

In addition to a data-intensive strategy, MSU also recognized holes in its supportive employment practices. As a result, we wrote and adopted a new university-wide mentoring policy (*Michigan State University Faculty Mentoring Policy*, 2011). The purpose of having such a policy was to provide an explicit expectation that all colleges "implement a formal mentoring program" to "help the university achieve its goals for a high-quality faculty, diversity, inclusive excellence and a respectful, positive work environment in which all members of the university community can thrive" (*Michigan State University Faculty Mentoring Policy*, 2011). The policy directed each college at the institution (e.g., Engineering, Natural Sciences, Social Science) to incorporate mentoring programs with a set of shared principles, but allowed for a variety of programmatic structures (according to unit-specific needs and norms). Central to this new policy was the idea that effective mentoring across differences was key to faculty success. This was not explicitly emphasized as a value prior to the grant, but including it in the mentoring toolkit led to a number of new initiatives such as faculty development programs that emphasize tactics for effective mentoring of women and faculty of color.

After reviewing the results from Year 1 of the project, our team recognized the degree to which faculty (broadly) did not know about or understand important academic human resource policies. As such, the ADAPP team developed, designed, and distributed a set of faculty toolkits[1] to create easier and broader access to both content of the policies as well as what these policies actually meant for the day-to-day lives of faculty. The team saw the production of these toolkits as a seemingly "basic" intervention (and not core to the project). However, they became a very visible and symbolic contribution of the project—they provided transparency and access to these otherwise dry policies. The toolkits contained both the actual policy as well as checklists for individual faculty, unit directors, and department chairs to use as they implemented or experienced the implementation of these policies.

For these new data-gathering strategies, supportive human resource policies, and new toolkits to make a difference in the lives of faculty at the department level, faculty themselves needed to lead and visibly promote the use of these resources. Knowing that staff in the Office of the Provost or CDO is not embedded in academic units on a day-to-day basis, we established the position of Faculty Excellence Advocate (FEA) in all colleges (not just STEM) across the institution. As originally conceived, each FEA was to serve as "a link between the College Dean's Office and the departments in providing input, guidance and resources to units on academic human resource procedures to ensure that these processes are objective, consistent and inclusive, and evaluation criteria used in faculty recruitment, retention, and advancement are aligned with the goals of the unit, college and university" (Michigan State University Faculty Excellence Advocate Position Description, 2009). The FEA role became instrumental to our process of *aligning* department-level policies and practices with the university-level policies and core values (at MSU, these values include quality, inclusiveness, and connectivity).

Faculty members do not receive training in inclusive human resource practice in graduate school. As a result, the role of the Office of the CDO and other support units on campus is critical to ensuring the effectiveness of these faculty leaders. At MSU, we spent significant time and resources helping FEAs and chairs learn how to: (a) conduct academic hiring and search processes; (b) mentor across differences; (c) develop faculty as leaders (in disciplines and institutional units); (d) minimize the role of bias (conscious and unconscious) in faculty hiring and promotion practices; and (e) create inclusive work environments.

We have used the NSF's support to help us build a solid foundation for structural change. However, it is now that the real work begins (again). Susan Sturm (2006) in her article "The Architecture of Inclusion" very aptly foreshadowed the future of this work at Michigan State University:

> A crucial step in this work is the move to institutions as the focus of analysis and intervention (as compared to the more conventional emphasis on individuals, groups, or policy). Interventions aimed at institutional practice have traction to improve the conditions shaping individuals' experiences and to connect local experimentation to national networks. Institutions, such as universities and their constituent departments, organize individuals' decision-making and activities. They shape how individuals participate in their workplace, and they manage the relationship of individuals to the broader profession and society. They often operate within a network of similar institutions, such as other universities, disciplines, and professional associations. Institutions are both lasting and permeable. They mediate how norms and policies are translated into practice. They are an important location for cultural meaning-making and for producing sustainable change.

Conclusion: Lessons Learned and Advice for Leaders and Change Agents

As this project winds down, there are many lessons learned—both personal and professional—that are relevant not only in the context of the grant project, but for sustainable structural change in achieving faculty excellence and diversity, and inclusiveness within the institution.

Integrate the Expertise of the CDO Early

CDOs, being on the front line, must be an integral member of the project team from start (proposal writing, planning meetings, etc.) to finish, and as a member of the team, one must bring his or her expertise, political savvy, networks, and office resources to the project to be regarded as a relevant "player" and "change agent." At the same time, the CDO must empower known allies (grant directors, faculty, and other administrators) who can also play a role in advocating for the mission of the project and the values and strategic aims of the office of the CDO.

Understand and Learn From What Came Before

Grant directors and grant authors must take the initiative to educate themselves about the years of effort the institution has taken prior to the award of the high-profile grant and the current efforts undertaken outside the grant umbrella. They must go beyond educating themselves; they must utilize this knowledge to inform strategic choices throughout the grant implementation period. They need to demonstrate respect for this historical work by engaging in real collaboration with the CDO and other colleagues working to promote inclusive practice, as well as by creating opportunities to make these collaborations visible. The need to implement these lessons learned is even more important when the CDO has not been integrated into the development and implementation of the project from the very beginning (see previous paragraph).

Build and Deepen Alliances

The project has the potential of transforming the institution if specific increases in structure will bring about changes in the work environment and perceived climate for women faculty and faculty of color through improved communication, increasing transparency, providing consistency, and adding measures of accountability in the employment processes. However, overcoming skepticism, cynicism, biases, and for some a resignation that "nothing is going to change" requires the CDO to be the diversity "champion" while engaging with strategic partners in continual efforts to create cultural change at the department level across campus—the places that climate and culture are most immediately experienced by faculty. If the grant leadership team is composed of faculty from around campus (this is often the case in NSF ADVANCE initiatives), they must publicly align the content and spirit of communication and interventions with the values and mission of the CDO and his or her colleagues. Individuals and the team as a whole must position themselves as a key ally to the CDO's office.

Accountability Matters

Structural change through a strategic human resource management (strategic HRM) approach is widely viewed as a "best practice" for promoting desired behavior and attitudes, increasing accountability, and reducing bias in faculty employment decisions. No other NSF institutional transformation grant has used this operational framework to advance project goals. The principles of strategic HRM are not inconsistent with the principles of affirmative action programs to remedy the effects of past discrimination, through consistency (or assuring that all employees/faculty are treated equitably), transparency (or assuring that the "rules of the game" are apparent to all), and adding measures of accountability that can influence substantive change and reduce bias and discrimination, which in turn enhances faculty excellence and diversity.

Administrators and Faculty Development: Doing the Work

While embracing the strategic HRM approach, make sure to not neglect the important role the CDO and his or her colleagues play in training faculty members and administrators at the institution on important topics such as implicit bias. People ultimately implement new policies and practices, and research has demonstrated the role that implicit bias plays in academic human resource practices such as hiring, annual review, and promotion and tenure (Dasgupta, 2012). It is also important that each collaborator engage in a rigorous examination of his or her own privileges and marginalities, and reflect upon how one's positionality impacts behaviors, assumptions, and interaction with others.

Build the Capacity of Others to Support an Inclusive Work Environment

Building the capacity of others to be responsible partners and leaders in diversity efforts beyond the CDO and his or her office must be regarded as a strategic imperative if we are to improve the work environment for diversity on our campuses that in turn will advance faculty excellence and diversity. This takes both patience and explicit intervention to build the capacity of colleagues not immersed in the day-to-day work of diversity initiatives on campus (e.g., faculty).

Support From the Top Matters

Challenges to the work are real, varied, and exist at all levels within an organization. Strategic diversity leadership can also exist within all levels of the organization, but leadership must be visible, consistently on message regarding the value of diversity and inclusion, and build accountability measures in employment processes if we are to succeed in changing the culture of the academy. The CDO must particularly encourage presidents, chancellors, provosts, and deans, to actively engage in strategic diversity leadership. While it has been Paulette's responsibility as a CDO to be a leader of change and articulate why underrepresentation and underparticipation by diverse members of our community is a problem that warrants sustained attention, it is a shared responsibility for achieving inclusiveness with those in a position to have an impact.

Be Strategic: Structural Change Does Not Happen Overnight

Organizations are, in the end, made of up people. The hard work we put into "walking the walk," being open to new approaches, and building deep trusting relationships with each other and other team members is not just invaluable—it is absolutely necessary. The real work continues!

Note

1. http://www.adapp-advance.msu.edu/annual-performance-review-tenure-system-toolkit; http://www.adapp-advance.msu.edu/Faculty-Mentoring-Toolkit; http://www.adapp-advance.msu.edu/Faculty-Search-Toolkit; http://www.adapp-advance.msu.edu/resource/reappointment-promotion-and-tenure-toolkit

References

antonio, a. l. (2002). Faculty of color reconsidered: Reassessing contributions to scholarship. *Journal of Higher Education, 73*, 582–602.

antonio, a. l. (2003). Diverse student bodies, diverse faculties: The success or failure of ambitions to diversify faculty can depend on the diversity of student bodies. *Academe, 89*(6), 14–18.

Arthur Jr., W., & Doverspike, D. (2005). Achieving diversity and reducing discrimination in the workplace through human resource management practices: Implications of research and theory for staffing, training, and rewarding performance. In R. L. Dipboye & A. Colella (Eds.), Discrimination at work: *The psychological and organizational bases* (pp. 305–327). San Francisco: Jossey-Bass.

Bowen, W. G., & Bok, D. (1998). *The shape of the river: Long-term consequences of considering race in college and university admissions.* Princeton, NJ: Princeton University Press.

Connerly, W. (2006). *With liberty and justice for all.* Retrieved from http://www
.heritage.org/research/lecture/with-liberty-and-justice-for-all

Dasgupta, N. (2012). *Mind bugs: How implicit bias affects faculty evaluations in academia* [PowerPoint slides]. Retrieved from http://www.adapp-advance.msu.edu/
implicit-bias-resources

Dyer, L., & Ericksen, J. (2005). In pursuit of marketplace agility: Applying precepts
of self-organizing systems to optimize human resource scalability. *Human Resource
Management, 44,* 183–188. doi:10.1002/hrm.20062

Edley, C. (1996). *Not all black and white: Affirmative action and American values.*
New York: Hill and Wang.

Evans, P., Pucik, V., & Barsoux, J. (2002). *The global challenge: Frameworks for international human resource management.* New York: McGraw-Hill/Irwin.

Fisher v. Univ. of Texas at Austin, 133 S. Ct. 2411 (2013).

Gratton, L., & Truss, C. (2003). The three-dimensional people strategy: Putting
human resources policies into action. *Academy of Management Executive, 17*(3),
74–86.

Gratz v. Bollinger, 539 U.S. 244 (2003).

Grutter v. Bollinger, 539 U.S. 306 (2003).

Gurin, P. (1999). Expert report of Patricia Gurin. In *The compelling need for diversity
in higher education,* presented in *Gratz* v. *Bollinger* and *Grutter* v. *Bollinger.* Washington DC: Wilmer, Cutler, and Pickering.

Hagedorn, L. S., Chi, W. Y., Cepeda, R. M., & McLain, M. (2007). An investigation
of critical mass: The role of Latino representation in the success of urban community college students. *Research in Higher Education, 4,* 73–91.

Knowles, M. F., & Harleston, B. W. (1997). *Achieving diversity in the professoriate:
Challenges and opportunities.* Washington, DC: American Council on Education,
and New York: Ford Foundation.

McGroarty, E., Jimenez, T. R., Linley, J., Li, Y., Russell, P. G., & Williams, K. P.
(2014). External funding: Impact of promotion and retention of STEM assistant
professors. *Journal of Academic and Business Ethics, 8.* Retrieved from http://www
.aabri.com/manuscripts/131645.pdf, pp. 1-16

Michigan State University Faculty Excellence Advocate Position Description. (2009).
Retrieved from http://www.adapp-advance.msu.edu/faculty-excellence-advocate-
position-description

Michigan State University Faculty Mentoring Policy. (2011). Retrieved from http://
www.hr.msu.edu/documents/facacadhandbooks/facultyhandbook/mentoring.
htm

National Research Council. (2007). *Beyond bias and barriers: Fulfilling the potential of women in academic science and engineering.* Washington DC: The National
Academies Press.

Regents of the Univ. of Cal. v. Bakke, 438 U.S. 265 (1978).

Ricci v. DeStefano, 557 U.S. 557 (2009).

Russell, P. G., Kilkenny, R. E., Ervin, A. W., Worthington, R. L., Rhys, R. S. A.,
& Reese, B. D. (2013). *Chief diversity officers: Leading and engaging in campus*

deliberations post-Fisher admissions strategies. Retrieved from http://www.nadohe
.org/public-policy#fisher

Shuford, R. T. (2009). Why affirmative action remains essential in the Age of
Obama. *Campbell Law Review, 31*, 503.

Smith, D. G., Wolf, L. E., Busenberg, B., & Associates. (1996). *Achieving faculty
diversity: Debunking the myths: A research report of a national study*. Washington
DC: Association of American Colleges and Universities.

Stanley, C. A. (2006). Coloring the academic landscape: Faculty of color breaking
the silence in predominantly White colleges and universities. *American Educational Research Journal, 43*, 701–736.

Sturm, S. P. (2006). The architecture of inclusion: Advancing workplace equity in
higher education. *Harvard Journal of Law & Gender, 29*(2), Columbia Public Law
Research Paper No. 06-114. Available at SSRN: http://ssrn.com/abstract=901992

Turner, C. S. V., Gonzalez, J. C., & Wood, J. L. (2008). Faculty of color in academe:
What 20 years of literature tells us. *Journal of Diversity in Higher Education, 1*(3),
139–168.

Umbach, P. D. (2006). The contribution of faculty of color to undergraduate education. *Research in Higher Education, 47*, 317–345.

Williams, D. A., & Wade-Golden, K. C. (2006, April 18). What is a chief diversity
officer? *Inside Higher Ed*. Retrieved from http://www.scribd.com/doc/14860557/
What-is-a-Chief-Diversity-Officer-by-Dr-Damon-A-Williams-and-Dr-Katrina-
Wade-Golden#scribd

Williams, D. A., & Wade-Golden, K. C. (2007). *The chief diversity officer: A primer
for college and university presidents*. Washington DC: American Council on
Education.

Williams, D. A., & Wade-Golden, K. C. (2013). *The chief diversity officer: Strategy,
structure, and change management*. Sterling, VA: Stylus.

9

CREATING INCLUSIVE ORGANIZATIONS

One Student Affairs Division's Efforts to Create Sustainable, Systemic Change

Kathy Obear and Shelly Kerr

M ost U.S. colleges and universities continue to experience increasing student diversity (Harper, 2008; Manning & Muñoz, 2011; Talbot, 2003), while also facing intensifying pressure to improve the academic success, persistence, and graduation of all students. Additionally, employers demand that students graduate with the skills and competencies to be successful leaders in increasingly diverse, global environments (Hart Research Associates, 2010; Hart Research Associates, 2013; Williams, 2013). To meet these challenges, colleges and universities must be better prepared to respond to the needs of all students across the full range of intersecting group identities (Talbot, 2003). Unfortunately, many campuses appear to fall short of this goal as campus cultures and climates continue to be unwelcoming and "chilly," (Whitt, Edison, Pascarella, Nora, & Terenzini, 1999) if not hostile, to members of historically underrepresented and underserved groups. In addition, too many students across all group identities do not yet fully demonstrate the depth of critical thinking, perspective taking, and multicultural competence required to work effectively on diverse teams that serve the increasingly diverse domestic and global populations.

The unexamined beliefs, norms, and preferences of privileged groups have become systemically, often unconsciously, embedded in daily policies, practices, and services in many student affairs divisions resulting in the privileging of dominant group members, the perpetuation of inequity, and the reproduction of oppression (Harper & antonio, 2008; Manning & Muñoz, 2011; Strange & Stewart, 2011). Campus change efforts have focused primarily on individual development through skill building and consciousness-raising activities. This focus on the individual tends to restrict these efforts to micro-level change (Pope & LePeau, 2012), and is an example of the "diversity as social good" approach which requires only a surface understanding and examination of systemic oppression (Watt, 2011). Whereas these efforts are necessary, they are not sufficient to create and sustain inclusive campus environments that advance the academic success of all students (Jackson, 2005; Jackson & Hardiman, 1994; Marchesani & Jackson, 2005). Increasing compositional diversity does not necessarily result in the necessary organizational culture change (Stewart, 2011). It reflects a sort of "magical thinking" on the part of participants (Chang, Chang, & Ledesma, 2005), a belief that the current campus climate and structures will support the academic success of the increasingly diverse student body without significant, systemic efforts to address the persistent, pervasive discrimination, alienation, and exclusion many members of marginalized groups experience on campus. It is imperative that all student affairs professionals develop the capacity and competence to lead macro-level organizational change efforts (Pope & LePeau, 2012). These efforts must address not only the systemic sources of inequity and oppression (Watt, 2011), but also transform organizational policies, practices, programs, and services to be fully responsive to the needs of all students across multiple, intersecting group identities (Manning & Muñoz, 2011).

What Is an Inclusive Campus?

It is important that campus leaders develop a clear, shared understanding of what both diversity and inclusion mean for their specific organization. The authors define an *inclusive organization* as one where students, staff, and faculty feel welcomed and affirmed for who they are across the full breadth of their multiple, intersecting group identities, including: age; race; ethnicity; nationality; English proficiency; gender identity and expression; ability; socio-economic class; generation to college; sexual identity; religion, spirituality, and ways of knowing; parental and relational status; and veteran status, among others. On an inclusive campus, all members are treated with fairness, respect, and dignity. There is a consistent effort to eliminate all barriers and forms of discrimination or negative differential treatment. Members of an inclusive organization experience a sense of belonging and mattering as full participants who are actively engaged in the campus community and are able to contribute to the success of the organization. They flourish and thrive in this environment where there is full access and equity for all as well as support to develop their full potential. Inclusive organizations actively seek out and value students, staff, and faculty who bring differing perspectives, life experiences, and group identities to the community. They leverage the wisdom and diversity of worldviews, talents, and competencies as a resource to prepare students for effective service and success in an increasingly diverse, global society. All members of an inclusive organization are responsible for revising policies, practices, curricula, programs, and services to align with the organizational mission and vision for inclusion and social justice (Cox, 2001; Elliott et al., 2013; Hurtado, Milem, Clayton-Pederson, & Allen, 1999; Jackson, 2005; Jackson & Hardiman, 1994; Marchesani & Jackson, 2005; Pope, Reynolds, & Mueller, 2004; Williams, 2013).

Multicultural Organization Development (MCOD)

The multicultural organizational development (MCOD) model developed by Bailey Jackson and Rita Hardiman provides a useful framework for designing and implementing long-term culture change efforts to create sustainable, meaningful inclusion for the full breadth of students on campus (Jackson, 2005; Jackson & Hardiman, 1994; Jackson & Holvino, 1988a; Marchesani & Jackson, 2005; Pope, 1993). Most campuses appear to have a haphazard, unplanned, and incremental approach to change, one that is often hastily constructed in reaction to the latest crisis or critical incident (Harper, 2011; Marchesani & Jackson, 2005; William, 2013). In contrast, the MCOD model provides a roadmap for developing an intentional, proactive "change process that involves all parts of the campus working towards eliminating barriers to full inclusion and creating pathways of success for all" (Marchesani & Jackson, 2005, p. 243). MCOD offers a process that first assesses the current culture, norms, policies, programs, priorities, and services in order to identify any structural inequalities where unintended bias or negative differential treatment occurs. MCOD then revises these, as needed, to "interrupt the usual" (Petitt & McIntosh, 2011, p. 201), and transform traditional campus culture and practices to support the academic success of the full breadth of students on campus (Manning & Muñoz, 2011; Watt, 2011).

What Is the Purpose of Multicultural Organizational Change Efforts?

The goal of MCOD change efforts is to transform the overall organization so that equity and inclusion are a "central and integrative dimension" (Watt, 2011, p. 132), and viewed as fundamental to achieving the mission, vision, and values of the organization (Watt, 2011; Williams, 2013). This requires weaving equity and inclusion into every aspect of student affairs practice (Grieger, 1996; Manning & Muñoz, 2011; Pope et al., 2004; Williams, 2013). The goal of institutional transformation necessitates a shift from an "additive to an integrated approach" (Manning & Muñoz, 2011, p. 297), one that requires all units and offices to develop the capacity and structures to serve effectively all students across all group identities.

A Multicultural Organization (MCO) is "a system that seeks to improve itself and/or enhance its ability to reach its mission by advocating and practicing social justice and social diversity internally and external to the educational system" (Jackson, 2005, p. 7). The MCOD model is based on several key assumptions: oppression is systemic and entrenched in U.S. organizations; systems, not just individuals, must be the focus of change; and a multi-facet approach is required that both increases social diversity, creating a balanced demographic representation throughout the organization, as well as eliminates discrimination and social injustices (Jackson & Hardiman, 1994).

MCOD Development Stage Model

The MCOD development stage model provides a developmental continuum of six stages that describes organizational states as they transform from a monocultural, exclusionary organization to a multicultural, inclusive organization (Jackson, 2005). It is important that leaders and staff develop a shared, comprehensive understanding of the stage(s) that best reflects the current state of the organization and each department so that they can collaboratively develop a change plan based upon an accurate diagnosis to move the organization toward the next stage of development (Jackson, 2005; Jackson & Hardiman, 1994).

The model is divided into three levels: Monocultural, Non-Discriminating, and Multicultural (Jackson, 2005; Jackson & Holvino, 1988b), with two stages at each level. Each of the six stages describes "the consciousness and culture of an organization with regard to issues of social justice and diversity and where the organization is relative to becoming an MCO" (Jackson, 2005, p. 144).

In Monocultural Organizations, leaders have no interest in becoming a Multicultural Organization (MCO) and focus on maintaining the privilege and access of those who have traditionally held power (Jackson & Holvino, 1988b).

- Stage 1, The Exclusionary Organization, openly maintains the power and dominance of members of privileged groups, and members of marginalized groups experience hostility and harassment.
- Stage 2, The Club Organization, stops short of explicitly excluding members of marginalized groups, but intentionally works to maintain the policies, norms, and practices that reinforce privilege of members of dominant groups (Jackson, 2005).

In Non-Discriminating Organizations, there is interest in bringing in members of marginalized groups so long as there is no change to the organizational culture and status quo (Jackson & Holvino, 1988b).

- In Stage 3, The Compliance Organization, some members of marginalized groups are hired into the lower levels of organizations or as tokens within the management ranks. The intent is to comply with external regulations and pressures for reform, yet there is no effort to shift the organizational mission, practices, or culture.
- Stage 4, The Affirming Organization, actively recruits members of marginalized groups and is committed to eliminating discriminatory practices. Structures are created to support the development of members of marginalized groups and increase their mobility in the organization. Awareness workshops are offered to encourage all members to behave in non-oppressive ways; however, members of marginalized groups are expected to assimilate and fit into the organizational culture (Jackson & Holvino, 1988b).

In Multicultural Organizations the focus is to increase the diversity of representation throughout the organization, shift structures to create equitable distribution of power and influence, and eliminate inequity and oppression inside and outside the organization (Jackson & Holvino, 1988b).

- Stage 5, Redefining Organization, is committed to the full participation, empowerment, and inclusion of all members across identity groups. Focus is on developing the internal capacity of all members to create inclusive environments. Policies, practices, services, and cultural norms are reviewed, revised, and changed to align with the organizational values and mission of inclusion and social justice (Jackson & Holvino, 1988b).

- Stage 6, The Multicultural Organization, is an aspirational stage and a vision for the organization to move toward (Jackson, 2005). In this ideal state all members are active participants in decisions and planning practices that impact the organization. The policies, programs, services, and culture are intentionally designed and continually revised to meet the needs of the increasingly diverse organizational membership and those they serve. The organization consistently acts on its commitment to eliminate oppression in all forms within the organization and in the local, regional, national, and global spheres.

The MCOD Change Process

Jackson (2006) identifies four components of the MCOD process:

1. Identify change agents (leadership team and internal change team);
2. Assess organizational readiness to determine if there is sufficient leadership and internal capacity to develop a successful MCOD change process;
3. Assess the current state (culture, climate, and organizational structures); and
4. Develop and implement a continuous improvement change cycle of assessment, diagnosis, planning, implementation, accountability, and evaluation.

What Are the Roles of the Leadership Team and the Inclusion Change Team?

The Leadership Team performs several critical roles in the change process: providing the direction, vision, sense of urgency, and expectations for change; outlining how creating an inclusive organization is integral to the institutional mission and strategic plan; giving authority to the internal change team; and providing active support and leadership throughout the change process (Cox, 2001; Jackson, 2006; Williams, 2013). The Inclusion Change Team, comprising a cross-section of both formal and informal leaders from throughout the organization, is responsible for managing the MCOD change process (Jackson, 2006). Significant team building and competency development is required to support the success of the change team. Core competencies include systems thinking, change management, foundational concepts and tools on inclusion and social justice, the MCOD model and change process, and navigating group dynamics and conflict.

How Does the Leadership Team Work With the Members of the Inclusion Change Team?

The leaders and members of the inclusion change team work in partnership to accomplish several key steps in the change process: clarifying the organization's mission and vision of inclusion and social justice; conducting a comprehensive assessment of the current state including strengths, issues of concern, opportunities, and challenges; completing a gap analysis between the current stage of development and the ideal state of a Stage 6 MCO; and developing and implementing a change plan that is aligned with the developmental readiness of the organization to move the organization toward greater inclusion and social justice (Jackson, 2006).

Complete a Cultural Audit

The purpose of the assessment phase is to determine the current state, identify how far the organization has to move to become an MCO, and establish a benchmark to measure progress over time (Jackson, 2006; Marchesani & Jackson, 2005). Common assessment methods include surveys, interviews, focus groups, and cultural audits. Cultural audits involve analyzing organizational data from a wide variety of sources, including student and personnel demographics, climate and culture surveys, recruitment and retention practices, critical incidents and grievances, service and program utilization studies, and performance management processes. It is critical to disaggregate the data by social identity groups, hierarchical level/position type, and organizational unit.

Develop a Shared Understanding of the Current State

In the next step of the change process, the leaders work with the inclusion change team to review, discuss, and analyze the data as they develop a shared understanding of the current state of the organization (Jackson, 2006). An important change management strategy is to involve a wide cross-section of the organization in this process by providing open forums or large group working sessions to review and discuss the data, identify the current state and issues needing attention, explore implications and unanswered questions for further assessment, and identify potential activities and strategies for change. The outcome of these assessment steps helps build ownership of the data, provide support for the change effort, and engage any potential resistance that exists (Chesler, 1994; Marchesani & Jackson, 2005).

Develop a Change Plan
The next key step is for the leaders and the inclusion change team to develop a plan for creating a more inclusive, socially just organization. Key elements of the plan include: identifying and prioritizing the issues and situations to be addressed; developing observable, measurable goals that will move the organization toward greater inclusion; identifying specific activities designed to achieve these goals; developing an accountability system including assignments, criteria to measure progress, resources required, and timelines for completion; and developing strategies to share the plan and invite feedback from members of the organization (Jackson, 2006).

Review Current Policies, Programs, and Services With an Inclusion Lens
A critical component in the implementation of the change plan involves reviewing and revising the policies and daily practices of every aspect of the organization (Williams, 2013). This includes: the mission and values; personnel profile; policies and practices related to recruitment, retention, orientation, professional development, planning and decision-making, budget allocations, supervision, and performance management; the programs and services for students, staff, and faculty; teaching and learning methodologies and curricula; and the culture and climate of the organization (Jackson, 2005). The goal is to ensure that the divisional units provide meaningful and relevant programs and services to meet the needs and support the academic success of students across the full spectrum of group identities (Pope et al., 2004).

Implement an Accountability Structure
Too often organizations fail to create any significant, lasting change. The initial urgency to create greater inclusion tends to dissipate as leaders and members of the organization realize both the depth of dysfunction and the amount of time, resources, and attention required to create sustainable change. A meaningful system of ongoing accountability helps to offset this tendency. Without an explicit structure to hold people accountable, most organizations experience a "natural pull back towards the status quo" (Jackson, 2005, p. 7). Effective accountability structures include published plans that identify responsible parties and clear timelines, regular updates in meetings of the leadership and the inclusion change team; and quarterly open forums to discuss progress and next steps with the entire organization (Jackson, 2006).

Plan for Continuous Improvement
A final critical element of the MCOD change process is annual formal evaluation processes that provide indicators of progress and data to inform

ongoing assessment and planning processes (Jackson, 2005). It is important that both leaders and members of the organization shift the cultural norms to embrace continuous learning, reassessment, and recalibration as foundational principles and practices for creating inclusive organizations (Jackson, 2006; Jackson & Holvino, 1988b). Creating sustainable, meaningful organizational change is an "enduring pursuit" (Petitt & McIntosh, 2011, p. 204), and a demanding, ever-changing process (Chang, Milem, & antonio, 2011), requiring courage, stamina, patience, and persistent leadership to effectively navigate the inevitable shifting contexts, challenges, and circumstances that occur over time.

A Multi-Year Systemic Change Process in a Student Affairs Division

In 2008, The University of Oregon Division of Student Affairs completed a five-year strategic plan in which it identified the goal of becoming a multicultural organization. The vice president for student affairs created the MCOD Implementation Team as an internal change team charged with identifying steps and strategies to achieve this divisional goal (Jackson, 2006). The MCOD Implementation Team spent its first year researching MCOD best practices, developing a simple and accessible definition of the Student Affairs multicultural organization, and writing a report to the vice president with initial perceptions and recommendations.

The MCOD Implementation Team described the Division of Student Affairs Multicultural Organizational Development as "the intentional creation of an organization that actively includes and engages everyone" (p. 2). The Implementation Team identified the following characteristics for the division to aspire to (a) a dynamic and ongoing commitment to the MCOD process; (b) creating a safe, welcoming, accessible, and fair environment; (c) advocating for social justice; (d) eliminating all forms of oppression; (e) having diverse representation throughout all levels of the division; (f) considering the multicultural impact in all decision-making processes; (g) understanding and engaging the advantages and strengths of a diverse organization; and (h) encouraging the contributions of all members of the division. The team also reported on Student Affairs' current multicultural efforts, MCOD best practices gleaned from the literature, changes needed for the division to become a multicultural organization, and barriers to becoming an MCO.

The MCOD Implementation Team developed a three-year action plan and implemented three key change strategies: (a) MCOD team members collaborated with Student Affairs department directors to train unit leadership teams on the MCOD model and key concepts; (b) team members integrated MCOD concepts into new employee orientation for unclassified and classified staff; and (c) the team developed a plan for each unit to conduct a Cultural "Snapshot" to assess the department's current state and areas for change.

Developing Internal Capacity of Division Leaders and Unit Change Teams

The MCOD Team hired an external consultant to facilitate a two-day Working Retreat to help increase internal capacity of leaders and staff to implement Cultural Audits and create inclusive organizations through long-term culture change. Because the word *audit* often connotes a negative experience, the Team used the phrase Cultural Snapshot instead of Cultural Audit. Each division leader attended the Retreat along with both formal and informal department leaders who reflected a "diagonal slice" of the unit and demonstrated a commitment to creating inclusion. These leaders and staff formed the nucleus of future Unit Inclusion Change Teams.

Intended Outcomes of the Working Retreat

The consultant designed learning activities to deepen the following competencies of participants: increasing clarity of the Leadership Team's vision and expectations for culture change; developing a shared understanding of common terms and concepts; understanding the MCOD change process; exploring key components and tools to conduct an MCOD Cultural Snapshot at the unit and divisional level; identifying next steps to create Unit Change Teams that successfully complete a Cultural Snapshot and identify recommendations for change. During this highly engaging, interactive retreat the facilitator reviewed several key models and competencies, including: the MCOD development stage model, Indicators of an Inclusive Organization, Multicultural Competencies for an Inclusive Organization, Discretionary Points Mapping, conducting a Cultural Snapshot/Audit, and Steps to Creating Organizational Change. In addition, participants experienced a wide variety of activities and tools they could use to train the members of their Unit Change Teams as they developed into high-performing teams. The retreat was successful in meeting its intended learning objectives and participant feedback was very positive.

Implementing a Cultural Snapshot

The MCOD Change Team developed and distributed a division-wide Cultural Snapshot survey based on the *Indicators of a Redefining/Multicultural Organization* (Obear, 2011). Each department then received data from the survey in the form of a report that included department-specific information and division-wide information. Each Unit Change Team used this information, in conjunction with other forms of assessment, to begin to analyze the current state of equity and inclusion in the unit. Each Team submitted a report of their findings to the department director and the vice president for student affairs. The following are the indicators used in the Cultural Snapshot assessment:

- **Departmental Mission**: Values such as diversity, equity and inclusion are (a) very important to my department; and (b) are articulated as central to the mission and focus of my department.
- **Leadership** (director, associate, and assistant directors): Department leaders (a) demonstrate a commitment to diversity, equity, and inclusion; (b) develop and communicate a clear and concise list of multicultural competencies that all staff members are expected to demonstrate in their daily work; (c) expect me to include diversity, equity, and inclusion goals in my work; (d) ensure that there are safe, confidential processes for reporting and resolving grievances, harassment, etc.
- **Supervision**: Supervisors (a) regularly discuss their commitment to issues of diversity, equity, and inclusion with direct reports, individually and as a team; (b) regularly assess the progress of direct reports on their diversity, equity, and inclusion goals; (c) provide opportunities to staff to participate in activities related to diversity, equity, and inclusion; and (d) immediately respond to reports of inappropriate and/or offensive behaviors from staff in their department(s).
- **Planning and Decision-Making**: My department intentionally includes input from staff and students who are affected by the potential decisions and those who are involved in implementing the decisions.
- **Policies and Procedures**: My department (a) has created policies and procedures that reflect a commitment to diversity, equity, and inclusion; (b) has reviewed its policies and procedures to assess their impact on those from underrepresented groups; and (c) intentionally creates forms and applications that are culturally inclusive.
- **Staff Recruitment and Hiring**: My department (a) always incorporates language expressing a commitment to diversity, equity, and inclusion in position/job descriptions; (b) always makes an effort to generate a diverse applicant pool for available positions; (c) always selects and interviews a diverse group of applicants; (d) has successfully hired staff from underrepresented identities;

(e) requires that applicants who will be hired by my department have a commitment to diversity, equity, and inclusion; and (f) follows processes for promotions and interim appointments that are transparent and aligned with diversity, equity, and inclusion goals.

- **Staff Orientation, Professional Development, and Retention**: My department (a) conducts orientation with new employees to review Division and Department priorities related to diversity, equity, and inclusion; and (b) has successfully retained staff from underrepresented identities; (c) ensures staff members from underrepresented identities receive mentoring, professional development opportunities, and professional and personal support in my department.

- **Physical Environment**: My department (a) displays physical artifacts (e.g., artwork, reading materials, decorations, photographs) that represent a diversity of cultural perspectives; (b) displays announcements for diverse/culturally inclusive programs/events/services in our public spaces (e.g., bulletin boards); and (c) the physical spaces in my department take into consideration different abilities, sizes, and physical needs.

- **Marketing and Communication**: My department's (a) publications (e.g., handbooks, brochures, flyers, resource guides, and announcements) are culturally inclusive in their use of language, photographs, and graphics; (b) web spaces (e.g., departmental website, social networking sites, and links to outside sites) are culturally inclusive in their use of language, photographs, and graphics; and (c) values and terms such as diversity, equity, and inclusion are always included in my department's written and visual materials (e.g., brochures, advertisements, websites).

- **Research and Assessment**: My department collects, analyzes, and shares data about the work environment for staff related to issues of diversity, equity, and inclusion.

Conducting a Gap Analysis and Developing Recommendations

Each department Inclusion Change Team analyzed the assessment information from the Cultural Snapshot to identify gaps between the current and desired state of the department, and then recommended strategies to achieve the desired state. Change Teams prioritized their recommendations and identified the strategies the department could commit to implement within the next 12–18 months. Inclusion Change Teams were required to submit brief progress reports to the MCOD Change Team at designated points in the process.

Next Steps in the MCOD Change Process

The MCOD Implementation Team intends to re-administer the division-wide Cultural Snapshot survey within a year of the completion of the initial Snapshot. Each department may decide to add new members to the Change Team to gain knowledge and expertise in MCOD as well as keep several former members on the Team to ensure consistency. Each Unit Change Team will analyze new data, conduct another gap analysis, and identify the next steps to create greater inclusion in the department.

The Student Affairs MCOD Implementation Team identified additional activities in its most recent action plan, including (a) continuing to offer new employee orientation programs twice annually; (b) providing an opportunity for current Student Affairs staff members to learn more about the division's MCOD initiative and the new Student Affairs strategic plan; and (c) providing two staff development trainings each year focused on incorporating issues of equity and inclusion into functional aspects of job roles (e.g., recruitment and hiring, front line student service/customer service, marketing, manager/supervisor responsibilities).

Lessons Learned for Implementing a Change Process in Other Student Affairs Divisions

The following recommendations reflect the authors' lessons learned from using the MCOD Model on college and university campuses. These key insights may help campus leaders develop a campus change process tailored to their specific needs and organizational context.

- **Align divisional activities within a larger organizational change effort.** The impact of using MCOD to create greater inclusion in a division of student affairs will be far greater at both two- and four-year institutions if the process is situated within a comprehensive institution-wide change effort. Aligning divisional strategies with campus-wide initiatives will help leaders and staff members recognize their responsibility to infuse issues of equity and inclusion into policies, practices, services, and programs.
- **Provide leadership for the MCOD Change Process.** Some student affairs divisions may not have leaders with the capacity (skills, resources, time) to lead a division-wide systems change effort. It may be possible to adjust a leader's current portfolio to include a 25% focus on leading the MCOD effort. Another possibility is to contract with external consultants to partner with internal leaders in this process.

- **Include at least one representative from each department on the Division's Change Team.** Departments without a representative on the Division's Team may have more difficulty understanding the purpose of, process for, and action steps toward developing a multicultural organization.
- **Develop a clear, written charge for Inclusion Change Teams.** Few division staff members may be familiar with the concept of an Inclusion Change Team. It is important to provide written structure regarding the composition, purpose, and scope of work to minimize confusion and time spent on activities not as relevant to the MCOD process.
- **Provide opportunities for Inclusion Change Teams to interact with each other.** It is important to provide opportunities for collaboration, exchange of ideas, and sharing of successes and challenges. Without these opportunities, much of this work happens in isolation at the department level, even when reported up to division leadership. It may be useful to create a combined Change Team across 2–3 smaller units. These cross-unit teams may offer a number of advantages: increased relationship building and knowledge about other units; opportunity for innovative, collaborative initiatives; and increased support and accountability across units.
- **Provide frequent communication about the MCOD process, deadlines, and expectations.** Regular, consistent communication will increase productivity and accountability throughout the organizational change process.

Conclusion

Manning and Muñoz (2011) argue that today's vision of educating the "whole student" necessitates a focus on issues of social justice, fairness, and equity. Student affairs practitioners need to increase their capacity to support students from underrepresented, marginalized groups while also equipping all students with the skills and competencies to be successful leaders in increasingly diverse, global environments (Harper, 2008; Harper & antonio, 2008; Hurtado & Guillermo-Wann, 2013; Manning & Muñoz, 2011). Implementing a long-term systems change process in the division of student affairs demonstrates leadership in achieving the academic mission of the university, provides staff with professional development opportunities to deepen their multicultural competencies, and sets the expectation that all staff are required to continually revise and improve policies, practices, programs, and services to create inclusive environments that support the academic success of the full breadth of students on campus.

References

Chang, M. J., Chang, J., & Ledesma, M. C. (2005). Beyond magical thinking: Doing the real work of diversifying our institutions. *About Campus, 10*(2), 9–16.

Chang, M. J, Milem, J. F., & antonio, a. l. (2011). Campus climate and diversity. In J. H. Schuh, S. R. Jones, & S. R. Harper (Eds.), *Student services: A handbook for the profession* (5th ed.; pp. 43–58). San Francisco: Jossey-Bass.

Chesler, M. A. (1994). Organizational development is not the same as multicultural organizational development. In E. Y. Cross, J. H. Katz, F. A. Miller, & E. W. Seashore (Eds.), *The promise of diversity: Over 40 voices discuss strategies for eliminating discrimination in organizations* (pp. 240–251). Arlington, VA: NTL Institute.

Cox, T. (2001). *Creating the multicultural organization: A strategy for capturing the power of diversity.* San Francisco: Jossey-Bass.

Elliott, C. M., Stransky, O., Negron, R., Bowlby, M., Lickiss, J., Dutt, D., . . . Barbosa, P. (2013). Institutional barriers to diversity change work in higher education. *Sage Open*: doi:10.1177/2158244013489686

Grieger, I. (1996). A multicultural organizational development checklist for student affairs. *Journal of College Student Development, 37*, 561–573.

Harper, S. R. (2008). *Creating inclusive campus environments for cross-cultural learning and student engagement.* Washington DC: NASPA.

Harper, S. R. (2011). Strategy and intentionality in practice. In J. H. Schuh, S. R. Jones, & S. R. Harper (Eds.), *Student services: A handbook for the profession* (5th ed., pp. 287–302). San Francisco: Jossey-Bass.

Harper, S. R., & antonio, a. l. (2008). Not by accident: Intentionality in diversity, learning, and engagement. In S. R. Harper (Ed.), *Creating inclusive campus environments* (pp. 1–18). Washington DC: NASPA.

Hart Research Associates. (2010). *Raising the bar: Employers' views on college learning in the wake of the economic downturn.* Washington DC: Association of American Colleges and Universities. Retrieved from http://www.aacu.org/leap /documents/2009_EmployerSurvey.pdf

Hart Research Associates. (2013). *It takes more than a major: Employer priorities for college learning and student success.* Washington DC: Association of American Colleges and Universities and Hart Research Associates. Retrieved from http://www .aacu.org/leap/public_opinion_research.cfm

Hurtado, S., & Guillermo-Wann, C. (2013). *Diverse learning environments: Assessing and creating conditions for student success—Final report to the Ford Foundation.* University of California–Los Angeles: Higher Education Research Institute.

Hurtado, S., Milem, J. F., Clayton-Pederson, A. R., & Allen, W. R. (1999). *Enacting diverse learning environments: Improving the climate for racial ethnic diversity in higher education* (ASHE/ERIC Higher Education Report, No. 8). Washington DC: George Washington University.

Jackson, B. W. (2005). The theory and practice of multicultural organizational development in education. In M. L. Ouellett (Ed.), *Teaching inclusively: Resources for course, department and institutional change in higher education* (pp. 3–20). Stillwater, OK: New Forums Press.

Jackson, B. W. (2006). Theory and practice of multicultural organization development. In B. B. Jones & M. Brazzel (Eds.), *The NTL handbook of organization development and change* (pp. 139–154). San Francisco: Pfeiffer.

Jackson, B. W., & Hardiman, R. (1994). Multicultural organization development. In E. Y. Cross, J. H. Katz, F. A. Miller, & E. W. Seashore (Eds.), *The promise of diversity: Over 40 voices discuss strategies for eliminating discrimination in organizations* (pp. 231–239). Arlington, VA: NTL Institute.

Jackson, B. W., & Holvino, E. V. (1988a, Fall). Developing multicultural organizations. *Journal of Religion and Applied Behavioral Science* (Association for Creative Change), 14–19.

Jackson, B. W., & Holvino, E. V. (1988b). *Multicultural organizational development.* Working Paper No. 11. Ann Arbor, MI: Program on Conflict Management Alternatives.

Manning, K., & Muñoz, F. M. (2011). Conclusion: Revisioning the future of multicultural students services. In D. L. Stewart (Ed.), *Multicultural student services on campus: Building bridges, re-visioning community* (pp. 282–299). Sterling, VA: Stylus.

Marchesani, L. S., & Jackson, B. W. (2005). Transforming higher education institutions using multicultural organizational development: A case study at a large northeastern university. In M. L. Ouellett (Ed.), *Teaching inclusively: Resources for course, department and institutional change in higher education* (pp. 241–257). Stillwater, OK: New Forums Press.

Obear, K. (2011). *Indicators of a redefining/multicultural organization.* Paper presented at American College Personnel Association, Baltimore, MD.

Petitt, B., & McIntosh, D. (2011). Negotiating purpose and context. In D. L. Stewart (Ed.), *Multicultural student services on campus: Building bridges, re-visioning community* (pp. 201–215). Sterling, VA: Stylus.

Pope, R. L. (1993). Multicultural-organization development in student affairs: An introduction. *Journal of College Student Development, 34,* 201–205.

Pope, R. L., & LePeau, L. A. (2012). The influence of institutional context and culture. In J. Arminio, V. Torres, & R. L. Pope (Eds.). *Why aren't we there yet? Taking personal responsibility for creating an inclusive campus* (pp. 103–130). Sterling, VA: Stylus.

Pope, R. L., Reynolds, A. L., & Mueller, J. A. (2004). *Multicultural competence in student affairs.* San Francisco: Jossey-Bass.

Stewart, D. L. (2011). Introduction. In D. L. Stewart (Ed.), *Multicultural student services on campus: Building bridges, re-visioning community* (pp. 1–10). Sterling, VA: Stylus.

Strange, C. C., & Stewart, D. L. (2011). Preparing diversity change leaders. In D. L. Stewart (Ed.), *Multicultural student services on campus: Building bridges, re-visioning community* (pp. 254–266). Sterling, VA: Stylus.

Talbot, D. M. (2003). Multiculturalism. In S. R. Komives & D. B. Woodard (Eds.), *Student services: A handbook for the profession* (4th ed., pp. 423–446). San Francisco: Jossey-Bass.

Watt, S. K. (2011). Moving beyond the talk: From difficult dialogues to action. In J. Arminio, V. Torres, & R. Pope (Eds.), *Why aren't we there yet: Taking personal responsibility for creating an inclusive campus* (pp. 131–144). Sterling, VA: Stylus.

Whitt, E. J., Edison, M. I., Pascarella, E. T., Nora, A., & Terenzini, P. T. (1999). Women's perceptions of a "chilly climate" and cognitive outcomes in college: Additional evidence. *Journal of College Student Development, 40*(2), 163–177.

Williams, D. A. (2013). *Strategic diversity leadership*. Sterling, VA: Stylus.

IO

DIALOGUE MATTERS

Applying Critical Race Theory to Conversations About Race

Sherri Edvalson Erkel

olleges and universities in the United States have made strides to improve structural diversity—the physical presence of a critical mass of underrepresented minority students—through affirmative action and other minority enrollment initiatives (Milem, 2003). U.S. college campuses have also been a place where race-based incidents have contributed to an environment that is marginalizing at best and at worst, hostile and unsafe to students from underrepresented minority groups (Vega, 2014). Yet there are no effective ways to address this issue. Off-campus, college educators see and hear evidence of the prevalence of racism in our society. Race is present in the current debate on immigration. It is present in the fact that our first African American President is also the first President whose citizenship was called into question. It is present when popular culture confronts us with questions such as, "Is Paula Deen (a Food Network star accused of making racist statements) a racist?" Perhaps most significantly, race is present as we try to make sense of tragedies such as the killings of Trayvon Martin, Jordan Davis, Eric Garner, and more recently, Michael Brown, all African American men reactively slain by fellow citizens or police officers who are White males (George Zimmerman identifies as Hispanic White).

When racist incidents occur on college campuses, student affairs practitioners and campus leaders grapple with the best ways to respond to the event in a way that will address the systemic nature of race and racism and not merely as reactions to specific events. The former is difficult; neither a formal apology nor a single forum on diversity can accomplish an understanding of the root causes of racism. This type of understanding requires that college educators improve competency with conducting conversations on race with colleagues and students in an effective way.

This chapter discusses how student affairs practitioners can use critical race theory to approach the issue of race on today's college campus. Race-based incidents both on and off campus continue to disrupt progress toward a more inclusive and equitable educational experience for our students. College administrators struggle with the most effective way to facilitate conversations about race. Applying critical race theory (CRT), in general, and the work of Richard Delgado and Gloria Ladson-Billings, in particular, is one way that we can leverage scholarship and practice against the persistence of racism on our college campuses. I offer strategies to help students reflect on their own experiences with race, to examine the impact of socio-cultural influences on their assumptions surrounding race, and to analyze their own understanding of the history of race and racism in the United States.

In this chapter, I frame race as a social construction that is a perception of difference based on certain physical characteristics. We learn about race through our relationships with family, peers, and other influencers throughout our lifespans (Harro, 2007). Race relations in the United States is complex and students from different racial groups have lived different realities. In addition, many have had limited opportunities to interact and have dialogues on these issues (Umbach & Kuh, 2006), the result of which can be developing defense mechanisms to cope with potential conflict about tension-filled topics such as race (Watt, et al., 2009). Socialization has led many students to avoid talking about race and consequently, they employ defenses against confronting the concepts of power, privilege, and oppression. These same students come to campuses where student affairs practitioners provide opportunities to live, learn, and engage with students with different racial identities.

Considering the impact that the concepts of power, privilege, and oppression can have on the various type of interactions students experience on a college campus, dialogue can be an effective tool in developing multicultural competence. Approaching the realities of race and racism with intention can help faculty, staff, and students have more meaningful dialogues and that can lead to a significant change in how they interact on campus and in the society at large. How often do students talk about their lived experiences with race and consider the possible influence it has on their ability or willingness to engage in dialogue on race? How often are students, faculty, and staff encouraged to reflect on their own racial identity, how their racial experiences are different from others, and how that understanding informs our work and life from day to day? How can we approach a deeper understanding of race?

This chapter will discuss ways that student affairs practitioners can consider dialogues related to race and understand how dialogue *matters* in our efforts to improve race relations on our campuses and in the world that our students will enter upon graduation. I conclude with suggestions for how to facilitate CRT-informed reflection, to share stories and counter-stories, and to use both as a means by which college educators can build multicultural competency for global citizenship.

Examining My Assumptions About Race

I am a White, college-educated, heterosexual, able-bodied woman, raised in a rural town in the Western region of the United States. I approach student affairs work through the lens of someone socialized in a predominantly White, rural community with little exposure to racial diversity. As many White students raised in a predominantly White community, my first meaningful interactions with peers with different racial identities than my own occurred when I entered college. Despite having few interactions with Difference prior to entering college, I unconsciously made assumptions about my new friends and acquaintances based on their race. How was this possible? After several years spent learning about diversity and multiculturalism, I began to understand that my previously held assumptions about race were shaped by many factors—media, conversations with family, my formal education—none of which involved taking into account my friends' lived experiences or asking to hear their stories.

I also learned that expressions of race and incidents of racism are part of a structure of inequality held firmly in place in the United States. Ideas and values that are associated with being White hold more power over ideas and values associated with the minority and with people of color (Reason & Broido, 2005). This system creates a way of relating where racial minorities are the target of prejudice, discrimination, and marginalization and the majority racial group reaps the advantages of benefits, elevated status, and centralized focus. Our perceptions of Difference (Watt, this volume) are based on our experiences with power and privilege versus oppression and marginalization based on race. Experiences with power and privilege or oppression and marginalization are one aspect of the larger concept of socio-cultural influences on the way individuals make meaning of their lives. Socio-cultural influences are the practices, beliefs, values, and interactions with others that inform the way an individual lives and makes meaning of his or her experiences (Vygotsky, 1978).

Critical Race Theory

Today, my views about race align more closely with critical race theory. CRT uses stories and counter-stories to gather evidence on the nature of race (Delgado, 1990; Dixon & Rousseau, 2005; Parker & Lynn, 2002). Scholars have used CRT to examine the relationship of race, racism, and power (Delgado & Stefancic, 1997, 2012). Delgado and Stefancic (1997) present a useful summary of the common understanding of CRT as it has evolved in the last decade in the first edition of their book on the theory. First, the theory assumes that racism is systemic in nature. Rather than consisting of isolated incidents, confronting racism is the common, everyday experience of people of color. Second, racism has benefits for members of the dominant group and, as a result, provides little incentive to change. Third, race, and the way that racism plays out in everyday experiences of both dominant and marginalized groups, is a product of social interactions, behaviors, and values. CRT's fourth assumption is that storytelling, or giving voice to previously silenced individuals, can contribute to the empowerment of marginalized individuals and the consciousness-raising of individuals from the dominant group.

Ladson-Billings and Tate describe the storytelling aspect of CRT as "the naming of one's own reality" (1995, p. 56). When students who identify as a member of a minority group exchange stories with members of the dominant group, they not only reveal the reality of oppression, but also help to reframe the reality, informed by systemic racism, constructed by White students. This type of story, which presents another reality opposed to the reality of the dominant group that is presented as a universal experience, is known as a *counter-narrative* or *counter-story*. By exchanging stories, members of both subordinate and dominant groups can engage in consciousness-raising on matters related to race.

CRT helps me to articulate my current assumptions about race, racism, and power. I assume that racism is a normal, everyday part of the experiences of minorities in the United States. I assume that the relationship tying together race, racism, and power is complex and that giving voice to both marginalized and dominant individuals in context is a first step in transforming the way that we approach the reality of race in contemporary society. Finally, I assume that giving voice to students by way of hearing their stories and counter-stories about race can transform the way we approach race and confront issues of racism on the college campus. Next, I will explain how giving voice to these stories and helping to raise consciousness about the realities of race and racism can create more intentional interactions that might improve how U.S. society handles contemporary problems.

How Telling Stories and Counter-Stories Can Improve Race Related Dialogue

I conducted focus groups with 22 undergraduate students with various racial identities at a predominantly White institution in the Midwestern United States as part of a study of socio-cultural influences on college students' conversations about race. I used CRT as the theoretical framework and identified themes related to students' experiences with race, racial identity, and the collective history of race in the United States. For minority students, sharing personal stories of discrimination or oppression offered a possible counterview to the dominant perspective on race at a predominantly White institution. White students in this study had the opportunity to hear everyday instances of oppression experienced by their peers who identified as one or more minority races. Within the framework of CRT, students' experiences served as stories and counter-stories about race in their individual lives and in this particular research setting.

The use of storytelling as a matter of everyday practice, rather than providing spaces only as a reaction to a specific incident can help students to have more authentic dialogues. Minority students who felt that their racial identity had to be invisible to persist in college were able to connect with students who identified as White/Non-Hispanic when they shared their experiences of oppression. White students who articulated various defenses in response to the stimuli were able to hear actual experiences from their peers in this setting.

Students in the study approached the complex and difficult issue of race in the interview setting by sharing their stories or counter-stories related to race. Questions about race elicited responses that invoked their ideas of privilege, power, and oppression, and described the influences on the way they thought about race. The White students in this study described the idea of diverse individuals coming together for common opportunities at the center of their discussion on race, focusing on the process of becoming "White." Both White students and the students who identified as a member of a minority group emphasized the idea of making race an invisible part of their identity and minimized the self as a racial being. Effectively facilitating dialogues on race can help to improve the campus climate for diversity and help students to see race as a social construction rather than as an individual experience or something located in the past but invisible in the present day.

Students who identified as White/Non-Hispanic seemed to privilege the invisibility of race in order to downplay or avoid their role in the system of oppression and seemed to exhibit defense mechanisms consistent with research on Privileged Identity Exploration (Watt et al., 2009). The most interesting defenses displayed in the conversations with the students in the present study included rationalization, minimization, benevolence, and intellectualization. Students demonstrated rationalization when they offered a logical explanation for racist acts or attitudes. I observed minimization when students attempted to reduce systemic inequality to simple facts. Students also displayed the benevolence defense when they described service trips or other instances where they believed they were helping those whom they believed to be less fortunate. Students who identified as White/Non-Hispanic also attempted to explain instances of race-based discrimination by offering intellectual arguments such as facts they learned in classes, such as Psychology or Sociology. It is possible that students who identified as one or more racial minority identities emphasized the invisibility of race as a way to minimize their experiences of oppression. Additionally, racial minority students talked about race as a way to describe how they persisted in predominantly White environments such as college through their counter-narratives explored in previous literature employing CRT (Ladson-Billings, 2005). These stories are important to hear. Students who identify as White/Non-Hispanic benefit from hearing the everyday, lived experiences of students who identify as racial minorities. Minority students benefit by having a space to voice their lived experiences where they have been previously silenced by the majority narrative on the college campus and in the larger socio-cultural context.

How College Educators Can Intentionally Place Race at Center of Dialogue

I found, at least among this particular group of students, that race does not occur just in a particular moment on campus or in U.S. society. Rather, race and race-related incidents are the results of students' individual experiences related to race, the collective racial history in the United States, and the extent to which they see themselves as racial beings (Figure 10.1). I found that providing spaces for students from various racial backgrounds to share stories and counter-stories could be a productive means of addressing the persistence of racism both on and off campus. Many college administrators have addressed race-based incidents as isolated acts committed by students who are the exception to an otherwise tolerant student body. Focusing on the historical, socio-cultural, and personal influences on the incidents and the overall climate for diversity can lead to a more productive response to race-based incidents on campus.

Figure 10.1 Critical Race Theory.

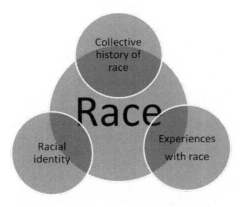

Student affairs practitioners can help students learn how to have conversations on race in ways that illuminate the influences of their pre-college practices, beliefs, values, and interactions with others on the way they make meaning of race. Influences such as these converge when students have dialogues on race or when race-based incidents occur on campus. Learning more about what students bring to the classroom, residence hall, student organization, or playing field can occur in structured opportunities to engage in dialogues on race. Effectively facilitating dialogues on race can help to improve the campus climate for diversity and help students to see race as a social construction rather than an individual experience or something located in the past but invisible in the present day. Facilitators who effectively facilitate dialogues on race are connecting the historical, socio-cultural, and personal influences on students' approaches to race.

Understanding the practices, beliefs, values, behaviors, and interactions with others that influence the way students make meaning of race is of particular salience for students and the way they view themselves as racial beings, and as members of a system of oppression in contemporary society. Whereas this current research demonstrates that increased interactions with diverse others has wide-ranging educational benefits and that intentional efforts to promote cross-racial engagement is an important aspect of promoting a positive climate for racial diversity, studying the socio-cultural influences on students' conversations on race can help practitioners to identify additional strategies for promoting diversity and inclusion. Identifying the socio-cultural influences on students' approaches to the issue of race can inform, for example, pedagogical strategies that focus on a more inclusive teaching of history and society in the curriculum and co-curricular programming.

Using Critical Race Theory in Practice

Engaging in personal reflection, articulating identities with peers, and using stimuli to facilitate discussion can help students across different racial backgrounds to have dialogue that is more authentic. Each of these strategies, when used together, can provide an anchor for CRT to centralize race in dialogues.

Personal Reflection

Personal reflection is an important first step because it can help students (and practitioners) recall their earliest interactions with racial difference. Reflecting on our personal experiences with race and our racial identity is the first step in developing a deeper understanding of the issue of race. Student affairs practitioners, particularly those who work with student leaders, routinely use reflection and sharing personal stories as a way to build community. These same activities—reflection and storytelling—can be facilitated using CRT as a framework. In this setting, facilitators could ask students to write a reflection about their earliest experience with someone from a different race. This exercise might be the first prompting to reflect on this particular aspect of their lives that many of these individuals have ever faced. Reframing this type of activity within the context of CRT can serve two purposes. As they reflect, they are at once recalling their early experiences with race and writing their stories to share with others. This activity can contribute to the empowerment of those who may not have previously had the chance to be heard, and revelatory to those who have never been in a position to listen to stories from peers from different racial identities than their own.

Articulating Identities With Peers

Students can also begin the process of personal reflection, framed in the context of CRT, by listing five to ten words that describe their identity in a series of "I am . . ." statements. This list then becomes the vehicle for articulating their story to a peer or a small group (three to five students). For a student who identifies as a racial minority, this provides a space to share her identity with a peer or group of peers who are offering undivided attention. For a White student, sitting face-to-face with a student with a different racial identity can be an effective first step in dismantling previously held assumptions about a particular racial group.

Using a Stimulus or Artifact for Dialogue

Another useful way to facilitate dialogue in the context of CRT is to present a stimulus with race as a central theme. Examples of stimuli include films (clips or full-feature depending on time), poetry, famous speeches on race (Presidential, other historical figures), or a common reading. After the stimulus, the students could be asked a series of open-ended questions to elicit responses related to the stimulus. Examples of these questions include: "What is your reaction to the film?" "Was there a particular part that struck you? Why?" and "In what ways, if any, do you relate to the character's treatment of race?" This technique can be particularly effective in groups that have not yet established a strong personal connection, such as the first weeks of a new learning community or new residents on a particular residence hall floor. Talking about the poem, film, or book chapter can be an avenue for building a safe space that can then lead to articulating personal stories in a more direct way.

Conclusion: Reframing Our Work With CRT

Student affairs practitioners can work within larger campus diversity efforts to construct cross-race groups when discussing issues of race and racism. Practitioners who are interested in transforming the way students approach issues of race must also review their current programs through a critical lens. Just as we ask our students to begin addressing race through personal reflection, practitioners can start the process of being a conscious scholar practitioner by examining the environment in which they work. Some questions to consider include: (a) how can you create space for students to share stories and counter-stories in your department, classroom, or program? (b) what makes talking about race difficult in your particular setting? (c) what is one thing you can do to address the challenges? and (d) who needs to be present at the table to address these challenges?

Responding to race-based incidents cannot be the first time that race is talked about on a campus. Introducing ideas, facilitating discussion, and encouraging reflections on race as part of everyday student affairs practice can provide a foundation upon which students can build their multicultural competence. Students who have had multiple opportunities to see how race plays out in their everyday lives and as part of learning to work with diverse others will likely be better equipped to confront prejudice and discrimination and to become effective allies on campus and in the worlds they will enter upon graduation.

Institutions of higher education find themselves increasingly called upon to address issues of race on campus as they relate to college access, campus climate, and effective teaching and learning (Hurtado, Milem, Clayton-Pedersen, & Allen, 1998). Campus administrators who answer this call often begin by initiating programs that seek to open dialogues on diversity issues including race (Chang, 2002). Dialogue has the potential to transform campus climates into positive spaces for diversity. These transformative efforts require that participants undergo changes in attitudes, beliefs, and the way they make meaning of their own position in the power, privilege, and oppression structures at the institution and in the larger community (Hurtado, 1992; Hurtado et al., 1998). CRT can be a useful theoretical frame to apply to practice when asking students to reflect on their own experiences and to share their stories with peers. Discussions about experiences related to race can expand to include more equitable exchanges among students from various racial backgrounds. Historically silenced populations need opportunities to tell their story and the historically dominant population needs to be placed within the conversation on race rather than viewing it from the outside. Within cross-racial groups, the telling and hearing of stories can not only empower marginalized identities but also enlighten those with privileged identities.

References

Chang, M. J. (2002). Impact of undergraduate diversity course on students' racial views and attitudes. *Journal of General Education, 51,* 22–42.

Delgado, R. (1990). When a story is just a story: Does voice really matter? *Virginia Law Review, 95,* 76–111.

Delgado, R., & Stefancic, J. (Eds.). (1997). *Critical White studies: Looking behind the mirror.* Philadelphia: Temple University Press.

Delgado, R., & Stefancic, J. (2012). *Critical race theory: An introduction* (2nd ed.). New York: New York University Press.

Dixon, A. D., & Rousseau, C. K. (2005). And we are still not saved: Critical race theory in education ten years later. *Race Ethnicity and Education, 8*(1), 7–27.

Harro, B. (2007). The cycle of socialization. In M. Adams, W. J. Blumenfeld, C. Castaneda, H. W. Hackman, M. L. Peters, & X. Zuniga (Eds.), *Readings for diversity and social justice* (2nd ed., pp. 15–21). New York: Routledge.

Hurtado, S. (1992). The campus racial climate: Contexts of conflict. *Journal of Higher Education, 63*(5), 539–569.

Hurtado, S., Milem, J. F., Clayton-Pedersen, A. R., & Allen, W. R. (1998). Enhancing campus climates for racial/ethnic diversity: Educational policy and practice. *The Review of Higher Education, 21*(3), 279–302.

Ladson-Billings, G. (2005). The evolving role of critical race theory in educational scholarship. *Race Ethnicity and Education, 8*(1), 115–119.

Ladson-Billings, G., & Tate, W. F. (1995). Toward a critical race theory of education. *Teacher's College Record, 97,* 47–68.

Milem, J. F. (2003). The educational benefits of diversity: Evidence from multiple sectors. In M. Chang, D. Witt, J. Jones, & K. Hakuta (Eds.), *Compelling interest: Examining the evidence on racial dynamics in higher education* (pp. 126–169). Palo Alto, CA: Stanford University Press.

Parker, L., & Lynn, M. (2002). What's race got to do with it? Critical race theory's conflicts with and connections to qualitative research methodology and epistemology. *Qualitative Inquiry, 8*(1), 7–22.

Reason, R. D., & Broido, E. M. (2005). Issues and strategies for social justice allies (and the student affairs professionals who hope to encourage them). In R. D. Reason, E. M. Broido, T. L. Davis, & N. J. Evans (Eds.), *Developing social justice allies.* San Francisco: Jossey-Bass.

Umbach, P. D., & Kuh, G. D. (2006). Student experiences with diversity at liberal arts colleges: Another claim for distinctiveness. *The Journal of Higher Education, 77*(1), 169–192.

Vega, T. (2014, February 25). Colorblind notion aside, colleges grapple with racial tension. *The New York Times.* Retrieved from http://www.nytimes.com

Vygotsky, L. S. (1978). *Mind in society: The development of higher psychological processes.* Cambridge, MA: Harvard University Press.

Watt, S. K., Curtiss, G., Drummond, J., Kellogg, A., Lozano, A., Tagliapietra, N. G., & Rosas, M. (2009). Privileged identity exploration: Examining White female counselor trainee's reactions to difficult dialogues in the classroom. *Counselor Education & Supervision, 49,* 86–105.

11

CONFRONTING SYSTEMS OF PRIVILEGE AND POWER IN THE CLASSROOM

Uses of Power

Bridget Turner Kelly and Joy Gaston Gayles

T o prepare the next generation of leaders in post-secondary education we must engage them in conversations about issues of *privilege* and *power*. The college classroom is an ideal place to foster these conversations and develop students' skills in understanding and managing difference. Conversations about privilege and power should be a central part of facilitating multicultural competence, defined as awareness, knowledge, and skills for effectively working with diverse populations (Pope & Reynolds, 1997). As college campuses become increasingly diverse it is critical for current and future campus leaders to increase their competence in negotiating conflicts related to difference on a personal, community, and/or societal level. In student affairs and higher education, multicultural competence is a clearly defined expectation for graduation preparation programs through the Council for the Advancement of Standards (CAS) as well as competencies publicly stated by professional associations such as the National Association of Student Personnel Administrators (NASPA) and the American College Personnel Association (ACPA).

Our discussion of multicultural competence centers on understanding key concepts such as privilege and power, and how they are used in the classroom setting. We first distinguish between important constructs related to privilege and power followed by a discussion of how they operate in society, including in the classroom, from a theoretical perspective. Next, we summarize a study conducted on faculty experiences teaching diversity and focus on power dynamics in the classroom. The chapter concludes with practical strategies for dealing with power dynamics and helping individuals recognize and name systems of power and privilege in a way that empowers us to interrupt larger systems of oppression.

Key Constructs Related to Privilege and Power

Before discussing how privilege and power operate in our society and in the college classroom, we differentiate related concepts such as stereotypes, prejudice, discrimination, and oppression. Often, the terms privilege and power are used interchangeably; however, they have very distinct meanings. Our aim is to be clear about the meanings of various terms to understand how they operate, and more importantly, how change can occur.

Stereotypes Feed Prejudice

Stereotypes are defined as characterizations about people based on incomplete, inaccurate, and or omitted information (Tatum, 2003). Stereotypes can be positive or negative, but the implications of stereotypes are usually negative. For example, the stereotype that all Asian people are smart has a positive undertone, but the effects of this "positive" stereotype have negative implications, particularly in a classroom setting. An Asian student struggling with an equation in math might go unnoticed because the teacher believes that all Asian people are smart and does not check the student's work because this student is assumed to have the answer correct. Stereotypes feed into people's judgments of others.

Prejudice Fuels Discrimination

Prejudice is collective preconceived judgment about groups of people informed by stereotypes and other forms of limited or inaccurate information (Bell, Love, Washington, & Weinstein, 2007). Prejudices may lead to discrimination, defined as the act of treating people differently based on judgments against them. Prejudice is often confused with discrimination, as is oppression.

Oppression Always Involves Power

Oppression is related to discrimination, but is deeper and characterized by the unjust exercise of authority and power by one group over another (Bell,

2007). The privileged or agent group imposes its belief system, values, and way of life onto the marginalized or target group. When oppression occurs, it sends negative messages to the marginalized group about their values, belief system, and way of life. When individuals who identify with marginalized groups begin to believe and accept negative messages about themselves based on value differences between groups, it can lead to self-hatred, low self-esteem, and internalized oppression. Internalized oppression is difficult to reverse once it settles in and it may take a lifetime to unlearn negative views of self and relearn positive ways of viewing one's self relative to the world around one. Unfortunately, internalization of negative messages is quite common. Scholars who study race and oppression have likened the internalization of negative messages about various groups in society to breathing smog in the air (Tatum, 2003): If you spend enough time outside it is inevitable that you will breathe in the smog whether you want to or not.

Defining *Privilege* and *Power*

We defined *stereotypes, prejudice, discrimination*, and *oppression* first because comprehending these terms and how they operate lays the foundation for understanding the definitions and operation of privilege and power in society. *Privilege* is a system of advantage that occurs in society based on membership and identification with the agent group (Bell, 2007). Privileges are unearned advantages and opportunities afforded to those who identify with agent groups, but not afforded to those who identify with target groups. Privilege has two defining characteristics: (a) benefits or entitlements are unearned; and (b) access to privilege brings about conferred dominance (i.e., *power*) of one group over another.

Privilege and Power as the Mythical Norm

To understand privilege and power we must be clear about how we define *target* and *agent groups* in society. Tatum (2003) identified agent and target groups according to the *mythical norm*. In her book *"Why Are all the Black Kids Sitting Together in the Cafeteria?" And Other Conversations on Race*, she characterized the mythical norm using seven categories of otherness: race, gender, sexual orientation, religion, class, disability status, and age. Each of these aspects of identity has an agent group, with all other group identities considered targets of oppression. Thus, the seven categories listed earlier— White, male, heterosexual, Christian, upper class, older individuals without a disability—represent the mythical norm. Unearned privileges and power over target groups accrue to individuals simply because they belong to one or many of the seven dominant identity groups.

Defining privilege as a system of unearned benefits and power can be difficult for some people to understand, particularly those who identify closely with the mythical norm. It can be difficult for individuals to understand or accept that they receive unearned advantages because of their dominant identities. This can be especially true for individuals who identify with both agent and target groups. Various aspects of an individual's identity can be privileged and oppressed simultaneously, which can lead to confusion about how privilege operates. One way to understand privilege and power is to reflect on the issue from an aspect of your identity that is considered target and think about all the ways in which society limits, discriminates, and/or oppresses you because of that aspect of your identity. Peggy McIntosh (1988), in her seminal article, discussed the ways in which privilege was accrued to her as a White woman. When you have aspects of your identity that are oppressed it is often easier to see privilege and power at work. In McIntosh's (1988) case, she used her target identity as a woman to connect with the 100 ways in which she benefited from being White and how she received these benefits without having to do anything to gain them. The reality is that individuals who have target identities must work hard to access these benefits, or worse, they do not receive access to the benefit at all. Lack of access to resources and benefits in society create and sustain the dynamics of power differentials between privileged and marginalized groups as well as outcome disparities between groups.

Racism and the Mythical Norm

Thinking about privilege in this way allows us to define *racism, sexism, classism*, and other aspects of the mythical norm in a more compelling way—one that can lead to real change. We use racism as our example; yet, we realize that this applies to all forms of "isms" associated with the mythical norm. A different way to define *racism* based on our understanding of how privilege and power work in society is as a system of advantages or benefits based on race. Using race as our example, White people benefit from advantages simply because they are White. People of color do not receive the same advantages and benefits, simply because they are *not* White.

One of the major issues with defining an "ism" in this way is that *racism*, for example, is typically defined as blatant or intentional acts of hatred and discrimination. Today, it is rare to see blatant acts of discrimination, and most acts are punishable by law. Does this mean that racism does not exist? Individuals who identify with target groups experience more passive and subtle acts of racism. Inappropriate jokes and discriminatory policies and practices (conscious and unconscious) are two examples of how racism exists today. Although subtle in nature, the effects of racism work against individuals in target groups and reinforce stereotypes and prejudices that lead to unfair treatment.

Racism can be further defined on three levels—individual, institutional, and cultural. Individual racism is characterized by beliefs, values, attitudes, and behaviors that perpetuate systematic advantages based on race. Institutional racism consists of policies and practices that systematically give advantages to White people while restricting access and mobility for people of color. Cultural racism is defined by beliefs that the cultural values of the privileged group are superior to others. One way this manifests is through cultural images in the media, in schools, and places of work that affirm the assumed superiority of White people and the assumed inferiority of people of color. One dominant media image is that there is a shortage of White males in colleges and universities. Is this image true? If so, what is the cause? Could affirmative action be one of the reasons? If the balance of power has shifted from less White males in the classroom to more students and faculty of color, what might the implications be?

Interlocking Systems of Privilege and Power in the Classroom

We view power dynamics in the classroom as a microcosm of systematic domination in the broader U.S. society (Feagin, Vera, & Imani, 1996; McKay, 1997). In *Writing Beyond Race: Living Theory and Practice*, hooks (2013) described the media as a system of domination at work in the United States that propagates imperialist, White supremacist, capitalist patriarchy. Hooks (2013) claimed that media is the most effective way this worldview or particular set of values spreads. For example, we believe that movies show professors largely in this dominant paradigm to such an extent of being White, male, middle- to upper-class (*Good Will Hunting, Legally Blonde, Paper Chase, With Honors*) that when faculty who do not share these identities enter the classroom they lose credibility, authority, and power. The system of domination connects not only to one's identity but also to parts of our institutional structure. Hooks (2013) argued that there is liberation in naming this structure and stated, "Time and time again critical theory has taught us the power of naming accurately that which we are challenging and hoping to transform" (p. 36). For the purpose of this chapter, we name the interlocking systems of power in which we are mired as faculty who hold subordinate identities and beliefs as we enter the university classroom. For instance, as Black women, we hold two target identities that are highly visible to students when we enter the classroom. From the construction of our syllabi and content of our courses, students learn quickly that we hold views that run counter to the dominant paradigm. We argue in this chapter that by virtue of our identities and worldviews, we do not wield as much power and privilege in the classroom compared to our White male peers who more closely identify with the mythical norm (Tatum, 2003).

Imperialism's Role in Systems of Power and Privilege

Unpacking the term imperialism provides a lens through which to describe how power is negotiated and wielded in the classroom. Imperialism can be defined as extending authority, influence, and power over others. From a U.S. perspective, imperialism involves thinking of the United States as the dominant empire in the world and one that can oppress others for its own gain. This thinking supports U.S. companies who set up clothing factories in what they deem third-world or underdeveloped parts of Asia because they can pay workers very low wages, pay zero to very little taxes, and construct unsafe buildings. Thus, what is valued is making the biggest profit margin rather than paying people a decent wage and ensuring they have safe working conditions. Confronting imperialism manifests in a classroom setting through upsetting power dynamics by teaching students to view issues from a cultural context that values people over profit. When I, Bridget, teach students about intergroup dialogue and they learn the purpose is to understand where another person is coming from and not to prove a point or come to consensus on how to solve a problem, some students see no value in the dialogue. I challenge imperialist thinking by focusing on people and their inherent value rather than objective or profitable outcomes. Consequently, I lost some credibility and power in the classroom. For example, one White female questioned the point of dialogue and when asked to expand upon her reasoning in our class discussion, she circumvented my authority by filing a formal charge against me to the dean and president of the university. The student did not make an appointment with me, e-mail me, or in any way alert me to her difficulty with me asking her a follow-up question in front of the class. By her not coming to me directly with her issue, my power in the classroom was undermined.

White Supremacy's Role in Systems of Power and Privilege

A second interlocking system of domination at work in the classroom alongside imperialism is White supremacy. White supremacy goes beyond racism and is inclusive of anyone, regardless of race, who believes light skin, blonde hair, and blue eyes are more desirable than dark skin, black hair, and brown eyes. White supremacy is about seeing White people, their values, and their actions as the norm and ideal, and seeing anyone who diverges from that ideal as undesirable. Hooks (2013) used the term *White supremacy* instead of *racism* because *racism* puts White people at the center of the discussion, where White people are seen as a superior race and therefore, they may hold views that people of color are subordinate. Conversely, White supremacy is not dependent on the actions and beliefs of White people to operate. Anyone can hold White supremacist views. From our experience, faculty who teach about internalized racism of people of color upset the dominant system of

White supremacy. When I, Bridget, as a Black woman, teach students that many people of color use bleach to lighten their skin or chemicals to make their hair straight I often draw anger from students of color who thought the conversation on race would center on White people and their actions. Thus, I lose some power and privilege in the class for naming White supremacy in a way that includes people of color as complicit.

Patriarchy's Role in Systems of Power and Privilege

Patriarchy works with imperialism and White supremacy to maintain dominance in society, and faculty can gain power by structuring their class to conform to patriarchy. Hooks (2013) defined *patriarchy* as:

> a political and social system that insists males are inherently dominating, superior to everything and everyone deemed weak, especially females, and endowed with the right to dominate and rule over the weak as well as the right to maintain dominance through various forms of psychological abuse and violence. (p. 35)

Recently, in a Women in Higher Education course, my authority and credibility as a professor came under scrutiny as a student questioned how I, Bridget, could design a course that did not contain any readings about males in higher education. The White female student wanted to compare how males were doing so she could judge the extent to which females had reached parity. I sought to shift the paradigm away from males at the center by exclusively including works by females about females in higher education. Doing so created discomfort for students who had grown accustomed to classes taught from a patriarchal perspective. One way the transfer of power manifested was this student confronting other students in the class and other White female professors to ask if my course should be more of a comparison between males and females. The student's attempt to discredit my approach to the course challenged my autonomy and power in the classroom.

Capitalism's Role in the Systems of Power and Privilege

We contend in this chapter that interlocking systems of imperialism, White supremacy, patriarchy, and capitalism operate together to form a dominant power structure. Capitalism, at its core, requires some people to be at the top and some people to be at the bottom of the socio-economic ladder. In a capitalistic system, the higher socio-economic classes are inherently dominant and superior to those in lower socio-economic classes. Thus, despite my target identities as a woman of color, students may find me, Bridget, credible in the classroom, in part due to my upper-middle class socio-economic status.

I dress, speak, and use cultural references (e.g., designer clothes, articulate speech, references to movies and plays I attend) such that students associate me with higher status in our capitalist society and grant me power and privilege because of this socio-economic class status.

System of Power and Privilege in the Classroom

We use hooks's (2013) dominant power structure concept to argue the more faculty resemble the mythical norm (Tatum, 2003) (e.g., U.S. citizen, White, heterosexual, Christian, middle- to upper-class, male, cisgender, temporarily able-bodied), and act in accordance with the dominant belief system, the more faculty are afforded deference, respect, and legitimized authority in the classroom. Conversely, the more faculty are different from this system of domination (e.g., immigrant to the United States, person of color, lesbian, Muslim, low socio-economic status, female, outside gender binary, person with a disability) or act in ways that subvert this system of domination, the less access to power and privilege they have in the classroom.

Power in the classroom is a source of negotiation between faculty and students, and is somewhat dependent on how students respond to faculty who act in alignment with or subvert the dominant system of power. Watt (2007) developed a theoretical framework that helps explain how students in diverse classrooms respond to dissonance, such as a faculty member who subverts the system of power by not situating men as dominant to women (patriarchy). Fear and entitlement are innate responses to this cognitive dissonance (Watt, 2007). We particularly focus on entitlement here as a lens to understand the classroom power dynamics experienced by faculty. Watt (2007) explained that entitlement "is an attitude that presumes ownership and power based on social/political contracts" (p. 119). The social/political contracts to which Watt (2007) referred are tied to the system of domination that hooks (2013) described. We believe students who are entitled have bought into imperialist White supremacist, capitalist, and patriarchy "contracts" that grant them power over people whose beliefs and identities run counter to this system of domination. Cognitive dissonance results then for some entitled students to grant power to faculty whose very identities and beliefs subvert the dominant power structure (Perry, Moore, Edwards, Acosta, & Frey, 2009; Watt, 2007).

Faculty Experiences Teaching Diversity Study

As faculty with experience subverting the dominant power structure, we were curious to hear about other faculty's experiences teaching courses embedded with concepts of oppression, privilege, and power. We conducted a study of faculty in graduate preparation courses who teach diversity courses, and sought to understand what they have learned about themselves, their students, and their teaching. The research questions that guided our study were:

1. What are the experiences of faculty who teach diversity courses?
2. How do faculty approach teaching diversity courses?

Methods

In this qualitative study, we collected data from 11 faculty who teach diversity-related courses within higher education programs across the country. We sought full-time, part-time, and adjunct faculty who taught diversity-related courses at least three times within the last 10 years for participation in the study. We conducted an initial search of graduate preparation programs who offered diversity courses as either a requirement or elective and identified faculty who taught those courses within the program. Diversity-related courses were defined as those designed to examine diversity and multiculturalism, race/ethnicity and other dominant/subordinate social identities, social justice issues, international and globalization, and religion and spirituality. Because the identity of the faculty member is closely tied to the multiple identities being taught in diversity classes, we were careful to include faculty from across a range of multicultural backgrounds to understand the potential role of the instructors' identities on the teaching and learning of diversity in graduate preparation programs. All of the participants chose pseudonyms to protect their confidentiality in the study.

The demographics of the 11 faculty participants consisted of seven females, four males, five White (Greg, Jane, Hillary, Elizabeth, Rick), one Asian-American (Melanie), one Hispanic (Robin), and four African American (Dora, Bryan, Michelle, Derrick). In addition, six of the faculty were assistant professors, three were associate professors, one was a full professor, and one was an adjunct faculty member. In terms of sexual orientation, six identified as heterosexual, three as lesbian, one as gay, and one as bisexual.

We used a semi-structured interview protocol and data were analyzed using hooks's (2013) conceptual theory of domination. This theory holds that imperialist, White supremacist, capitalist, patriarchal systems interlock and work together to reinforce power in the United States. Though hooks's (2013) theory did not explicitly address sexual orientation, her definition of patriarchy covers people who receive disdain or unequal treatment from those in power. There is great cultural evidence that people who are not heterosexual are poorly regarded in U.S. society (Watt, 1999) and there is greater evidence that people who identify as gay, lesbian, or bisexual experience oppression and marginalization, and lack access to power in many aspects of society (e.g., marriage equality, insurance, and death benefits). We included sexual orientation in our data analysis to unpack notions of patriarchy. We were unable to collect data on socio-economic class for every participant, so our discussion that follows mostly centers on sex, race, and sexual orientation, and whether the faculty held power or lacked power across these aspects of their identities.

Next, we used Watt's (2007) theoretical perspective that fear and entitlement are innate responses to cognitive dissonance. We examined how students in these classrooms responded to faculty whose identities and/or teaching challenged the dominant power structure of the United States.

Uses of Power in the Classroom

As we focused on uses of power in the classroom through hooks's (2013) and Watt's (2007) conceptual framework, we found the closer faculty were to the dominant paradigm and mythical norm, the more power and privilege they were afforded compared to faculty who diverged from the norm. In addition, students responded with varying levels of fear and entitlement to cognitive dissonance in the classroom, tempered by faculty's perceived access to power in the classroom. Faculty identity and students' responses to faculty are discussed under one broad category of "give and take of power dynamics."

Give and Take of Power Dynamics

Faculty in our study had different experiences with power in the classroom. Those who had more access to the dominant power structure as outlined by hooks (2013) often held a teaching philosophy that focused on active student engagement, gave students autonomy over their learning experience, and ceded power to students. Out of the 11 faculty, three discussed tempering their power and privilege in the classroom. Two were White heterosexual males and one was a White lesbian female. Greg described how students deferred power and authority to him in the classroom as he is "a person who identifies with a great many privileged categories" and "can't be assured that my students are always gonna challenge me." Rick explained that he comes from a privileged background and used the classroom as a democratic space where he handed a lot of power over to students to make decisions about assignments, points, and grading. Elizabeth said it is important for her to locate her "own privilege as White, as upper middle class, but also as a professor" and try "really hard not to have that overtake the classroom experience." In addition, she relayed how students defer power to her in that they "take you on faith that you're trying to do the right thing and then will forgive you if you screw up even in ways that possibly they shouldn't forgive me."

Thus, whereas some faculty with access to the dominant power structure outlined by hooks (2013) gave power to students or were granted power by students, other faculty experienced students taking power from them. Melanie and Michelle, two heterosexual females of color, both discussed their power and authority being challenged in the classroom. For instance, a White female student in Melanie's class got up and left during a discussion on White privilege. Melanie described several examples of the manner in which her power and credibility were usurped in the class:

> Usually students tell me if they have to leave early and so on, but for some reason she just left. So later I received an e-mail from her and she says to me that she did not enjoy the class because she didn't feel like talking about White privilege had anything to do with a diversity class. . . . I felt disrespected also because I started to think again on my position as a woman of color teaching this class, there's definitely some things that—there's perceptions that people hold of me and I wondered how this would have been perceived by this woman had I been maybe a White professor who's male.

Melanie later described that the student returned to class but did not respond to Melanie's request to speak with her one-on-one about why she was uncomfortable. Michelle similarly discussed students wielding power in her classroom because of her identity as a female of color. She remarked:

> [P]eople abuse me in the classroom because they are disrespectful of my experiences. And that's the other thing that is very frustrating about teaching these courses. I feel like it's an abuse. I feel like they come from that place of privilege and they won't let go.

Thus, Melanie and Michelle discussed students as disrespectful and abusive in their efforts to discredit and disavow these females of color of their power in the classroom.

Six faculty described moderate resistance to their teaching and to their identities in the classroom. Bryan, an African American heterosexual male, like many of the faculty of color in this study (Derrick, Melanie, Michelle), encountered those who thought he might be biased because of his race and side with students of color in discussion and/or berate White students for being racist. Derrick, an African American gay male, said students questioned whether his assignment to the diversity class was just because he was a person of color.

Jane and Dora specifically referenced the power students have when they feel challenged by concepts discussed in diversity courses. Jane, a White lesbian female, remarked: "[Y]ou are always wondering, How are students going to respond to this? Are they gonna get frustrated, and then rate me lower because I've challenged them in a way that they weren't prepared to be challenged?" Students have power to write negative course evaluations, which can damage faculty members' promotion opportunities, but they also have power to disrupt the classroom. Dora, an African American lesbian, recalled a student who had a "contrarian approach to whatever was happening in class and he just debated . . . . He said 'he's (author of class text) wrong about this, and he's wrong about that' and you know, [that] was distracting in many ways." Thus, students could discredit the faculty member's judgment and lessen his or her power simply because they feel challenged by the material.

Hillary and Robin discussed vulnerability, another aspect of teaching that disrupted their sense of power in the classroom. Hillary, a White bisexual female, shared her sexual orientation in class and a student who had sat next to her every day up until that point sat far away from her after that. The student later disclosed he had difficulty reconciling his religious beliefs with her sexual orientation. Hillary questioned her ability to connect with all students in future classes. Robin, a heterosexual Latina and immigrant to the United States, felt disempowered and unprepared to teach her diversity course because it was assigned to her simply due to her identity as a female of color. Faculty in our study with target identities were vulnerable both to students and to being essentialized by faculty assignments. Vulnerability and disclosure can lead to power dynamics in which students disrespect the professor, dismiss what the professor has to say, or withdraw from the class all together.

Discussion and Practical Suggestions

In terms of theme one, we learned from our study that power and privilege dynamics are at play in the diversity classroom. Three faculty out of 11 reported the most direct access to the dominant power system in the United States. In reference to hooks's (2013) theoretical concept, all three were White, two were heterosexual and male, and one was a lesbian female. In order for White supremacy to operate, students and faculty have to buy into the idea that White is the ideal norm for faculty. This can be intensified by patriarchy, which comes with the belief system that males are "endowed with the right to dominate and rule" (hooks, 2013, p. 35). The two White male heterosexual men, Greg and Rick, were reportedly granted the most power and credibility by students. One other participant, Elizabeth, discussed the power and privilege afforded to her in the classroom, which she attributed to her race as a White person, status as a professor, and her socio-economic status as upper-middle class. From hooks's (2013) framework, we saw White supremacy and capitalism operating together such that Elizabeth said students assumed she had good intentions and forgave her for any mishaps she might have had in class. Elizabeth did not discuss any instances where her sex as a female or her sexual orientation as a lesbian affected her credibility or power in the classroom. This demonstrates that the giving and taking of power by students and faculty is complex and not solely attributable to identities one holds.

In terms of theme two, students responded differently to faculty based partly on their utilization of the dominant power system in the United States. Watt's (2007) theoretical concept of fear and entitlement being innate responses to cognitive dissonance was evident in the experiences of eight participants (all faculty of color and two faculty with non-dominant sexual orientations) who lacked full access to the dominant power structure (hooks, 2013). Students wielded power in the classroom by physically removing themselves from the classroom environment or avoiding the faculty. In both cases, the manifestation of cognitive dissonance experienced by students was a fear of confronting something counter to their belief system, whether that was a White male student's religious opposition to bisexuality or a White female student challenging the notion of White privilege. These two examples highlight the role of patriarchy in males being "superior to everything and everyone deemed weak" (hooks, 2013, p. 35) and the role of White supremacy in White students' entitlement. Watt (2007) explained: "When facing what it means to be privileged, individuals may unconsciously fear giving up power, and use defenses to retreat back to the comfort that exists within their dominant identity" (p. 119). Other examples of fear and entitlement rooted in White supremacist and patriarchal power dynamics came from students challenging faculty's choice of readings and challenging whether the faculty member could be unbiased in teaching students from agent and target identities. Through the lens of the dominant power structure (hooks, 2013) and fear and entitlement responses to cognitive dissonance (Watt, 2007), faculty participants in our study who held dominant identities were afforded power and those who held non-dominant identities had power usurped. Although nuanced in terms of faculty holding multiple dominant and subordinate identities, those who were White and male experienced the most privilege in the classroom.

Garcia and Hoelscher (2010) labeled incidents the least-privileged faculty in our study experienced as *diversity flashpoints*—defined as uncomfortable, potentially explosive situations that involve differences in attitudes, values, and behaviors of people from different multicultural backgrounds. The result of a diversity flashpoint is equivalent to the old adage of an elephant being in the room. Everyone is aware that something is wrong, but no one is willing to accept responsibility and address the issue in a healthy productive way. Garcia and Hoelscher (2010) suggested the "4 R" system for effectively dealing with diversity flashpoints. The four Rs stand for recognize, reflect, react, and reassess. In order to acknowledge and name systems of power and privilege when they occur, faculty and students must recognize that a flashpoint has occurred. This is not as simple as it seems because individuals who identify with agent identity groups do not often recognize when they say something inappropriate or behave in a way that is insensitive. Because they are entitled and may have never experienced what it is like to experience a marginalized identity, individuals remain unaware of how their attitudes and behavior can affect someone different from themselves. The ability to recognize flashpoints when they occur comes with increased awareness about issues of privilege and power in society.

Below we offer a few practical suggestions for managing diversity flashpoints that operate in the college classroom, as well as in society generally.

- Acknowledge and name loss of power or credibility as systems of domination and use them as teaching moments.
- Engage in dialogue around diversity flashpoints no matter how uncomfortable it may be.
- Do not avoid conflict. Successfully resolving, unlearning, and relearning information that is incorrect, incomplete, or flat out wrong may begin to break down age-old systems of power and privilege that exist in the classroom.
- Do not stop with an apology. Apologizing for making an insensitive comment does little to interrupt systems of power and privilege in society. Engage in a deeper discussion about what happened in the class, workshop, or training session and how one's actions are tied to systems of privilege and power.
- Address the "elephant" in the room in a timely manner because the opportunity for learning is often limited to a short timeframe.
- Revisit the incident and outcome in terms of how well the resolution worked in addressing the issue for all of the parties, not just those with privilege and power.
- Co-teach with colleagues who identify with dominant groups or someone of a different identity than yourself. Sometimes hearing the same message from more than one individual can be meaningful.
- Find peers at other institutions who also teach diversity courses. Discussing issues with a colleague can lend support and ideas for effectively resolving diversity flashpoints when they occur.

- Incorporate content on power structures and privilege into the course. Students are at various levels in terms of their multicultural competence and not all students will understand how power and privilege work the first time they experience it.

We offer these suggestions because they have been useful to us as educators and because they are supported by the data and research we covered in this chapter. Having taught diversity courses for over a decade, we liken teaching diversity to planting seeds. Life experiences will occur over time that will stimulate growth. Often, our own presence of non-conformity to the mythical norm may stimulate growth for students. The timing is different for everyone—it may take a month, a year, or a lifetime for individuals to understand fully the manifestations of privilege and uses of power in society. Understanding this principle gives us great hope in the face of diversity-related challenges experienced in the classroom.

Recommended Reading List

Adams, M., Bell, L. A., & Griffin, P. (Eds.). (2007). *Teaching for diversity and social justice*. New York: Routledge.

Barratt, W. (2011). *Social class on campus: Theories and manifestations*. Sterling, VA: Stylus.

Cuyjet, M. J., Howard-Hamilton, M. F., & Cooper, D. L. (Eds.). (2012). *Multiculturalism on campus: Theory, models, and practices for understanding diversity and creating inclusion*. Sterling, VA: Stylus Publishing.

Garcia, J. E., & Hoelscher, K. J. (2010). *Managing diversity flashpoints in higher education*. Lanham, MD: Rowman & Littlefield Publishers.

Goodman, D. J. (2011). *Promoting diversity and social justice: Educating people from privileged groups*. New York: Routledge.

Johnson, A. G. (2001). *Privilege, power, and difference*. Boston, MA: McGraw-Hill.

Kivel, P. (2002). *Uprooting racism: How white people can work for racial justice*. Gabriola Island, BC: New Society Publishers.

Tatum, B. D. (2007). *Can we talk about race?: And other conversations in an era of school resegregation*. Boston, MA: Beacon Press.

Winkle-Wagner, R. (2014). *Diversity and inclusion on campus: Supporting racially and ethnically underrepresented*. New York: Routledge.

References

Bell, L. A. (2007). Theoretical foundations for social justice education. In M. J. Adams, L. A. Bell, & P. Griffin, (Eds.), *Teaching for diversity and social justice* (2nd ed., pp. 1–14). New York: Routledge.

Bell, L. A., Love, B. J., Washington, S., & Weinstein, G. (2007). Knowing ourselves as social justice educators. In M. J. Adams, L. A. Bell, & P. Griffin, (Eds.), *Teaching for diversity and social justice* (2nd ed., pp. 381–393). New York: Routledge.

Feagin, J., Vera, H., & Imani, N. (1996). *The agony of education*. New York: Routledge.

Garcia, J. E., & Hoelscher, K. J. (2010). *Managing diversity flashpoints in higher education*. Lanham, MD: Rowman & Littlefield.

hooks, b. (2013). *Writing beyond race: Living theory and practice*. New York: Routledge.

McIntosh, P. (1988). *White privilege and male privilege: A personal account of coming to see correspondences through work in women's studies* (Working Paper No. 189). Wellesley, MA: Wellesley College Center for Research on Women.

McKay, N. (1997). A troubled peace: Black women in the halls of the white academy. In L. Benjamin (Ed.), *Black women in the academy: Promises and perils* (pp. 12–22). Gainesville, FL: University Press of Florida.

Perry, G., Moore, H., Edwards, C., Acosta, K., & Frey, C. (2009). Maintaining credibility and authority as an instructor of color in diversity-education classrooms: A qualitative inquiry. *Journal of Higher Education, 80*, 80–105.

Pope, R. L., & Reynolds, A. L. (1997). Student affairs core competencies: Integrating multicultural awareness, knowledge, and skills. *Journal of College Student Development, 38*(3), 266–277.

Tatum, B. D. (2003). *Why are the Black kids sitting together in the cafeteria?: And other conversations about race*. New York: Basic Books.

Watt, S. (1999). The story between the lines: A thematic discussion of the experience of racism. *Journal of Counseling and Development, 77*, 54–62.

Watt, S. (2007). Difficult dialogues, privilege and social justice: Uses of the privileged identity exploration (PIE) model in student affairs practice. *The College Student Affairs Journal, 26*(2), 114–126.

12

THE TRANSFORMATIONAL POTENTIAL OF ACADEMIC AFFAIRS AND STUDENT AFFAIRS PARTNERSHIPS FOR ENACTING MULTICULTURAL INITIATIVES

Lucy A. LePeau

Higher education, faculty, researchers, and student affairs (SA) practitioners promote student participation in high-impact practices (HIP) such as study abroad, undergraduate research with faculty members, and service-learning (Kuh, 2008; National Survey of Student Engagement [NSSE], 2013). Depending on how faculty and SA practitioners design these HIPs, students are intentionally poised to learn across differences, find plausible solutions to complex issues with more than one response, and integrate learning from multiple disciplines (Kuh, 2008; NSSE, 2013). Faculty and SA practitioners *also* need to engage in these types of learning experiences in order to implement robust multicultural initiatives to promote student success. Kezar and Lester (2009) defined *collaborations* or *partnerships* as: "Individuals working together toward a common purpose, with equal voice and responsibility" (p. 138). Therefore, it is essential to create academic affairs (AA) and SA partnerships whereby faculty, practitioners, staff, and students can work together and make cultural shifts happen on college campuses.

Watt (2013) raised the question: "How can we design initiatives that set in motion social change on an individual, institutional, and/or a systemic level?" In a grounded theory study, I examined participants engaging in AA and SA partnerships in order to promote diversity and inclusion at four different institutions (LePeau, 2012). This study revealed some important qualities of a functional relationship between AA and SA. The purpose of this chapter is to offer extended insight into the ways in which partnerships between AA and SA can represent a "standard operation of the entire campus" (LePeau, 2012, p. 222). When I refer to AA and SA, I am including all faculty, administrators, staff, students, and student affairs professionals who inhabit college educator roles in either AA or SA functional domains. In this chapter, I discuss common barriers to collaboration, share effective strategies, offer guidance for how a campus might build a working partnership between AA and SA to better students, and provide examples from the different types of institutions I studied. Finally, I share recommendations for how institutions can sustain AA and SA partnerships.

Common Barriers to Collaborations

There is a wealth of literature outlining barriers to developing partnerships between AA and SA. Researchers point to the cultural differences between AA and SA as the primary barrier (Blake, 1996; Kuh, 1996; Magolda, 2005; Schroeder, 2003; Smith, 2005). Researchers also outline ideas such as the perception that AA and SA college educators are rewarded differently (Kezar & Lester, 2009). That is, faculty members' reward system is for activities such as generating single-authored publications and giving academic presentations to national audiences, while SA college educators are rewarded for working in collaboration and bridging partnerships with AA to accomplish learning goals (Kezar & Lester, 2009). As a faculty member and student affairs professional, I have heard statements that reinforce these cultural barriers.

For instance, I have heard SA college educators state that "Faculty members will never come to my programs, especially after 5 p.m.," "Faculty members just want me to do all of the administrative tasks and so they belittle me," or "Faculty members say that they value student learning about diversity, but if the activities do not help them get tenure why would they participate?" I also hear faculty members make comments such as: "They (SA) know how to do the student life stuff—that's their strength. I'll let them do their thing and I'll do my thing" or "I don't know how SA supports the academic mission of the institution." I wonder, where are the limiting beliefs coming from? Are the beliefs supported by evidence or are the beliefs based on stereotypes? Granted, I have also heard remarkable accounts about how AA and SA college educators collaborate, such as in living learning communities, service learning projects, and study abroad experiences.

AA and SA college educators can benefit from opportunities to learn from each other and to recognize that their diverse thoughts and social locations are assets to the fabric of the institution. Yet, AA and SA college educators find it difficult in the current pace of higher education to make time for these types of joint learning experiences. AA and SA college educators are encouraged to reflect on whether or not learning with AA and SA partners is a priority at their respective institution. If the immediate response or excuse people make is that they are too busy, too overworked, and/or do not have adequate time in their jobs to complete priorities as it is, AA and SA college educators need to name that these barriers exist.

Further, all parties need an awareness and understanding of navigating political dynamics at the institution in order to benefit from relationships when doing collaborative work toward implementing multicultural initiatives. If AA college educators have more actual or perceived power than SA college educators, partnerships for implementing multicultural initiatives are more difficult to forge (Fried & Associates, 1995; Kuh, 1996; Schroeder, 1999, 2003; Smith, 2005). To truly transform institutions through multicultural initiatives, I am focusing on presenting AA and SA partnerships as mechanisms for the culture of the institution to support multiple and simultaneous efforts. AA and SA college educators can implement initiatives in classrooms, curriculum designs, co-curricular initiatives and more to strive for the multi-level changes Watt (2013) described. It is critical, therefore, to examine how AA and SA college educators employ strategies to transform barriers to collaboration.

Strategies for Building a Working Partnership Between AA and SA

All campus community members play a role in student learning. As Watt (2013) described, a conscious scholar practitioner affirms and engages differences in ways that influence their individual and community behaviors. Harper (2008) also described a conscious and courageous educator as someone who recognizes "–isms (racism, sexism, heterosexism, ableism, etc.) and oppressive conditions in campus environments, call(s) them to the attention of several others, and respond(s) with deliberation" (p. 11). AA and SA college educators, operating in functional partnerships, see everyone as an "academic" in their campus community and this language is important (LePeau, 2012). If everyone is an "academic" who contributes to student learning, then there is something to learn from each other. Partnerships between AA and SA can be a powerful tool particularly when thinking about them as a standard operating practice so that all "academics" contribute to more than a singular initiative for a learning community or study abroad program. Thus, AA and SA college educators can design multicultural initiatives to dismantle marginalization that faculty, students, and staff from underrepresented groups experience on college campuses and to create multi-level transformations.

However, a caveat is for AA and SA college educators to design multicultural initiatives that do not benefit faculty, students, and staff solely from dominant groups. I present key strategies for AA and SA college educators to break down barriers and build working partnerships between AA and SA. These strategies include implementing processes for examining the historical context of the institution, interrogating power dynamics between AA and SA, and developing deep relationships with counterparts in AA and SA. These strategies may compel AA and SA college educators to delve more deeply into the benefits of building partnerships for multi-level multicultural changes.

Examine the Historical Context of the Institution

Everyone in the institution can ask key questions to understand whether diversity is a value at the institution and recognize where tensions between people operating from dominant and subordinate paradigms exist (Watt, 2013). The first step is for AA and SA college educators to consider the historical context and mission of the institution because this examination will offer greater insights about systems and institutional structures that have lingering counterproductive influence on the current campus culture (Hurtado, Milem, Clayton-Pedersen, & Allen, 1999; Milem, Chang, & antonio, 2005). For example, a Hispanic-serving institution in my study outlined in its mission that every student needed to take courses that prepared them for participating in a diverse democracy. An accrediting body evaluated the curriculum, however, and unearthed that the general education curriculum was rooted in White European male history. As a result, the AA and SA college educators at the institution acknowledged the gap between the stated and enacted objectives; their work then related to altering the curriculum. The process took into account not only evaluating one's individual teaching practices but also the institution's design of the general education program (LePeau, 2012).

Some additional questions to consider when outlining institutional goals are: How are AA and SA college educators designing curriculum that is culturally relevant for students? Are systems in the environment reinforcing White privilege? Are faculty, students, and staff from underrepresented groups experiencing sexism, classism, and other intersecting "isms" in the environment? What is the compositional diversity of the institution? When AA and SA college educators collaboratively identify institutional goals and objectives for multicultural initiatives, then working in a partnership toward that end seems more palatable. Finally, AA and SA college educators are encouraged to construct institutional goals that cut across the entire institution to alter the curriculum, campus climate, and culture (Bensimon & Malcom, 2012; Hurtado et al., 1999; Milem et al., 2005).

Interrogate Power Dynamics Between AA and SA

In order to support diversity as a social value at any institution (Watt, 2013), all individuals need to believe in their capacity to enhance the environment. As noted earlier, a common barrier to collaborations is power dynamics between AA and SA whereby the perception is that AA partners have more power than do their SA counterparts. Therefore, AA and SA partnerships represent a social justice initiative in and of itself because they inherently represent a sharing of power. Designing initiatives to alter inequities between AA and SA becomes part of the work of contributing to multi-level change. AA and SA college educators operating from functional partnerships will take on this challenge of interrogating power dynamics at the institution because they have realistic views of power and find creative ways to share power.

For example, SA college educators may voice frustration that faculty members are protected by academic freedom and SA college educators are not. Therefore, faculty members may have power to name issues of exclusion that SA college educators might experience in the campus environment without fear of retribution. Faculty members who study labor unions, organizational change, and/or the law may have different insights about the institutional policies than SA college educators. AA and SA college educators working through a functional partnership model may invite these faculty members to build coalitions with them to better understand their rights and responsibilities and construct opportunities for change (LePeau, 2012). Thus, AA and SA college educators' partnerships may generate multiple ways to create new organizational systems and structures to support cultural change.

As another example, some institutions are implementing digital portfolios as mechanisms for students to display their academic accomplishments online. AA and SA college educators can work together and consider how to encourage students to map their academic progress with their co-curricular work in the digital portfolio; this process might include AA and SA college educators changing current systems or structures. If AA college educators outline student-learning objectives such as global interdependence, critical thinking, and intercultural learning, then they will find digital portfolios offer platforms to connect student learning across the institution (Association of American Colleges and Universities [AAC&U], 2007). This example is a way for AA and SA college educators to promote student learning inside and outside of the classroom and serves as a way to co-construct a system (e.g., the digital portfolio) that demonstrates how everyone is an "academic" at an institution.

To push the efforts of altering inequitable organizational systems, policies, and structures, AA and SA college educators must track and report data; college educators can use research from Bensimon and Malcom (2012) pertaining to the Equity Scorecard to inform the design. Key questions AA and SA college educators must ask through disaggregating data include: Who is actually enrolled and retained in academic programs? Who is enrolled and retained in co-curricular programs? What is the institutional climate like for students and college educators from different backgrounds? How do you know? Institutional leaders such as provosts, faculty, and deans of students can collaborate and then have a better sense of the effectiveness of programs and consider whether proposed institutional objectives align with the data. Further, AA and SA partnerships may also challenge themselves to learn from their counterparts, which will enhance their own work.

Develop Deep Relationships With Counterparts in AA and SA

It is important for AA and SA college educators to develop deep relationships in order to enact multi-level changes. AA and SA college educators want to ensure that the commitment to social change is more than talking about diversity as a good but that colleagues are living out diversity as a value (Watt, 2013). In order to exemplify this ongoing commitment, AA and SA college educators need to find ways to develop more than cursory relationships with their counterparts. For instance, at a minority-serving institution AA and SA college educators operating in functional partnerships gathered in regular teaching and learning meetings (LePeau, 2012).

More specifically, if AA and SA college educators are interested in developing culturally relevant pedagogy for students both inside and outside of the classroom, the topics for the meetings might directly relate to this point. One example is how to select readings or how to facilitate difficult dialogues (i.e., dialogues where people deeply discuss conflicting views related to diversity issues like heterosexism and racism) in curricular and co-curricular learning experiences (Watt, 2007, 2013). AA and SA college educators may discuss how they select literature for particular classes or generate examples for classroom engagement activities. They may use this discussion venue to suggest new books and media for the library. This practice is an example of AA and SA college educators talking about how seeing the assignment of authors in curriculum (broadly in and out of class) matters for affirming one's identities (Quaye & Harper, 2007).

However, *how* facilitators construct these meetings with AA and SA college educators is critical to their success; sometimes the facilitators may be insiders to the institution and sometimes it is more effective to enlist external facilitators. It is natural for AA and SA college educators to resist talking across differences. These college educators have the capacity to address biases and assumptions and learn new perspectives from each other. Often, facilitators construct ground rules for participants such as "be respectful" or "talk openly by using 'I' statements to take ownership for missteps." However, ground rules can be potentially harmful to participants engaging in difficult dialogues if facilitators do not take into consideration privileging one individual or another's group norms (Arao & Clemens, 2013; Watt, 2007). Arao and Clemens (2013) presented the idea of facilitators working with students to create brave space where differences are discussed regularly and ground rules might evolve as participants of difficult dialogues get to know each other differently. Facilitators working with AA and SA college educators talking across differences for the purpose of implementing multicultural initiatives could revisit ground rules with an acknowledgment that consensus-building is not the end goal and that ongoing work is required to continue learning about each other's differences (Arao & Clemens, 2013).

Recommendations for Sustaining AA and SA Partnerships on College Campuses

The strategies I presented for building AA and SA partnerships may seem simple. However, making the commitment to doing these practices may shift the operating practices at institutions. AA and SA college educators who adopt limited beliefs about the potential for AA and SA partnerships on college campuses in relation to implementing multicultural initiatives may stalemate the opportunities before they start. Thus, AA and SA college educators developing sustained functional partnerships at their institution requires great perseverance. One of the participants in my study described his commitment to multiculturalism as "something that is in your gut." The participants faced opposition and experienced challenges, but their commitment and camaraderie helped them sustain their efforts in reaching some institutional objectives. They developed deep relationships with colleagues across campus that shared their perspective that student learning is enhanced by diversity. As AA and SA college educators look at their own institutions, I offer three recommendations for sustaining AA and SA partnerships:

1. **Include both AA and SA college educators in designing institutional goals.**

   When senior level administrators such as presidents and provosts include representatives from *both* AA and SA as well as students to develop institutional priorities for diversity, this practice communicates to members of the campus community that everyone contributes to student learning. AA and SA college educators will more likely commit long-term to something they helped design. Senior-level administrators may intentionally or inadvertently reinforce a power differential of an us-versus-them mentality between AA and SA through these practices (Kuh, 1996) if they do not include students and SA college educators in the institutional planning. Therefore, the composition of campus-wide committees needs to represent all campus community constituents. A functional partnership involves effective communication among representatives from AA and SA in designing institutional goals.

2. **Blur the lines in your work between AA and SA.**

   Blurring the lines between AA and SA college educators increases the possibility of functional partnerships for multicultural initiatives. For example, create positions where the job description includes AA and SA college educators co-teaching and facilitating in study abroad experiences. When AA and SA college educators transfer their skills in different job responsibilities, they may be more equipped to see everyone on campus as "academic."

3. **Involve catalysts (both internal and external) to keep initiatives going.**

   Senior-level administrators such as provosts and deans of students look to external constituencies to provide different perspectives and expertise about how to design multicultural initiatives. Oftentimes people not immersed in the day-to-day politics of the institution have the capacity to name issues of exclusion or tensions related to difference (Watt, 2013) differently than people in the institution. It might be difficult for an SA college educator to tell a provost an institutional policy is racist or sexist. It might be difficult for a faculty member to state that although family leave policies exist, the culture of the institution makes it difficult for him or her to take leave without feeling that there is the perception that he or she is less committed to the job. AA and SA college educators should examine who might serve as a catalyst for their institution to make changes in enacting multicultural initiatives. For instance, the Association of American Colleges and Universities (AAC&U) orchestrated a national initiative called American Commitments to focus on working with college educators to infuse tenets related to diversity in both the curriculum and co-curriculum (AAC&U, 1995a, 1995b, 1995c). Participants from both AA and SA attended institutes to talk about their efforts and learn about initiatives occurring at different institutions. AA and SA college educators conversing with colleagues at these institutes may generate ideas for campus to manage more effectively these challenges with structural inequity.

It is possible to seek out people who can catalyze initiatives on campus as well. For instance, AA and SA senior administrators can seek out researchers within their institutions who study organizational change, diversity issues in higher education, and/or intergroup relations to share their expertise with members of the campus community. AA and SA college educators can apply for internal grants to initiate change within the institution. Similarly, there may be SA college educators on campus who serve as facilitators for programs like the Social Justice Training Institute through ACPA—College Student Educators International or LeaderShape. SA college educators can work with AA faculty members to replicate programs that happen outside or within the institution in relation to institution-specific partnerships. AA and SA college educators still benefit from getting outside of one's day-to-day environment to meet different people and have space to reflect deeply about one's own practices through attending professional conferences and institutes. Too often, however, members of our own institutions do not even know these national programs exist or that AA and SA college educators in their respective institutions are leaders of these programs.

Conclusion

Demonstrating functional partnerships between AA and SA will undoubtedly have a positive impact on students. Students are looking for hope and want to make positive contributions to social change. In previous chapters of this book, authors provided suggestions for how to conduct ongoing assessments and adjust strategic plans when there are differences between the stated objectives and the actual outcomes in enacting multicultural initiatives. The suggestions in this chapter regarding how to sustain a functional partnership may also be helpful. Robust partnerships between AA and SA will challenge college educators to look inward and acknowledge ways to enhance the total college environment for students (Watt, 2013). Thus, college educators have the potential to improve multiculturalism and to revolutionize "how things are done here" in higher education by committing to making cultural shifts through strengthening AA and SA partnerships.

References

Arao, B., & Clemens, K. (2013). From safe space to brave spaces: A new way to frame dialogue around diversity and social justice. In L. M. Landreman (Ed.), *The art of effective facilitation: Reflections from social justice educators* (pp. 135–150). Sterling, VA: Stylus.

Association of American Colleges and Universities. (1995a). *American pluralism and the college curriculum: Higher education in a diverse democracy*. Report prepared for American commitments: A national initiative of the Association of American Colleges and Universities. Washington DC: Author.

Association of American Colleges and Universities. (1995b). *Liberal learning and the arts of connection for the new academy*. Report prepared for American commitments: A national initiative of the Association of American Colleges and Universities. Washington DC: Author.

Association of American Colleges and Universities. (1995c). *The drama of diversity and democracy: Higher education and American commitments*. Report prepared for American commitments: A national initiative of the Association of American Colleges and Universities. Washington DC: Author.

Association of American Colleges and Universities. (2007). *Liberal education and America's promise*. Report prepared for college learning for the new global century. Washington DC: Author.

Bensimon, E. M., & Malcolm, L. E. (Eds.). (2012). *Confronting equity issues on campus: Implementing the equity scorecard in theory and practice*. Sterling, VA: Stylus.

Blake, E. S. (1996). The yin and yang of student learning in college. *About Campus, 1*, 4–9.

Fried, J., & Associates. (1995). *Shifting paradigms in student affairs: Culture, context, teaching and learning*. Lanham, MD: University Press of America.

Harper, S. R. (Ed.). (2008). *Creating inclusive campus environments for cross-cultural learning and engagement*. Washington DC: NASPA.

Hurtado, S., Milem, J., Clayton-Pedersen, A., & Allen, W. (1999). Enacting diverse learning environments: Improving the climate for racial/ethnic diversity in higher education. In A. J. Kezar (Ed.), *ASHE-ERIC Higher Education Report* (Vol. 26, No. 8). Washington DC: The George Washington University, Graduate School of Education and Human Development.

Kezar, A., & Lester, J. (2009). *Organizing higher education for collaboration: A guide for campus leaders*. San Francisco: John Wiley & Sons.

Kuh, G. D. (1996). Guiding principles for creating seamless learning environments for undergraduates. *Journal of College Student Development, 37*, 135–148.

Kuh, G. D. (2008). *High-impact educational practices: What they are, who has access to them, and why they matter.* Washington DC: American Association of Colleges and Universities.

LePeau, L. (2012). *Academic affairs and student affairs partnerships promoting diversity initiatives on campus: A grounded theory* (Doctoral dissertation). Available from ProQuest Dissertation and Theses database. (UMI No. 3543589).

Magolda, P. M. (2005). Proceed with caution: Uncommon wisdom about academic and student affairs partnerships. *About Campus, 9,* 16–21.

Milem, J. F., Chang, M. J., & antonio, a. l. (2005). *Making diversity work on campus: A research-based perspective.* One in a series of three papers commissioned as part of the making excellence inclusive initiative from the Association of American Colleges and Universities. Washington DC: Author.

National Survey of Student Engagement (NSSE). (2013). *A fresh look at student engagement: Annual results 2013.* Retrieved from http://nsse.iub.edu/NSSE_2013 _Results/pdf/NSSE_2013_Annual_Results.pdf#page=22

Quaye, S. J., & Harper, S. R. (2007). Faculty accountability for culturally inclusive pedagogy and curricula. *Liberal Education, 93,* 32–39.

Schroeder, C. C. (1999). Partnerships: An imperative for enhancing student learning and institutional effectiveness. In J. H. Schuh & E. J. Whitt (Eds.), *Creating successful partnerships between academic and student affairs* (pp. 5–18). San Francisco: Jossey-Bass.

Schroeder, C. C. (2003). Using the lessons of research to develop partnerships. In S. R. Komives, Woodard, D. B. Jr., & Associates (Eds.), *Student services: A handbook for the profession* (4th ed., pp. 618–636). San Francisco: Jossey-Bass.

Smith, K. K. (2005). From coexistence to collaboration: A call for partnership between academic and student affairs. *Journal of Cognitive Affective Learning, 2,* 16–20.

Watt, S. K. (2007). Difficult dialogues, privilege and social justice: Uses of the privileged identity exploration (PIE) model in student affairs practice. *College Student Affairs Journal, 26,* 114–126.

Watt, S. K. (2013). Designing and implementing multicultural initiatives: Guiding principles. In S. K. Watt & J. Linley (Eds.), *Creating successful multicultural initiatives in higher education and student affairs* (pp. 5–15). San Francisco: Jossey-Bass.

PART FOUR

CONSCIOUS SCHOLAR PRACTITIONERS' REFLECTIONS ON IDENTITY, POWER, AND PRIVILEGE

How do conscious scholar practitioners face the challenges within the convergence of identity, power, and privilege that are inherent to multicultural initiatives and campus organizational change?

13

POLITICS OF INTERSECTING IDENTITIES

John A. Mueller and Craig S. Pickett

When we define ourselves, when I define myself, the place in which
I am like you and the place in which I am not like you, I'm not
excluding you from the joining —I'm broadening the joining.
—Audre Lorde (1984, p. 11)

Implementing multicultural initiatives on campus is exciting and rewarding work. It can vary in form and content from campus to campus,
department to department, and person to person. In general, though,
it involves efforts we make to promote multiculturalism and inclusion at
our institutions through policies, programs, and services. Multicultural initiatives can take many forms: They may be diversity workshops we deliver
to our students or staffs; strategies to increase and retain diversity in our
department staffs; the creation and coordination of campus-wide programs
(e.g., mentoring, leadership); or policies that guide decisions with respect to
financial support, curriculum development, academic support, assessment,
student retention, and staff evaluation, to name a few. Furthermore, multicultural initiatives may target any or all levels of the campus: the individual,
the group, the department, and the institution itself (Pope, Reynolds, &

Mueller, 2014), and may reflect some combination of "diversity as good" or "diversity as a value" ideologies (Watt, 2013). The work is indeed stimulating, insightful, and inspiring. But it is not without challenges; it can be fraught with confusion, questions, and cautions.

Our identities and the meanings we attach to those identities can become one challenge in implementing multicultural initiatives. When we develop a program, or design a workshop, or implement a policy, how we identify in terms of race, gender identity, sexual orientation, ability—whether we are aware of it or not or whether we choose to or not—will likely influence how we go about these tasks and/or how they are received or perceived by others. We regard this latter aspect—how our work is received or perceived—as the politics of identity.

Most of us embrace the notion that we cannot do our work from a "color-blind" perspective or one that ignores race, gender, sexual orientation, class, ability, veteran status, and religion (Manning, 2009). Typically, though, we tend to adopt this perspective with respect to those who are the beneficiaries of our work. When it comes to our own identities, we rarely consider them. Whereas elite athletes are encouraged to "leave your ego at the door" as they enter the gym for a workout, we cannot "leave our identity at the door" as we enter into this work. As authors of this chapter, we argue that one's identity is inescapable in this work. As such, the sign outside the metaphorical door of this work urges us to acknowledge, celebrate, and bring our identities into the room.

In this chapter, we explore the implications of identity in the process of designing and implementing multicultural initiatives. In particular, we unpack the politics of identity inherent in doing this work. To accomplish this, we first introduce ourselves and our identities as these become essential to the examples and experiences we share later in the chapter. This chapter explores the politics of identity guided by these essential questions: What do we mean by the politics of identity? What are some examples? How do multiple and intersecting identities overtly and/or covertly influence the implementation of multicultural initiatives? Finally, we close with some recommendations for negotiating the politics of identity in designing and implementing multicultural initiatives.

Introductions and Identities

In writing this chapter, we elected not to leave our own identities at the door. To the extent that this chapter (and this book) is a multicultural initiative, we believe that we must model this imperative in writing this chapter. Therefore, as authors, we engaged in a revealing conversation about our identities and, in the process, uncovered how our intersecting identities compel us to engage in multicultural initiatives and also become a source of tension in some instances.

Craig

Craig is the Coordinator for Student Life and Diversity at a large public institution in Tennessee. He has worked in student affairs since 2010 (when he completed his graduate studies). He comes from a middle class, African American family. Both of his parents have college degrees, his father having also earned a master's degree. Craig is the middle child among three brothers. All three hold college degrees. Craig, however, was the first child in his family to complete a graduate program. His father served 11 years in the army and, as a result, his family moved numerous times during Craig's childhood; still Craig strongly identifies as Southern. He is able-bodied and identifies as heterosexual. Craig was born and raised in one of the largest African American Pentecostal Christian denominations in the nation (Church of God in Christ). His father served as a church deacon and minster at their local church for many years before being appointed as a pastor. Craig strongly identifies with his Christian faith and considers it the most important aspect of his identity, ensuring that it guides all aspects of his personal and professional life.

John

John is a professor in a student affairs graduate preparation program with 15 years of prior practitioner experience, largely in residence life. He comes from a middle class, Midwestern family and was a first-generation college student. John identifies as White and male. Since his late 20s, he has publicly and professionally identified as gay. John was born and raised Catholic and for most of his life strongly identified with his faith, keeping his faith and sexual orientation identities separate and distinct. He now publicly identifies as an atheist. John does not identify in any significant or meaningful way as a person with disability. Influenced largely by his education in psychology and education, his early participation in progressive Catholic communities, and his professional experience in student affairs, John has made a commitment to social justice and to developing his multicultural competencies.

Identity in the "Politics of Identity"

Identity is a complex concept but is probably best understood as the organization of life experiences into images and characteristics that give us a sense of self and distinguish us from one another while, at the same time, connecting us to members of particular social groups who share those characteristics (Erikson, 1959; Kroger, 2004; Rummens, 2003; Turner & Oakes, 1986; Widick, Parker, & Knefelkamp, 1978). The latter part of this definition is most relevant to the discussion in this chapter as it speaks to one's self-concept based on perceived or actual membership in certain social groups based on race, country of origin, gender, religion, sexual orientation, socio-economic status, age, ability, and language among others (Bula, 2000; Jones & McEwen, 2000; Tatum, 1997). We refer to this, as others do, as social identity (Reynolds, 2001; Torres, 2011).

For years, researchers assessed and explored social identity development from a singular, one-dimensional perspective. However, over the past two decades, scholars have emphasized the need to consider multiple social identities and examine how these identities intersect to create the human experience (Ferguson, 2007). In today's society, many people place themselves in numerous social identity groups, with a large number identifying with both a dominant group and a marginalized group (Ferguson, 2007). For example, a White gay woman may find herself in several groups—White (dominant), gay (marginalized), and female (marginalized). Most identity models that focus on a single dimension of identity tend to ignore experiences related to how these singular identities converge, or intersect, to create the human experience. Therefore, we must embrace the reality that humans form their identity through the intersection of multiple identity factors and groups (Abes, Jones, & McEwen, 2007; Ferguson, 2007; Jones & McEwen, 2000; Renn, 2008, 2011).

Social identity, identity development, and intersectionality all have implications for multicultural initiatives. How we identify, the degree to which we identify with a particular social group, and the recognition of our multiple identities may all factor into our work to create multicultural change. Yet, many of us are not as conscious of identity and consequent pitfalls or challenges that may result: the political aspects of our identities.

Politics in the "Politics of Identity"

Whereas there may be many different definitions of the term *politics*, most seem to agree that the term describes "the occurrence of certain forms of behavior associated with the use of power or influence" (Gandz & Murray, 1980, p. 237). More broadly, politics involve attitudes, perceptions, and maneuvers and mechanisms to gain control, power, or influence.

In settings where we are attempting to create multicultural change, there will be politics. Change requires openness to new ideas, flexibility in one's worldview, and a willingness to try out new behaviors. All of this involves some degree of giving up or suspending power and control. This perceived (or real) loss of control—even momentarily—is perhaps the most challenging part of change and is likely the reason most of us are resistant to it at one time or another.

Raising our awareness to the politics of identity is not an easy task. Politics of identity, like other elusive phenomenon, are hard to identify and describe. The difficulty of doing so is similar to the challenge the U.S. Supreme Court faced in determining what obscenity was. Perhaps when it comes to these perplexing concepts, it is best to apply Supreme Court Justice Stewart's pithy observation, "I know it when I see it" (*Jacobellis v. Ohio*, 1964). This observation may apply to the politics of identity in multicultural initiatives. We may not be aware of them until we are in the midst of the diversity training program, the staff recruitment process, or the policy implementation and we become aware of the struggle for control and influence.

Politics of Identity in Action

As we approached writing this portion of the chapter, we struggled to identify and codify the politics of identity. We finally decided that the best approach was to share with one another our individual stories of implementing multicultural initiatives. In doing so, we began to see certain themes emerge in our own storytelling. Interestingly, each of these stories seem to raise questions that get at the heart of the politics involved: (a) What's in it for me? (b) Who am I to be doing this work? (c) How much should I reveal about myself? (d) Can I or should I be neutral and value-free? (e) How much can I admit about my own weaknesses? (f) What if I make a mistake? (g) How do I overcome others' stereotypes of me? (h) What are the implications of my intersecting identities?

Following we present the eight questions that we believe characterize the various politics of identity in implementing multicultural initiatives. Threaded through each of these are our own stories as well as stories of others we have met and worked with along our journeys.

What's In It for Me?

One of the more sensitive issues when it comes to the politics of identity, particularly when one's marginalized identity is salient, is dealing with the perception that the initiative is self-serving. By definition, identity politics are political arguments that articulate and address the perspectives and self-interests of those linked to the civil rights movements, the gay and lesbian movement, the feminist movement, etc. (Heyes, 2002). Indeed, initiatives that are designed to effect change when it comes to racism, or sexism, or heterosexism are largely launched to advance the circumstances of those most negatively affected by these forms of oppression. Unfortunately, when it is a person of color, or a woman, or a gay or lesbian practitioner who is implementing or leading the initiative, they may be viewed as doing so only for their benefit.

Take, for example, the following situation involving Craig. While attending his undergraduate institution, Craig served as the Peer Mentor Coordinator for a first-year program for minority students. Although the program consistently produced positive retention results amongst its participants, many of his White peers vehemently opposed the program, adamantly arguing, "Craig is only passionate about the program because he is Black—if he was White, he would see our point of view!" After repeatedly hearing this argument, Craig found himself going through a soul-searching process, in an effort to locate his true motives and intentions. He came to the conclusion that his passion for the program's continuation went beyond his own racial identity or skin color. Although some students refused to change their perspectives on the program, Craig and other participants of the program were able to convince a majority of the campus community to support the initiative.

Another example of this politics of identity question occurred when John was asked to chair a committee that examined the possibility of a domestic partners policy for graduate and "married" student housing at his university. Although he was assured that he was asked to lead this initiative because of his organizational skills, his follow-through, and his ability to bring together different perspectives and come up with a cohesive and articulate proposal for a policy change, he wondered if others might perceive that he had accepted this responsibility simply to help himself and those who identify with him (i.e., other gay and lesbian people). The committee was successful in developing a more inclusive policy and although no one articulated it, John was mindful throughout the process that he needed to treat this committee in such a way that no one could accuse him of doing this for his own (and others like him) personal benefit and gain.

Members of marginalized groups most often contend with this politics of identity question when they are intimately engaged in a multicultural initiative. We can also look at this from the perspective of one's dominant identity. For example, a White woman may be engaged in a multicultural initiative that challenges or disrupts racism. In this instance she may encounter the question from others: "What's in it for *her*?" Inherent in this question may be a suspicion that she is doing this out of self-interest to enhance her self-image or to allay White guilt.

Although this particular politics of identity question may be problematic, the reality is that many of us engage in multicultural initiatives that are, to some degree, self-serving. Historically, marginalized groups have had to advocate for themselves and build alliances with dominant group members in the process. To be motivated by self-interest is not an entirely bad thing. But it can be disruptive to the initiative if we become consumed with and question the motivation for the initiative—by others or ourselves.

Who Am I to Be Doing This Work?

Racism is a White problem (Katz, 2003). Logically, then, White people should be actively involved in multicultural initiatives that address racism. Following this line of reasoning, men should be engaged in initiatives that address sexism and heterosexual people should be addressing heterosexism. Yet, it often seems that when members of one identity group are engaged in initiatives that are intended (at least on the surface) to address the issues of another identity group, questions may be raised about whether or not they are the right people to be doing this. People in this situation may be asking themselves: Do I have credibility? Am I qualified? Will I be accepted? Will I be trusted? What if I come across as patronizing? In fact, inquiries that center on these questions have been discussed by a number of scholars. For example, Mio and Iwamasa (1993) explored the issue of White researchers studying counseling outcomes in communities of color and Washington (2011) tackled the question of a White person leading a multicultural center on campus. Next we share some more personal examples from our own experiences.

John was once doing an anti-racism training workshop for a largely African American and Hispanic audience. Throughout the workshop, he found himself struggling with an internal dialogue centered on: "Who am I to be teaching these professionals about racism?" What credibility do I have?" He decided to share with them the theory of racism as essentially a White problem accompanied by the equation: prejudice + power = ism/oppression. Given John's White identity, the logical conclusion of this equation was that he could not avoid his racism. After the session, one of the audience members (an older, African American woman) came up to John, thanked him for the insightful program, and observed that in discussing his White racism, John came across almost proud of his White racism. That led to a lengthier private discussion afterward, riddled with some discomfort, defensiveness, and intellectualizing on John's part. The long-term effect was that John reflected carefully and regularly on his capacity to do this type of work with and for certain audiences.

Craig had a similar experience while completing an internship in graduate school. He was given the task of working with six Asian Greek associations to coordinate an Asian Student Leadership Conference. His initial enthusiasm quickly turned to fear, as he questioned his own ability (as a Black man) to connect with a different minority group (Asian students). In his mind, he could imagine the students questioning his competency and skillset: "How can an African American coordinate an Asian student leadership conference? What does he know about the Asian student experience? Is he aware of the issues and problems that we face on a college campus?" Despite his initial fears and self-sabotaging mindset, Craig discovered that the student leaders quickly connected to his ideas, personality, advising skills, and leadership style. He was able to put his own fears to the side, collaborate with the student leaders, and successfully implement a student conference for over 125 Asian students.

This politics of identity question, although challenging, is not necessarily a bad thing. It causes us to be reflective about the work we are doing and to think about our audience. It reminds us of the importance of being in touch with our own identity and to learn as much about the culture we are entering into so that, ultimately, we are more effective and respectful in executing the initiative.

How Much Should I Reveal About Myself?

For many of us, certain aspects of our identities may not be visible or they may be assumed. Sexual orientation, class, religion, and ability are among those identities that may not be as visible as others. Likewise people may assume and, by default, attribute dominant identities to those they interact with: heterosexual, middle class, Christian, and without a disability. When engaged in multicultural initiatives, we sometimes find ourselves in the position of having a hidden identity that may be relevant to the topic at hand and we question whether or not to disclose that identity.

John, for example, was doing training on lesbian, gay, and bisexual (LGB) issues (transgender was hardly discussed at the time) earlier in his career. Although he is now publicly out, John was more selective about to whom he disclosed his sexual orientation. As he conducted these workshops, he wondered if he should have been out or if it was safer to look like the "cool heterosexual ally." Would he have more credibility with the heterosexual students in the room who were struggling with the topic? What about the gay and lesbian students who might benefit from an open and out role model? Looking back now, he realizes he was capitalizing on heterosexual privilege, but at the time he was engaged in an honest struggle with this politics of identity question. Today, in a similar way, John has had to deal with his openness about his atheism when engaged in multicultural initiatives that address religion and spirituality.

Can I or Should I Be Neutral and Value-Free?

When engaged in multicultural work, one may question *if* or *should* one's identity matter. A host of related questions then emerge: Does my identity matter or factor into the work that I am doing? In the name of neutrality, should I leave my identity at the door when I enter to do multicultural work? Are there some aspects of my identity that are more value-free than others?

For example, in a class on social justice in education, the instructor, a Korean man who identifies as heterosexual and Christian (but non-religious), strives to create an environment of respect and openness in the class. He finds that as students struggle through readings and discussions where class, gender, religion, and sexual orientation are the topic, he is able to guide and facilitate the discussion and "stay above the fray." However, when the topic of racial stereotypes and racial oppression is on the table, he can feel his passions rise and his ability to guide the discussion becomes far more challenging, especially as some students' comments hit a nerve with him.

Although we may not be aware of it, when our privileged identities are the focus of discussion, one of the unseen privileges is that we do not have to think about our identity, even when the discussion becomes passionate or contested. Whether we are aware of it not, we can (or appear to) be neutral, rational, and open in the discussion. This may not be the case when one of our non-privileged statuses is up for discussion. Depending on the degree to which we identify with that identity and the salience of it at that point in our lives (or in that particular context), our passions might be stirred. In this situation, we may be (or appear to be) irrational, biased, and closed off.

Doing multicultural work needs to involve both our heads and our hearts, but balance between the two is key (Watt, 2013). Too much head can lead to over-intellectualizing; too much heart can lead to emotions that, if not managed, can disrupt the work. We propose that rather than try to avoid the role of identity altogether—we acknowledge and honor our identity in all multicultural interventions and try to avoid the impulse to think that we can (or should) treat our identities as neutral players in the game.

How Much Can I Admit About My Own Weaknesses?

With each of our identities (and our level of identity within those identities) come benefits and liabilities. Consider, for example, both John and Craig and their male privilege. Depending on the level of their understanding of their privilege (see Hardiman & Jackson, 1997), there may be biases each is struggling with or privileges each must account for. Although John, for example, may be working to deal with these, he may question how open and honest he can be about them. Will openly admitting to these liabilities help or hinder the work he is trying to do? Does it model helpful behaviors for other men or does it undermine one's efforts to effect change?

As with the other politics of identity questions, this is not one faced only by those with privilege. For example, John recalls being in a diversity training session conducted by a woman during which she was explaining the concept of collusion as a mechanism that maintains oppression. She described collusion as attitudes and behaviors that involve going along with the oppressor's jokes, assumptions, assertions, etc. To illustrate her point, she shared an example that had just occurred as she was flying to the training session from across the country. Already fearful about flying, not to mention doing so under deteriorating weather conditions, she heard the captain announce that the plane was ready to pull away from the gate. The captain's voice was a woman's voice. She confessed that her immediate reaction was fear—"a woman is flying this plane!" She caught herself engaging in collusion. In sharing this example, some might say she lost credibility with the audience; others might say she was modeling self-reflection and self-awareness.

Recognizing that our level of development within each of our identities can yield certain strengths and weaknesses is an important step in handling this politics of identity question. The more open and comfortable we are with this, the more likely we can address and enhance our development within our own social identities.

What If I Make a Mistake?

Multicultural initiatives involve human interactions and human interactions, inevitably, will involve mistakes. Pope, Reynolds, and Mueller (2004) proposed that one of the multicultural skills necessary for effective practice is the ability to bounce back from making cultural errors when engaged in multicultural initiatives. Still there is a political dimension to this. Making a mistake might be over-interpreted or misinterpreted by others as saying something more about your social identity than about you (e.g., all men are misogynists, all heterosexual people are homophobic, etc.). In other words, one may question if a mistake will be attributed to the individual or will it be attributed to one's identity group.

For example, John, while teaching an experimental course on Spirituality in Higher Education, was engaged in a vigorous class discussion. During the conversation, he rather aggressively questioned a student about a point she was making in defense of her Christian faith. John's line of questioning did little to open up the conversation; in fact, it silenced her (and others) which was hardly an objective of the course. Reflecting on this after class, John contacted the student to apologize for his behavior and at the start of the next class apologized to the class for his behavior. Underlying this situation was a question that was needling John: Would his mistake be attributed to all other atheists now and would it contribute to a stereotype that all atheists are aggressive and angry, set on ridiculing Christians?

This politics of identity question is especially prominent for oppressed identities. As McIntosh (1995) notes, one of the privileges dominant group members have is that they can make a mistake without it being attributed to their identity group. The mistake is regarded as isolated to that individual. So when, in the course of engaging in a multicultural initiative, if someone who is a member of the oppressed group (a woman, person of color, gay man, or lesbian) makes an error of some kind, they run a greater risk that the mistake will be attributed to their identity and generalized to other members of that identity. This is how stereotypes persist.

How Do I Overcome Others' Stereotypes of Me?

One of the most insidious politics of identity questions involves overcoming others' stereotypes of oneself. When each of us enters a space, others will perceive or make certain assumptions about our race, ethnicity, gender, sexual orientation, belief system, class, ability, etc. With those perceptions come a variety of stereotypes. Even when stereotypes are considered positive (e.g., good at sports, good at sciences, sensitive, creative, etc.) they can still be limiting and in many cases, simply wrong. Every time Craig or John walks into a class or into a workshop, each has to contend with what others perceive, know, or eventually learn about him. With that come all the stereotypes people will have, in John's case, about White people, men, gays and lesbians, and atheists, or in Craig's case about African Americans, men, heterosexuals, and Christians.

Whereas some may be open-minded, willing to suspend their stereotypes, and able to incorporate new information that challenges their stereotypes, others will perceive everything John or Craig does and says through the lens of their own stereotypes, seeking (and finding) the thinnest shreds of evidence to support their stereotypes. What is necessary here is for the facilitator to be aware that these stereotypes are present consciously or unconsciously and that they may affect one's ability to effect change. Again, balance is key—to have awareness of the presence of other stereotypes without letting it immobilize you in your work.

What Are the Implications of My Intersecting Identities?

As discussed earlier, we each have more than one identity and this phenomenon has implications for the politics of identity. First, these identities can stack on one another. Craig, as noted earlier, is not just male, but he is

Christian, and African American, and heterosexual. The cumulative effect of these identities, and the stereotypes that come with them, can weigh heavily on the work Craig tries to do. Second, some identities may seem inconsistent or contradictory with one another. For example, Craig was asked to participate in a two-day Safe Zone training session. He found himself wrestling with the idea of participating in a program that clashed with his Christian identity. He reluctantly participated in the program after convincing himself that it would further his opportunity to serve as a catalyst for change on campus. However, he found himself wrestling internally again at the end of the program, when the instructors asked him to place the Safe Zone sticker (a rainbow) on his office door. He asked himself: "What would the students on campus who attend my church think when they visited my office and saw a rainbow sticker on the door?" As a personal compromise between his values, his identity, and his passion for student development, he decided to place his name on a resource electronic mailing list. With this, members of the LGBTQ community knew that they could reach out to him for guidance and support, without publicly informing the entire campus community.

Third, people's inability to see all dimensions in another's identity may result in reducing someone to an identity that fits their expectations. This was powerfully illustrated in the popular HBO drama *The Newsroom*. In an episode aptly titled "Bullies" (Podeswa & Sorkin, 2012), the host of a cable news show interviews a fictional aide of a conservative presidential candidate. The aide, who is Black, Catholic, and openly gay, is questioned relentlessly about how he can possibly support the candidate. Having had enough, the political aide fires back: "I am more than one thing. How dare you reduce me to the color of my skin! I am not defined by my Blackness. I am not defined by my gayness. And if that doesn't fit your narrow-minded expectation of who I'm supposed to be, I don't give a damn because I'm not defined by you either."

Conclusion and Recommendations

Ken (2010) observed that race, class, gender, and other social identities—sources of both privilege and oppression—organize, structure, and shape all aspects of our lives. Consequently, the inherent politics of identity are present in all our interactions, not just multicultural initiatives. However, they can become even more amplified in that line of work.

Being aware of our privileged and our non-privileged identities (and the associated politics of those identities) can ground and anchor our multicultural initiatives in the "diversity as a social value" perspective (Watt, 2013, p. 9). When we ask and answer the difficult questions about our identities in doing this work, we are able to more substantially understand and address systems of oppression—how we perpetuate them, how we are targeted by them, and how we can leverage our identities to disrupt them.

As we conclude this chapter, we offer a few recommendations, reminders to ourselves and helpful hints to others as they manage in their own work the politics of identity.

- **Accept the politics of identity.** One of the realities of this work is that it inevitably involves the politics of identity. Avoiding or denying them will not make them go away or cease to exist. If anything, this strategy may worsen the situation. The politics of identity must be encountered if they are to be successfully negotiated.
- **When in doubt, check it out.** If you find yourself in a situation where you suspect your identity is the source of tension, internal conflict, or resistance from others, consult with colleagues or with the person(s) directly involved. It is natural and appropriate to question the potential or likely influence of the politics of identity when doing multicultural work. Getting answers to these questions can offer very useful insights on how to proceed.
- **Stay on the learning curve.** Continually increase your knowledge about oppression and how it operates and affects your marginalized and your privileged identities. Oppression is the stage on which the politics of identity play out and a greater understanding of oppression theory can be very beneficial in negotiating the politics of identity.
- **Don't expect easy answers.** Recognize that there is no single response or cookbook answer to the challenges that the politics of identity pose in multicultural initiatives. There are many variables involved: your intersecting identities, the identities of those you are working with, the political environment in which the initiative is playing out, etc. That said, the principles explicated in this book can become valuable resources helping you come to a resolution that works for you and your particular situation.

As we have noted throughout this chapter, the politics of identity can raise many questions and uncertainties in implementing multicultural initiatives. Although we need be aware of them and attend to the questions they raise, we must have confidence in our ethics, our knowledge, our competencies, our practice and, yes, our unique social identities. These are what we bring to the process of facilitating change. As noted in Chapter 2, we cannot predict or control the outcome of our efforts; but we do have a responsibility to bring self-awareness, expertise, and skill to the process. The work that we are doing is too important to be derailed by the politics of identity.

References

Abes, E. S., Jones, S. R., & McEwen, M. K. (2007). Reconceptualizing the model of multiple dimensions of identity. *Journal of College Student Development, 45,* 612–632.

Bula, J. F. (2000). Use of the multicultural self in effective practice. In M. Baldwin (Ed.), *The use of self in therapy* (2nd ed., pp. 167–189). New York: Haworth Press.

Erikson, E. (1959). Identity and the life cycle. *Psychological Issues Monograph, 1*(1), 1–171.

Ferguson, A. (2007). Intersections of identity: Navigating the complexities. *Forum on Public Policy: A Journal of the Oxford Round Table, 2007*(1), *1–15.*

Gandz, J., & Murray, V. V. (1980). The experience of workplace politics. *Academy of Management Journal, 23*(2), 237–251.

Hardiman, R., & Jackson, B. (1997). Conceptual foundation for social justice courses. In M. Adam, L. A. Bell, & P. Griffin (Eds.), *Teaching for diversity and social justice: A sourcebook* (pp. 16–29). New York: Routledge.

Heyes, C. (2002). Identity politics. *Stanford encyclopedia of philosophy* (Metaphysics Research Lab, Stanford University). Retrieved from http://plato.stanford.edu/entries/identity-politics/

Jacobellis v. Ohio, 378 U.S. 184 (1964).

Jones, S. R., & McEwen, M. K. (2000). A conceptual model of multiple dimensions of identity. *Journal of College Student Development, 41,* 405–414.

Katz, J. H. (2003). *White awareness: Handbook for anti-racism training* (2nd ed.). Norman, OK: University of Oklahoma Press.

Ken, I. (2010). *Digesting race, class, and gender: Sugar as a metaphor.* New York: Palgrave Macmillan.

Kroger, J. (2004). *Identity and adolescence: The balance between self and other* (3rd ed.). London: Routledge.

Lorde, A. (1984). *Sister outsider: Essays and speeches.* Berkeley, CA: Crossing Press.

Manning, K. (2009). Philosophical underpinnings of student affairs work on difference. *About Campus, 14*(2), 11–17.

McIntosh, P. (1995). White privilege and male privilege. In M. L. Andersen & P. H. Collins (Eds.), *Race, class and gender: An anthology* (pp. 76–87). New York: Wadsworth.

Mio, J. S., & Iwamasa, G. (1993). To do, or not to do: That is the question for White cross-cultural researchers. *The Counseling Psychologist, 21,* 197–212.

Podeswa, J. (Director), & Sorkin, A. (Writer). (2012). Bullies [Television series episode]. In A. Sorkin & S. Rudin (Producers), *The newsroom.* United States: HBO.

Pope, R. L., Reynolds, A. L., & Mueller, J. A. (2004). *Multicultural competence in student affairs.* San Francisco: Jossey-Bass.

Pope, R. L., Reynolds, A. L., & Mueller, J. A. (2014). *Creating multicultural change on campus.* San Francisco: Jossey-Bass.

Renn, K. A. (2008). Research on bi- and multiracial identity development: Overview and synthesis. In K. A. Renn, & P. Shang (Eds.), *Biracial and multiracial college students: Theory, research and best practices in student affairs* (pp. 13–21). San Francisco: Jossey-Bass.

Renn, K. A. (2011). Mixed race millennials in college: Multiracial students in the age of Obama. In F. A. Bonner, A. F. Marble, & M. F. Howard-Hamilton (Eds.), *Diverse millennial students in college: Implications for faculty and student affairs* (pp. 227–242). Sterling, VA: Stylus.

Reynolds, A. L. (2001). Embracing multiculturalism: A journey of self-discovery. In J. G. Ponterotto, J. M. Casas, L. A. Suzuki, & C. M. Alexander (Eds.), *Handbook of multicultural counseling* (pp. 103–112). Thousand Oaks, CA: SAGE.

Rummens, J. A. (2003). Conceptualising identity and diversity: Overlaps, intersections, and processes. *Canadian Ethnic Studies, 35*(3), 10–25.

Tatum, B. D. (1997). *"Why are all the Black kids sitting together in the cafeteria?" And other conversations about race.* New York: Basic Books.

Torres, V. (2011). Perspectives on identity development. In J. H. Schuh, S. R. Jones, & S. R. Harper (Eds.), *Student services: A handbook for the profession* (5th ed., pp. 187–206). San Francisco: Jossey-Bass.

Turner, J. C., & Oakes, P. J. (1986). The significance of the social identity concept for social psychology with reference to individualism, interactionism and social influence. *British Journal of Social Psychology, 25*, 237–252.

Washington, J. (2011). Working with the majority. In D. L. Stewart (Ed.), *Multicultural student services on campus: Building bridges, re-visioning community* (pp. 245–253). Sterling, VA: Stylus.

Watt, S. K. (2013). Designing and implementing multicultural initiatives: Guiding principles. In S. K. Watt & J. Linley (Eds.), *Creating successful multicultural initiatives in higher education and student affairs* (pp. 5–15). San Francisco: Jossey-Bass.

Widick, C., Parker, C. A., & Knefelkamp, L. (1978). Erik Erikson and psychosocial development. In L. Knefelkamp, C. Widick, & C. A. Parker (Eds.), *Applying new developmental findings* (pp. 1–17). San Francisco: Jossey-Bass.

14

TOXIC ENVIRONMENTS

Perseverance in the Face of Resistance

Mary F. Howard-Hamilton

Toxic environments exist in every organization and in particular the violent assaults are most often felt by marginalized multicultural scholars in the academy (Cuyjet, 2011; Feagin & Sikes, 1994; Harris-Perry, 2011; hooks, 1995; Howard-Hamilton, Morelon-Quainoo, Johnson, Winkle-Wagner, & Santiague, 2009; Patitu & Hinton, 2003). What is a toxic environment, what is the definition of *violence*, what types of harm are inflicted upon people of color, how do environments respond to overt and covert hostility, what initiatives and policies can be implemented to create institutional environments that support diverse ideas and people?

A toxic environment creates a stagnant, stifling, and poisonous atmosphere for individuals who are members of a marginalized group. These environments not only mute and anesthetize the oppressed, they also damage the oppressor because there is no dialogue, communion, and mutual understanding (Freire, 1987). Neither group grows or becomes fully human because of the exploitation of power and control. The voices of the oppressed in toxic environments will be the central focus of this chapter. The counter-stories shared could open the door for the oppressors, thus creating an opportunity for them to be informed and enlightened transformational change agents. For example, Latina(o) students on a predominantly White campus who are constantly taunted and asked if they are in this country legally are immersed in a toxic environment that causes mental, emotional, and physical stress (Minikel-Lacocque, 2013). The toxicity occurs when there are degrading comments or hate speech spoken in the environment, the lack of safe spaces for the students to congregate and be culturally immersed, and few role models who look like them or have a sensitivity to their needs. When referring to indignities or slights projected toward oppressed groups, the term most often used to describe these assaults is a *microaggression* (Delgado & Stefancic, 2012). Moreover, an *environmental microaggression* is when "racial assaults, insults and invalidations . . . are manifested on systemic and environmental levels" (Sue et al., 2007, p. 278). This definition and the examples provide a vivid description of how an environment can be toxic for underrepresented groups.

Feagin and Sikes (1994) discuss the concept of home as a place of refuge, and for Black families, "home represents one of the few anchors available to them in an often hostile White-dominated world" (p. 224). The outside world, which includes one's place of work or study, constantly bombards marginalized groups with microaggressions (Delgado & Stefancic, 2012) and racial maltreatment (Feagin & Sikes, 1994). However, Blacks can control their home environment and make it safe and comfortable. A Black student who attended a predominantly White institution went home continuously during his freshman year because "everything in the environment here [at school] causes stress" (Feagin & Sikes, 1994, p. 225). Going home allows a person of color to get replenished and come back to face the challenges, hostility, and violence in the world of the dominant culture.

The constant exchange of an "engage, fight, replenish, engage" method of coping with the challenges in a dominant society leads to racial battle fatigue (Smith, 2004). The exposure to toxic environments leads to psychological and physical damage in the form of high blood pressure, emotional outbursts, headaches, inability to sleep, and extreme fatigue to name just a few behaviors. These symptoms, according to Smith, are similar to veterans returning from war resulting in post-traumatic stress syndrome.

Although the language being used to describe a toxic environment is graphic and strong, Paulo Freire (1987) proffered that "violence is initiated by those who oppress, who exploit, who fail to recognize others as persons—not by those who are oppressed, exploited, and unrecognized" (p. 41). Thus, there is no need to see bloodshed for a violent act to have occurred; violence is the pain and dehumanization of a person's spirit, soul, and identity.

Introduction

Throughout this book you have read about designing multicultural initiatives, understanding and observing organizational systems with direct consequences for underrepresented groups, as well as connecting various theoretical models to our practice of creating non-toxic environments for everyone. I have served in three capacities at various institutions as a student affairs administrator, academic affairs administrator, and faculty member. It is Watt's (2013) metaphorical connection to our professional lives as gardeners that closely connects to my philosophy of why we do this type of work. She states that it is because "these professionals view their work as if they are tending to a garden where they plant seeds, fertilize soil, and facilitate the growth of the people and the organization" (p. 5). I also find that our toxic environments with their systemic oppression are likened to fighting a harmful pest that has attacked what we have nurtured. Thus, "Systemic oppression frames the way that privilege and marginalized groups exist and interact in society. It results in unhealthy organizations and damaged relationships between members of the community" (Watt, 2013, p. 5). The cases that follow are to provide some perspective on toxic environments, microaggressions, and systemic oppression. The first case, "We Love You; We Hate You," is a recreated situation based on a typical situation I have observed repeatedly throughout my career. The second case, "Prove Yourself," is my story with excerpts from journal entries made after I received my doctorate and began my career as a professor at the University of Florida.

"We Love You; We Hate You"

Amazing University has a new president and she has guided the university toward a strategic plan created to make significant and bold strides toward the implementation of a diversity initiative to increase the number of Black faculty by 50%. The diversity initiative includes "opportunity hires" or opportunities for departments to forego the formal process of screening all the applications in order to target a specific candidate to interview immediately. The campus is buzzing over this aggressive plan to increase Black faculty from its current count of 9 to 14. The most forward thinking unit on campus is the College of Education and there are several searches underway. The Department of Educational Leadership is looking for a person to teach in the K–12 administration area and invited an African American woman, Dr. Angel Patterson (pseudonym), to interview.

Dr. Angel Patterson is the "opportunity hire" who had been an assistant professor at a comparable institution, received her doctorate from a top-tier research university, and had several years of full-time experience as a K–12 teacher. When Dr. Patterson arrives on campus the faculty rail against her candidacy and begin questioning her credentials, as well as making inappropriate statements during the entire interview process. Dr. Patterson meets a Black faculty member during her tour of the College and reaches out to her during a break. Dr. Patterson walks in with a dazed look, closes the door, and collapses into tears while asking "What is wrong with these people? They are so evil." An overall account of the day was the incessant critique of her references, interruptions during her research presentation, and overt reminders that she was not their first choice because they felt coerced to bring her on campus.

Dr. Patterson's interview process is an example of the mental toll placed upon marginalized groups in the academy because regardless of the amount of education, publications, and service they have, it is still not enough for their colleagues to "love them." Instead, the faculty at Amazing University "hate her" because of what they believe is the unfair advantage she has as an applicant "skipping over other highly qualified applicants"; thus, she is not a "good fit" for the department. Institutions say that they need to diversify the environment (we love you) but again there is a tax levied when the presence of marginalized groups appear on campus (we hate you). When the interview process ended, the faculty wrote negative evaluations about Dr. Patterson stating that she did not have the skills or credentials to teach courses in their department. Because they needed someone to teach in the fall a decision was made to hire a doctoral candidate in their program who was scheduled to complete her degree within a year. The new faculty member was hired at the instructor level until she completed her degree. No one at the college or university level intervened to assess the interview process or challenge the decision of the faculty in the department. It is also important to note that the department has never had a person of color teaching their courses and this is a K–12 teacher preparation program area.

"Prove Yourself"

I have been a professor for 23 years, teaching at four universities. Throughout my career, journaling has been an important part of my emotional catharsis after working in the toxic systemic environment of higher education. I perused my journal entries written in 1991, the year I began interviewing for faculty and administrative positions. Several examples of survival in a toxic environment are provided. Early in my professional career I will never forget the following question asked by a member of the interview committee: "What does your husband think about the possibility of you teaching here?" I was stunned however quickly processed his question and asked: "Tell me how that question is relevant to the position I am seeking?" There was silence, and then the committee moved on to another question. Later that evening I recounted this thought in my journal as: "Is this an institution and faculty I want to begin my professional career with and at what cost if I must endure insensitive questions on a regular basis?" I decided to accept the position and the oppressive actions continued. Here is a personal account from my journal entry on September 25, 1991:

> Joe, he is so paternalistic! Good ole' Joe walked into my office and proceeded to tell me that new professors do not get tenured when there's too much contact with students. How can you write, research & prep your articles if you have interaction with your students similar to that of grand central station?! Well, I was stunned and embarrassed. I opened my door and in pops a student and one of my colleagues. Then Joe . . . who said that he had been watching me all day and there were too many students around . . . all day! I'm tired of being watched and I do know that the student personnel scholars are starved for attention. Additionally, the female scholars in the program need a female role model.

This encounter with a full professor was a constant interaction, invited and uninvited, on a daily basis. I found myself persevering in the face of resistance because I knew that the university did not embrace African American women and I had to be an exemplary scholar because the expectations of my colleagues were minimal. The environment was similar to being a fish in a fishbowl, there was nowhere to run or hide, all eyes were on me like the day I was heading to class and like most new professors, I had a ton of books, my attaché, and back up materials when a voice from behind said "leaving early?" My journal entry reflecting on this microagression says: "Again, I was stunned, embarrassed, and felt like I was an infant who needed her moves guided or else she may stray off the appropriate professorial track. I couldn't say much except that I was heading to class and not 'home.'" The encounters with my colleagues made me stronger and more persistent. I remember saying to myself "I am better than this" and overcoming these obstacles could be accomplished. The most difficult battle was fighting the invisible demon, covert sexism and racism which were internalized by faculty who thought that their actions were supportive. Sometimes the demon was covert by its verbiage that was the intellectual form of bullying. For example, a colleague said: "Mary doesn't know when to quit" as a group of faculty were milling in the office one morning. My journal entry reflects my confusion from that statement in which I wrote: "Where the hell did that come from? They just want you to feel inferior and always be in a state in which you question your motives and behaviors."

What I love the most is teaching and mentoring students so that they can become future scholar researchers. Unfortunately, it seems as though there are covert and overt challenges to "prove myself" in the classroom—specifically, to prove that I have experience as an administrator, prove that

I have experience as a researcher, prove that I have experience as a faculty scholar, and prove that I have experience as a teacher.

The first day of class means that I must share my professional story and journey so students can relax and absorb what I expect from them during the semester. The students still challenge, question, resist, and block when they are in my class because there is a sense of privilege when there is a Black woman teaching them. "How can she know more than me?" "What, if anything, can she teach me?" and "I know she is going to talk about Black and White issues only . . . she just wants me to feel guilty!" My journal entries typically include quotes from scholars who understand the importance of creating an empowering environment for all students so that they can intellectually and realistically see themselves purposefully transforming the world (Edelman, 1992; Freire, 1987). For example, one quotation from my journal asserts that if students are excluded from being fully represented in the curriculum materials and classroom dialogue, then they are being miseducated.

My greatest resistance comes from the students who take the multiculturalism course. I have taught some form of a diversity course to master's students in student affairs graduate preparation programs for 22 years and I have always received poor teaching evaluations upon completion of the course. I have tried every teaching method and textbook available to help the students relax and open their minds, and rarely do they "get it" during the semester the course is being taught. They do not "get" that their actions toward me are oppressive and disrespectful, they do not "get" that shutting down the discussion about marginalized groups silences everyone, and they do not "get" that they have created a hostile and violent environment. There was one time when I asked my graduate teaching assistant to count the number of times I referred to "Black and/or White student issues in my class." The graduate student said that I did not refer to Black or White students at all during the three-hour class. However, when I asked several White students about our discussion they said that I talk about race all of the time and the conversation centers on Black students. When you have a passion for diversity, multiculturalism, and issues related to race, racism, and ethnicity there is a sense of hope that others can be taught to believe and embrace similar ideas.

The challenges and questions from students happen continuously when you are a faculty member of color. I often ask students if they would engage in this level of inquiry in a classroom with one of the White male professors in order to push back on their toxic behaviors. Many students come without ever experiencing a teacher of color in the K–12 system who could help shift their perspective to be excited about a teacher of color instead of being overtly confrontational.

The environment that was the most hostile to me as an administrator was when I became an associate dean for graduate education in the School of Education at a previous institution. Within the first three months of my tenure as the dean, two of the White female administrative assistants "retired" and one decided to transfer and with them went nearly 60 years of institutional memory. I could not prove my worth in this situation because it was clear that they did not want to be supervised by a Black woman and I clearly did not know what I was doing. This scenario is similar to what President Obama is experiencing with politicians who ask him to prove his birth status and shutting down of the government (walking out or leaving the work environment) so his policies will fail.

The embedded systemic nature of racism and hostility within the environment leads one to believe that there is very little that can be done to eradicate the violence inflicted on marginalized groups. There is a personal tax that takes its toll on teachers, administrators, and facilitators who engage in diversity initiatives. The theoretical concepts that provide a framework for the environmental stressors can assist in explaining the coping strategies needed to persist.

Theories Linked to Cultural Issues in the Environment

Paulo Freire's (1987) germinal definition of violence gives us a different lens to see how everyone is impacted when the oppressed are rendered helpless within their own environment. Specifically, he states that violence does not necessarily require bloodshed. It is the act itself which is used to dehumanize another and oppress her/him psychologically, spiritually, and emotionally which leaves the person anesthetized. When a multicultural champion is rendered mute, incapacitated, and alienated the violence incurred upon her does not impact just one person, it impacts an entire community.

Those who inflict violence must go through a revolutionary transformation of consciousness and personality from the right to the left (Spring, 1999). The difference between the two revolutions are as noted in Table 14.1 (Spring, 1999, p. 149).

Behaviors on the Right must be ameliorated so that the behaviors on the Left can be heard and respected. It is the beginning of a cultural environment that can be humanized and mutually respectful.

The case studies that were provided at the beginning of the chapter are prime examples of the Revolution to the Right and Left. Angel Patterson, in "We Love You; We Hate You," wants to find answers to the reason why she is being treated so rudely and placed in a domesticated stance. The faculty organized to render her silent and to support the traditional bureaucratic

TABLE 14.1.
Revolutionary Consciousness of the Liberated and the Oppressor

Revolution to the Left	*Revolution to the Right*
People are the subjects of history	Leadership knows the future
Leadership and the people work together	People are domesticated
Biophilic	Necrophilic
Love as liberation	Love as possession
Dialogue	Mutism
Reflective—Problematizing	Slogans
People who organize	Organization people
Revolution continuous	Bureaucracy

nature of the search process by screening all applicants to find the person that is a good fit.

Similarly, my story, "Prove Yourself," is an example of a Revolution to the Left. I attempt to create an environment in the classroom and my office space that engages people to think freely and compassionately about our society. The Revolution to the Right would be reflected in the behaviors of my colleagues who are necrophilic by limiting communication in retaining or failing to share information that would lead to a comfortable work environment. I must be domesticated and rendered helpless. The toll on the psychic and physical well-being of the multicultural faculty member can be damaging if one does not resist systemic oppressive messages.

Racial battle fatigue is the tax that is paid when there is continuous micro and macro assaults toward a person on a daily basis (Smith, 2004). The faculty of color who teach race-based or ethnic classes "often treat White students as if they are tabulae rasae" (p. 179). However, as faculty of color we learn quickly that students come with their own backpack full of slogans, stereotypes, and prejudices which are difficult to eradicate in a 16-week semester. As Smith (2004) describes, students are racially primed for the classroom. The toll these micro and macro assaults take on a person's energy and physical levels is devastating. Often even the expectation of a racist act engenders battle fatigue. Moreover, who will listen and believe that such symptoms are experienced and exist? The skepticism involved with the reporting of these behaviors is an additional source of stress for African Americans in the academy. When we revisit the case of "We Love You; We Hate You," we see Angel Patterson found herself seeking out the one person who would listen to her interview horror story without repudiation, another scholar of color. During the emotional catharsis of telling her story she was in shock and cried, which are signs of racial battle fatigue.

Perseverance in the Face of Resistance

For a seed to achieve its greatest expression, it must come completely undone. The shell cracks, its insides come out, and everything changes. To someone who doesn't understand growth, it would look like complete destruction.

— **Cynthia Occelli**

The garden metaphor shared by Watt (2013) provides a framework for learning how to nurture the seeds we are working with at our institutions and challenges us to be astute gardeners in a complex environment replete with toxins and inconsistent soil that could endanger the growth of new and creative ideas. Watt (2013) shared three lessons when implementing multicultural initiatives that apply to perseverance in toxic environments. The lessons include: (a) focusing inward, not outward; (b) partnering and scheduling opportunities for renewal and reflection; and (c) managing defensive reactions. Each lesson can be accompanied by a specific coping mechanism that may help with persistence and ameliorate resistance and I see this as an act of becoming completely undone.

My story of facing difficulties without fear is borne out of Watt's first lesson of focusing inward, not outward. If I had focused on Joe's intellectual bullying tactics this would have left me defeated and drained. However, one of my main survival techniques was journal writing and reframing the microaggressions that were part of my day-to-day interactions with individuals on campus. The journal writing was an opportunity to reframe the situation and place it in the context of a counter-story. This method of meaning making allowed me to respond to the situation in a reflective manner and not have my future determined by others. Overall, it is imperative for faculty and practitioners to *find the reflection time and focus on their strengths*. As faculty, *focus on the positive course evaluations* rather than ruminating for days over the few that were a bit cynical. You will find that the majority of the evaluations are stellar and there are less than a handful noting any weaknesses. Practitioners should *find time to engage in professional development activities* that improve upon an attribute that could lead to enhanced leadership skills. *The attention to one's faults can block or inhibit the development of strengths.*

When I was talking to an African American woman who is a tenured associate professor, she shared with me her trepidation about going through the promotion process for full professor. I thought about my promotion process and how lonely it was because there were no other Black women to share my thoughts and anxieties with in the field of higher education. It then dawned on me that there were four other Black women who planned on transitioning from associate to full professor within the next three years. Partnering and scheduling opportunities for renewal and reflection would be an avenue in which we could all lean on each other and speak about our fears without being scrutinized. We have started our conference call counter-story conversations and next year the plan is to take the dialogue to the beach. Watt recommends "going for a walk, or taking some time to rest and read, and/or going on a multiday retreat" to travel the path to renewal.

The most difficult lesson, for me, is managing defensive reactions. As I have matured in this profession, my responses to uncaring and unkind people are to use the dialogue as a teaching moment if at all possible and try to help them become "undone" in their perception of who I am. You cannot be a prophet in your own land and unfortunately the people will not benefit from your knowledge. Most scholars of color are respected and sought after for consultations off campus rather than on campus. In order to hear the voices of diversity experts, a suggestion is to create opportunities for scholars of color to share their expertise. This could be done by establishing workshops periodically throughout the year on various diversity topics and inviting the campus to participate in the dialogue. Another effort to increase communication about diversity issues is to find an individual to be a diversity liaison in each college/school. This scholar would act as a consultant when difficult conversations need to be mediated. Moreover, the liaison would be available for teaching moments that could be in the form of a seminar or guest lecture in a classroom. Last, find ways to reward those who are staying engaged with the diversity initiatives. Create ways for students to be part of the faculty member's diversity activities and create scholarly outlets to share what is being learned, perhaps a weekly column in the campus paper on diversity, conducting institutional climate and environmental assessments on the faculty and staff of color. If there are more people recognized, rewarded, and respected for their support of diversity initiatives and teaching moments, others may model their behavior similarly.

Conclusion

Toxic environments that employ individuals who have a mindset geared to a Revolution to the Right are pervasive in business, schools, colleges, and universities, as well as in places we consider to be safe and supportive such as churches and family domiciles. So the unanswered question that remains a conundrum for me is: Where can we find institutions that are sane and safe places to grow as facilitators of multicultural dialogue as well as encourage the transformational Right Revolutionaries?

The spaces that need to be examined are those that are the cultivators of new ideas and innovative programs—educational institutions. The best and brightest minds are walking among us every day and we have the tools to impact the canon as it relates to what is written about marginalized groups, concomitantly we can change to make the campus more like "home" and a place that does not cause stress. Our institutions and the students are gardens and seeds respectively; we must tend to them carefully and begin to change the landscape from barren (in thought) to lush (with dialogue, reflection, and action). Watt (2013) stresses that "higher education administrators, faculty, and student affairs professionals must understand that better decisions are made for all involved when intentional effort is given to balancing the head, heart, and the hands when engaging in Difference—whether doing so in the classroom, in campus programming, or as it relates to administrative policy decisions" (p. 14).

References

Cuyjet, M. J. (2011). Environmental influences on college culture. In M. J. Cuyjet, M. F. Howard-Hamilton, & D. L. Cooper (Eds.), *Multiculturalism on campus: Theory, models, and practices for understanding diversity and creating inclusion* (pp. 37–64). Sterling, VA: Stylus.

Delgado, R., & Stefancic, J. (2012). *Critical race theory: An introduction* (2nd ed.). New York: New York University Press.

Edelman, M. W. (1992). *The measure of our success: A letter to my children and yours.* Boston, MA: Beacon Press.

Feagin, J. R., & Sikes, M. P. (1994). *Living with racism: The Black middle-class experience.* Boston, MA: Beacon Press.

Freire, P. (1987). *Pedagogy of the oppressed.* New York: Continuum.

Harris-Perry, M. V. (2011). *Sister citizen: Shame, stereotypes, and Black women in America.* New Haven, CT: Yale University Press.

hooks, b. (1995). *Art on my mind: Visual politics.* New York: New Press.

Howard-Hamilton, M. F., Morelon-Quainoo, C. L., Johnson, S. D., Winkle-Wagner, R., & Santiague, L. (2009). *Standing on the outside looking in: Underrepresented students' experiences in advanced-degree programs.* Sterling, VA: Stylus.

Minikel-Lacocque, J. (2013). Racism, college, and the power of words: Racial microaggressions reconsidered. *American Educational Research Journal, 50*(3), 432–465.

Patitu, C. L., & Hinton, K. G. (2003). The experiences of African American women faculty and administrators in higher education: Has anything changed? In M. F. Howard-Hamilton (Ed.), *Meeting the needs of African American women* (pp. 79–93). San Francisco: Jossey-Bass.

Smith, W. (2004). Black faculty coping with racial battle fatigue: The campus climate in a post-civil rights era. In D. Cleveland (Ed.), *A long way to go: Conversations about race by African American faculty and graduate students* (pp. 171–188). New York: Peter Lang International Academic Publishers.

Spring, J. (1999). *Wheels in the head: Educational philosophies of authority, freedom, and culture from Socrates to human rights*. Boston, MA: McGraw Hill.

Sue, D. W., Capodilupo, C. M., Torino, G. C., Bucceri, J. M., Holder, A. M. B., Nadal, K. L., & Esquilin, M. (2007). Racial microaggressions in everyday life: Implications for clinical practice. *The American Psychologist, 62*, 271–286.

Watt, S. (2013). Designing and implementing multicultural initiatives: Guiding principles. In S. K. Watt & J. L. Linley (Eds.), *Creating successful multicultural initiatives in higher education and student affairs* (pp. 5–15). San Francisco: Jossey-Bass.

15

FACING THE PROVERBIAL
LION OF RACISM

Jodi L. Linley and Sherry K. Watt

> I feel like I've been hit in the head by the invisible elephant in the room.
> —White faculty statement after a contentious exchange in a faculty meeting
> about the value of diversity and inclusion

Whereas my White faculty colleagues may notice the "elephant in the room," I (Sherry) always experienced these types of exchanges as the "proverbial lion" of racism. What is the difference? The "elephant in the room" is awkward and uncomfortable; it takes up space and makes some people sweat. The "proverbial lion" is regal and quietly commands respect. As it lies in the room, groaning, yawning, showing its teeth, and licking its mouth, the power that it possesses does not have to be acknowledged to exist. The power of White supremacy (Potapchuk, Leiderman, Bivens, & Major, 2005) is inherent in structural racism. I likened the "proverbial lion" to White supremacy because the belief reigns highest. It is the belief that White people and their ways of being in the world are not only superior, but also correct. This belief shapes the relationship between historically marginalized and dominant groups. It is present in the cultural underpinnings of every faculty meeting, campus program, and large campus community gathering. The lion is always present and threatens to raise its large paw to show force if anyone displaces its power. I notice the lion when I teach classes on the topic of multiculturalism as an African American faculty member. The lion does not always utilize its standard power as long as I do not fully exercise my authority as a faculty member. When the "proverbial lion" feels threatened, however, it exerts power by lashing out violently, leaving its prey and witnesses emotionally and sometimes physically wounded. I experience the threat of this lion in both power struggles as an academic and when I face professional scrutiny from my colleagues about the worth of my research.

Once I shared my metaphor with Jodi, a White woman, friend, and colleague, she recalled also seeing that lion in her own experiences. In this chapter, we recall conversations and experiences from the last 15–20 years of our lives working in higher education with a wide variety of multicultural initiatives and the times we observed and/or felt the "proverbial lion" of racism. Through these pages, we both share our encounters with the "proverbial lion." This chapter is written in three sections: (1) a brief review of the contexts for thinking about the "proverbial lion"; (2) our reflections on actual situations where we both have seen the lion bare its teeth; and (3) practical suggestions for conscious scholar practitioners who wish to confront the lion without losing their lives. We realize "losing their lives" may sound extreme, but considering the physical health and emotional consequences of racial battle fatigue (Smith, Hung, & Franklin, 2011), facing the "proverbial lion" really is as dangerous as it sounds.

Contexts for Exploring the "Proverbial Lion"

In higher education, faculty, staff, and/or consultants often facilitate multicultural initiatives. One's position on campus certainly invokes varying levels of authority, but more important than position is one's facilitation toolkit. According to Griffin (1997):

> Social justice education requires a simultaneous awareness of content and process, as well as an ability to both participate in the process and remain outside of it to assess interactions in the group as a whole and among individuals within the group. (p. 279)

Facilitator readiness can be assessed in terms of personal resources one brings to the initiative, including support network, passion, awareness, knowledge, and skills (Griffin, 1997). These five areas of resources, when well-stocked, can make facilitating multicultural initiatives incredibly rewarding. Nevertheless, having these resources does not preclude one from experiencing the "proverbial lion." For example, targets of microaggressions must constantly assess and interpret the meanings of these subtle actions and whether or not, and how, to respond (Smith et al., 2011; Solorzano, Ceja, & Yosso, 2000).

There is very little literature about staff and consultants as educators or facilitators of multicultural initiatives; most literature in this area is about faculty of color and their classroom experiences. A recent collection of essays titled *Presumed Incompetent: The Intersections of Race and Class for Women in Academia* (Gutierrez y Muhs, Niemann, Gonzalez, & Harris, 2012) provides a rich, meaningful understanding of the experiences of women of color in academia, and the reader gains a true sense of the prevalence of being presumed incompetent across all contexts in U.S. higher education. Several of the essays in *Presumed Incompetent* paint a troubling portrait of the expectations for women of color in academe to match deeply rooted racist and sexist stereotypes, such as the "nurturing mammy" and the "acquiescent servant," in every corner of the academy. "Institutional paternalism did not seem simply to be the style of a single, particular administrative unit but occurred across the entire organizational structure" (Shields, 2012, p. 35). Other essays focus on women faculty of color as "more vulnerable to student perceptions as a professor lacking in objectivity and pushing my own agenda" when the subject matter was multicultural in nature (Onwuachi-Willig, 2012, p. 146). The first-person narratives that comprise *Presumed Incompetent* confirm extant research. One study found that students consistently inappropriately questioned the authority and credibility of faculty of color in the classroom (Stanley, 2006). Women faculty of color in another study reported that White male students challenged and questioned their authority and teaching competency, disrespected their academic expertise, and communicated intimidating and threatening messages (Pittman, 2010). That has certainly been the case for Shannon Gibney, the English professor whose situation made national headlines in 2013. Several White male students charged Gibney, a Black professor teaching about systemic oppression in an introductory journalism course, with racial discrimination. This was not the first time. Gibney's reflections on her constant challenging from White students includes important historical context. She stated:

> The thing is, I was never supposed to be there; these institutions were not built for Black women, or anyone of color for that matter, to live or work in. In fact, they were built to keep us out. I know this, intellectually, being a student of history, but every time I come up against the blunt-end truth of it, I still shiver. (Gibney, n.d.)

Questions of credibility do not come exclusively from students, however. Gibney was also charged with racial and gender discrimination by a White male colleague who felt the department's search for a faculty member with expertise in critical race theory discriminated against him (Gibney, n.d.). Challenges such as those Gibney has faced repeatedly take a toll on one's spirit. For example, consider these reflections from a group of scholars of color that coalesced their experiences to present a common case:

> It was difficult not to feel as though my performance in seminars and dur-
> ing casual hallway conversations was intended to gauge my worthiness to
> the field. I always wondered, "At what point are they going to realize I am
> an impostor?" I began doubting my abilities as a scholar, a writer, and a
> teacher. (Tuitt, Hanna, Martinez, del Carmen Salazar, & Griffin, 2009,
> p. 68)

The effects of a constant presumption of incompetence result in what has been dubbed "racial battle fatigue," a phenomenon referring to the psychological, emotional, and physical toll that everyday racial battles take on people of color (Smith et al., 2011; Solorzano et al., 2000). For conscious scholar practitioners who facilitate multicultural initiatives when the subject is Difference, we wonder if the fatigue is elevated.

Sherry's Encounters With the Proverbial Lion

I apply my scholarly and professional expertise through teaching multicultural courses, and have done so over the span of my 20-year career. The "proverbial lion" establishes its position right in the center of the room, be it a faculty meeting, a national conference, or my classroom. However, following I will focus my reflections on how that lion disrupts my teaching. In the context of teaching in the academy, colleagues and students of both dominant and marginalized identities question my authority and intentions.

Roaring to Mark the Territory

I approach teaching in ways that invite students to share power with me as we explore contentious issues. Sharing power as an African American female faculty member is tricky. There is always a threat to my authority because there are very few African American faculty members, so I am an anomaly. The majority of the students I teach have not encountered an African American teacher during their entire educational careers. Students perceive me through their preconceived notions of African Americans. Their impressions may be positive, but generally tainted by the negative images plastered over news media and in the social consciousness of America. Due to all of these factors, students respond to my sharing and asserting authority in different ways.

I can recall numerous positive experiences. Yet, there are occasions when both the students and I fall over that huge lion sitting in the middle of the room and he lets out a roar that reverberates for miles. The roar of both the male and female lion reaches the ear from five miles away. The responses to the echo of the lion's roar results in students abusing that shared power by undermining me. This undermining comes in the form of "checking out" my assignments by asking my colleagues for their advice or questioning my authority by asking me to repeat instructions repeatedly to be certain that I know what I am talking about. I noticed that the "proverbial lion" shouts out a roar from its position in the center of the room to mark its territory whether it is a White student or a student of color that complains. I noticed that White students sometimes depend on their same-race relational power with my White faculty colleagues to prod the lion. This use of power in this way manifests in a colleague coming to me to confirm my thinking on a particular assignment or classroom exchange. Even worse, my colleagues at times passively or verbally acquiesce, thereby giving the students permission to withdraw from the process of exploring their dissonance through the learning process.

Do not get me wrong—I am a process teacher. I want my students to explore their dissonance. I am open to feedback from colleagues. I want students to find space to work through the complex ideas around race and other social issues. I do want them to seek out my colleagues for support in their developmental progression toward understanding complex concepts I teach around race. However, because that lion sits there all the time, it creates a mistrust and the roar sounds like an attempt to put me in "my place." I hear the roar as a shout that arises from the positioning of dominance that White people have historically held in U.S. culture. This shout doubts my abilities and intelligence. I feel the roar as a pushback on me stepping out of the degradation and powerlessness that is rooted in African Americans' history in this country. Some students, in their dissonance, use the lion to escape from deeper exploration of their own racism and entangle me in the attack. The attack takes the form of students using the grievance process to question grades. My responses to this roar of the lion are to doubt my abilities and experience or to respond aggressively to the constant questioning. I am not suggesting that I am a perfect teacher. I am human and I make mistakes. I am also an award-winning teacher (three times) and there are no substantiated student grievances against me. Yet, the lion can overshadow all of that with one of those reverberating roars.

Although I teach classes that have mostly White students, there are also students of color. The irony is that students of both dominant and marginalized identities question my authority and intentions. The times when I teach courses that include students of color and the lion lashes out at me, it startles me when I hear the roar through the actions and words of a cub from my own pride. It reminds me though of the pervasiveness of White supremacy. It prompts me to think about how the lion holds everyone hostage and how aggressive he is in establishing his territory. I believe the lion's roar coming through mouths of students of color comes from the same shock. They expect me to protect them from the intellectual/emotional roller coaster that comes with examining social oppression in a room that feels hostile because it is predominantly White. They are under the illusion that the classroom is my territory and that I can keep the lion out. Indignation arises when the lion's roar prompts them to move. They question my approach, my identity, and discount my credentials. They want to know if I am part of their pride or the other one. They do these checks to see if I hold the "people of color card" that proves that I am on their side. They too ask me to tell them about my training, but mostly they search for clues about how I grew up. If they determine I did not grow up "Black enough," they discount what I am trying to teach, they file angry grievances too, and they disengage from the process. I recognize that the lion is vicious and threatens the life of everyone. I understand these students retreat and put up defenses to protect themselves from the historical traumas of racism in a space where they think that I can protect them from the lion or at least provide shelter to give them a break. Even when I can see the lion, I cannot stop him from exerting his power. I am its victim too. After all, the lion is the king of the jungle. I, too, am working around him.

As I think about the "proverbial lion," it is interesting to note that the female lion does the hunting for the pride. She does it at night; she creeps up on her prey unsuspectingly and pounces. At times, the "proverbial lion" is tough to see, other times she is hard to name, and she is definitely difficult to quantify. Her cloak of inherited power and conferred dominance can cause so much disruption. And she is an excellent hunter.

Jodi's Encounters With the Proverbial Lion

In this section I discuss ways I have witnessed the "proverbial lion" from inside the cage as a White woman. Specifically, I share my reflections on ways I have seen power, privilege, and positionality engaged to subversively exploit the process of a multicultural initiative and disempower people of color. As a conscious scholar practitioner, I have personally found agency in education contexts. As a lifelong learner, I seek opportunities to further my education about Difference, primarily through reading, reflection, dialogue, and professional development. As an educator, I seek to embed multiculturalism throughout all of my courses and workshops, seeing each of them as a multicultural initiative through which I can engage with my students in deepening all of our understandings of power, privilege, and oppression. It is imperative that conscious scholar practitioners "pay careful attention to their own and others' racialized and cultural systems of coming to know, knowing, and experiencing the world" (Milner, 2007, p. 388), and over the years I have spotted the "proverbial lion" in a variety of settings. In this section, I describe three ways the lion has appeared from my positionality as a White woman. It is important to note that my recollections of these moments may differ from others' recollections because how we experience life is influenced by our positionality. One's social identity "has an epistemically significant impact on that speaker's claims" (Alcoff, 1991, p. 7). As such, the retelling of these experiences is in my voice and from my memory alone.

The "Go-Around" Jaw Snap

I have worked on a handful of multicultural initiatives whose top leaders were people of color. In my work with those initiatives, whose missions and goals were all somehow related to increasing persistence of underrepresented folks in higher education, I have experienced the "proverbial lion" in a specific capacity, what I am calling the "go-around" jaw snap. This manifestation of the lion happened when a constituent, usually a White person in a position of authority, "goes around" the involved people of color directly to me, when it would have been more appropriate to go directly to the person or people of color in the unit's leadership.

In Organization A, I was part of a six-person leadership team for an undergraduate retention initiative. Three of our executive leaders were people of color, and three were White. Five of us held master's degrees and we all had significant work experience in higher education and student affairs; we were professional peers. At one point during year three, I realized that the institution's central administrators primarily called on me to represent the program, either in meetings with high-level officials or to provide program updates to university administrators. When I had this realization, I first spoke with another of the White leaders, who argued that central administration knew of my reputation as a doer and simply wanted fast results. I am a doer, but two of the people of color on the executive leadership team were also known as doers on our predominantly White campus, so why did they not receive a call to represent the program? By "going around" my peers on the leadership team and speaking exclusively with me about the multicultural initiative, the central administrators sent a message to our team that some (White) individuals' work on the initiative was more valued and respected than others.

In Organization B, the "go-around" jaw snap did not happen to my peers, it happened to my supervisors. In this unit, I reported directly to two people of color, both of whom were tenured faculty in prestigious research programs and gave a small but significant amount of their effort to our initiative as directors. As an interdisciplinary multicultural initiative, our program bounced from location to location around campus. In fact, we had at least seven different office locations. I say "at least" because I lost count. Space at a research university is at a premium, and decisions about space are not made lightly. Decisions are driven by revenue streams and our multicultural initiative did not generate revenue, so the university faced challenges when attempting to balance its espoused values of inclusion and diversity with its business motivations. On two different occasions, a high-level White administrator approached me about the program's space (or future space) and cornered me into conversations that were certainly above my pay-grade. Those experiences left me in the tough position of relaying what happened to my supervisors. The image that resonates with these experiences is one in which the lion sneaks around its prey, snapping its jaw of racism from the side.

The Lion's Pride: Pack Mentality

I am not an animal expert, but I have taken my kids to the zoo enough times to know that lions are the only large cats that form social groups. The pack mentality of social groups can be dangerous. One individual can establish harmful norms for the whole group, and it is that image of the "proverbial lion" I wish to describe next. I have been to graduate school twice (master's and doctorate) with many years in between. In both of my graduate experiences, my peers and I celebrated the completion of our comprehensive exams. On one of these occasions, we sat at a local greasy spoon for breakfast, processing the exam questions and the different approaches we each took to answering them. One White person in the group, whose attention and approval mattered to most of the class, made an off-hand comment about hoping a certain Black faculty member would not grade her exam. This person's comment sparked a series of negative comments from my (mostly White) peers. It was as if the alpha group member gave everyone else permission to spout racial microaggressions about a Black professor. Before this occasion, I had not heard most of these people mutter a word about the professor, which led me to believe that their underlying racism was just waiting for an opportunity to rise up in what they thought was solidarity among the lion's pride.

Easy Prey of Silence

One phrase I have heard many times over the years that I find particularly troubling is that I am overly sensitive about issues of privilege and power. "No people of color have complained about this; you're too sensitive!" Silence is complicity, and White folks cannot sit by, putting the burden on people of color to make noise about racism. A few years ago, I was rifling through an engineering school's publication and came upon a racist image. A White male post-doctoral researcher had developed groundbreaking facial recognition software, and the photo in the publication included this White man next to a large computer screen that showed arrest mugshots of men of color. I sent a message to the associate dean of the school about the implicit message of exclusion to prospective students of color and the perpetuation of the stereotype of men of color as criminals. The associate dean's reply indicated he had not heard any complaints about the image, and perhaps I was overanalyzing it. Although the reply was not what I had hoped for, I was glad that I said something.

Another example of this manifestation of the lion involves a graduate course I took in which each student designed her or his own multicultural initiative, and we provided each other with peer feedback as we developed our initiatives. One of my classmates, another White woman, was developing a multicultural initiative that I found troubling. Her initiative was a tutoring program through which White suburban students would go to an inner-city school and save the poor kids of color who needed help. Reading this peer's proposal was hard, and I centered my written feedback on privilege and power, hoping it would help raise her awareness about the deficit model within which she was functioning. I was also very aware of my positionality in providing feedback—one White woman to another. I was able to use my identity to (hopefully) provide a level of criticism that she may not accept from our professor, a Black woman. I reflected for days about my positionality. Was I usurping my professor's authority and overstepping the bounds of peer feedback by accessing and using White privilege in this way? Ultimately, I decided to provide the critical feedback. Silence makes for easy prey for the "proverbial lion," and I do not intend to feed the lion.

Preparing for the Lion's Pounce

This chapter is about naming and discussing the viciousness of the "proverbial lion" of racism, but it is also about strategies for facing and surviving the lion as conscious scholar practitioners. In this section, we discuss ways that readers engaged in multicultural initiatives can face the lion. This is not an exhaustive discussion by any means, but taken with the other excellent chapters in this book, we hope you can find utility in some of these strategies.

- **Develop "color insight."** Armstrong and Wildman (2012) describe "color insight" (p. 233) as the antithesis of colorblindness. It is a process that engages people in reflecting on their understandings of race by having regular dialogue about race. Discuss current events as racialized experiences by noticing race instead of ignoring it. Doing so helps us examine systems of privilege, unmask perspectiveless-ness (in ourselves and others), and combat stereotypes (Armstrong & Wildman, 2012). Armstrong and Wildman (2012) describe color insight as a useful process for workplaces, and we would add that color insight could also be useful as a reflection activity. For example, if you journal, processing experiences or observations using color insight can help you examine how your own understandings of race have changed over time.
- **Identify and write down your pedagogical principles.** Thinking about who we are and what matters to us as facilitators helps us remain centered on the learning outcomes we develop for each multicultural initiative. Adams's (1997) five principles of social justice education may provide a starting point. Those principles are: (a) balance the cognitive and emotional components of the learning process; (b) support the personal while revealing the systemic; (c) manage social relations in the initiative group; (d) draw on reflection and experience as learning tools; and (e) adopt social awareness, personal growth, and social action as learning outcomes (Adams, 1997).
- **Develop a support network.** Anecdotally, many conscious scholar practitioners who do multiculturalism work describe feelings of isolation. We think Griffin (1997) put it best with, "Teaching social justice education courses is more rewarding if you have colleagues and friends who can discuss issues, challenge your awareness, provide help, and commiserate when things don't go as planned" (p. 279). If you are on a campus where you are isolated, reach out to regional colleagues or folks you have met at professional conferences to develop a virtual network and establish regular meetings to discuss your work and current events.
- **Find a compatible co-facilitator.** One of the best pieces of advice Jodi ever received about facilitating multicultural initiatives was to consider her positionality in reference to participants' social identities. "Some parts of the content and process . . . are more appropriately addressed by a facilitator from the agent group, and others are best dealt with by a facilitator from the target group" (Griffin, 1997, p. 281). Co-facilitating multicultural initiatives with colleagues whose social identities are different from our own has been beneficial for

participants who seek to identify with a facilitator. These experiences have also been personally beneficial, as we have gained awareness, knowledge, skills, and some of our closest friends by co-facilitating multicultural initiatives.

- **Know what defenses to expect.** An awareness of the ways people react to difficult dialogues about Difference can help the facilitator be ready for participants' defenses. As you read in an earlier chapter, Watt's (2007) privileged identity exploration (PIE) model identified eight defense modes. Learning about these defense modes and discussing them with your support network will help you to be ready to address the defenses as they arise, rather than getting stuck in that place we have found ourselves too often, thinking, "What just happened?" and feeling unable to move the dialogue forward in a productive way.

Conclusion

The "proverbial lion" is present in our everyday lives. Through this chapter, we sought to name the phenomenon and explore the ways we have experienced and witnessed the lion. By briefly reviewing the contexts for thinking about the "proverbial lion," sharing our personal experiences with the lion, and offering suggestions for conscious scholar practitioners, we hope we have provided our readers with reflections that help them identify where and when they have spotted the lion and strategies for surviving its presence.

References

Adams, M. (1997). Pedagogical frameworks for social justice education. In M. Adams, L. A. Bell, & P. Griffin (Eds.), *Teaching for diversity and social justice: A sourcebook* (pp. 30–43). New York: Routledge.

Alcoff, L. (1991). The problem of speaking for others. *Cultural Critique, 20,* 5–32. doi:10.2307/1354221

Armstrong, M. J., & Wildman, S. M. (2012). Working across racial lines in a not-so-post-racial world. In G. Gutierrez y Muhs, Y. F. Niemann, C. G. Gonzalez, & A. P. Harris (Eds.), *Presumed incompetent: The intersections of race and class for women in academia* (pp. 224–241). Boulder, CO: University Press of Colorado.

Gibney, S. (n.d.). *Teaching while black and blue.* Retrieved from http://gawker.com/teaching-while-black-and-blue-1473659925

Griffin, P. (1997). Facilitating social justice education courses. In M. Adams, L. A. Bell, & P. Griffin (Eds.), *Teaching for diversity and social justice: A sourcebook* (pp. 279–298). New York: Routledge.

Gutierrez y Muhs, G., Niemann, Y. F., Gonzalez, C. G., & Harris, A. P. (Eds.). (2012). *Presumed incompetent: The intersections of race and class for women in academia*. Boulder, CO: University Press of Colorado.

Milner, H. R. (2007). Race, culture, and researcher positionality: Working through dangers seen, unseen, and unforeseen. *Educational Researcher, 36*(7), 388–400.

Onwuachi-Willig, A. (2012). Silence of the lambs. In G. Gutierrez y Muhs, Y. F. Niemann, C. G. Gonzalez, & A. P. Harris (Eds.), *Presumed incompetent: The intersections of race and class for women in academia* (pp. 142–151). Boulder, CO: University Press of Colorado.

Pittman, C. T. (2010). Race and gender oppression in the classroom: The experiences of women faculty of color with White male students. *Teaching Sociology, 38*(3), 183–196.

Potapchuk, M., Leiderman, S., Bivens, D., & Major, B. (2005). *Flipping the script: White privilege and community building*. Silver Springs, MD: MP Associates, Inc., and the Center for Assessment and Policy Development (CAPD).

Shields, S. A. (2012). Waking up to privilege: Intersectionality and opportunity. In G. Gutierrez y Muhs, Y. F. Niemann, C. G. Gonzalez, & A. P. Harris (Eds.), *Presumed incompetent: The intersections of race and class for women in academia* (29–39). Boulder, CO: University Press of Colorado.

Smith, W. A., Hung, M., & Franklin, J. D. (2011). Racial battle fatigue and the miseducation of black men: Racial microaggressions, societal problems, and environmental stress. *Journal of Negro Education, 80*(1), 63–82.

Solorzano, D., Ceja, M., & Yosso, T. (2000). Critical race theory, racial microaggressions, and campus racial climate: The experiences of African American college students. *Journal of Negro Education, 69*(1/2), 60–73.

Stanley, C. A. (2006). Coloring the academic landscape: Faculty of color breaking the silence in predominantly white colleges and universities. *American Educational Research Journal, 43*(4), 701–736.

Tuitt, F., Hanna, M., Martinez, L. M., del Carmen Salazar, M., & Griffin, R. (2009, Fall). Teaching in the line of fire: Faculty of color in the academy. *Thought & Action*, 65–74.

Watt, S. K. (2007). Difficult dialogues, privilege and social justice: Uses of the privileged identity exploration (PIE) model in student affairs practice. *College Student Affairs Journal, 26*(2), 114–126.

16

THE ART OF REFLECTIVE TEACHING

Ellen E. Fairchild

My 25-year career in higher education is split evenly between student affairs administration (12+ years) and teaching faculty (12+ years). As I reflect on my experience working with university students (both positions were in the same large, public institution), a few observations have impacted my views of multicultural initiatives and how I proceed when fashioning one to suit the needs I have at the time.

During my student affairs career as the program coordinator for non-traditional and off-campus students, much of what I dealt with was advocacy for students in tenant–landlord situations. These types of circumstances are fraught with power and privilege, usually on the side of the landlord, but, at times, with roommate situations as well. Because of the time period during which I held this position, off-campus housing was not uniformly available to all types of students. In many cases the discrimination was aimed at students in general, but more often it was specifically aimed at LGBTQA students. Although there are now laws and codes in place for some of these obstacles, there are still many ways landlords can and do discriminate against students in their housing search. Each case was unique, but discrimination ranged from student status, along racial and sexual orientation lines, to whether children were welcome in an apartment complex. Knowing and applying legal strategies was the typical solution for students as they fought for their rights as tenants in a town that favors large land holders and management companies that have great power on city boards. In my role, providing education about systemic uses of power and broad oppressive practices was key in helping students obtain the self-advocacy needed to fight for themselves.

I am now a faculty member in a School of Education, preparing students to be teachers in a diverse society. The difference in these students versus the ones I advocated for in my student affairs position is that they are pre-dominantly White. However, what they have in common with the students of color that I worked with previously is that they do not fully understand the complexities of power and privilege. I teach first-year students in courses in the foundations of education in the United States. Other course content areas I teach include multiculturalism and social studies methods. All of these classes are part of the core requirements to become a licensed teacher in the state in which we reside. In all, I touch the lives of over 300 students every academic year over two semesters. What I have learned about our students has further solidified my views of the possibility of multicultural initiatives and how practices inside and outside of the classroom can help students become change agents in society.

In this chapter, I reflect on the challenges I face as I design and implement multicultural initiatives. I will share key questions I use to guide my thought process and planning as I work with students around difference. Finally, I will illustrate how I use these key guiding questions to design a transformational experience for my students and discuss what it means to me.

Facing Privilege, the American Dream Myth, and Complacency

What students tell me (both in words and actions), is that they believe our society has solved some of our worst problems with race, class, gender, and ability (these are the typical lenses through which I format my classes). They believe that they, as the current generation, are better at dealing with these social problems (especially sexual orientation). Although I recognize that there has been some progress in some of these areas, I cannot, and do not agree with them when they pose this argument. There is a form of conceit that leads to complacency on their parts as they fight against hearing "again" about the racism, sexism, homophobia, ableism, and class warfare that is currently being played out in U.S. society. Unexplored, this privilege goes unchallenged as they live in a society that has been formed around them as members of the dominant group.

They believe they know the answers because their parents have "always told them that they should love everyone the same, and that we are all the same on the inside," (student quote, Fall 2012); this fails on many levels. It fails to recognize the widespread and lasting history of discrimination and prejudice that forms the foundations of this society. It fails to realize the disparity of opportunity this long-lasting history has created for many and does not recognize the myths of the American Dream and "pulling oneself up by one's bootstraps." Yes, these are just myths. This belief fails to recognize unevenness of opportunity and the realities of multiple perspectives. Finally, and potentially the most costly for them, is that their complacency toward these big issues facing U.S. society may one day envelop them as the divide deepens between U.S. economic classes. Our college students simply must see the world around them as the complex, fascinating, frightening, harsh, wonderful, and diverse creature it is. It is our job, as student affairs professionals and faculty members, to reveal this world through our multicultural initiatives. When we deal directly with these failures in beliefs then *everything* becomes a multicultural initiative, because we are asking our young people to think about how society affects everyone . . . some of us differently than others.

Addressing the Challenges: Key Guiding Questions

How we manage these beliefs and behaviors makes every educational endeavor a multicultural initiative, from advocacy in a tenant–landlord issue to a freshman foundations of education course; all can, and should, be multicultural initiatives. What I have come to utilize over my years of multicultural work are three questions that I ask myself when planning presentations, speeches, or university courses. First, I ask, "What do I want them to know?" Then, "What do I want them to feel?" And finally, "What do I want them to do?" It is not a formula because formulas do not work; we must be free to react to our participants and the background they bring with them. They are specific enough to force me to think about what I am planning, but general enough to allow me to be agile in my selection of information and activities. These questions have served me well regardless of whether I am planning a student affairs symposium or a semester-long class.

These questions help me think about who and what I am teaching. My inherent optimism leads me to hope that ultimately, because of what they have thought, felt, and committed to do, someone in the audience will change society in extraordinary ways. Realistically, I know this is not the case, but I am prepared to foster small actions across many individuals that collectively matter a great deal.

The following is an example of a series of four lessons. This unit on poverty and social class is consistently successful and illustrates how I use the three guiding questions to plan as I challenge the myths and disrupt the privileges present in my classroom.

What Do I Want Participants to Know?

It is important for me to use a mix of historical and contemporary content. The historical content builds the foundation upon which we can challenge our assumptions of today. Without the history, critically thinking about today's realities is harder and not as complete.

Though they hate it while they are in the middle of it, students say historical knowledge is essential to their understanding. For the first time they are able to see the roots of poverty within the United States and how seemingly ordinary processes were manipulated to keep groups of people from realizing the same potential as other groups. I view historical background in multicultural initiatives as a necessary step because so many do not know or understand what went on before to bring us to where we are now. This foundation-building allows me to make direct connections between past events and current issues.

A person's worldview is built on a lifetime of experience; therefore, it is essential to build a foundation of knowledge on the subject in order to establish an emotional and behavioral connection later on. In this instance, I have several readings that the students complete and discuss in small and large groups. Written reflections, conversation starters, and reading guides all help students to scaffold their learning into something that makes sense. Time and event lines help them to build context and decipher time periods about which they have little comprehension. I also use a series of charts and graphs to illustrate current poverty realities as national wealth becomes more and more concentrated in fewer and fewer individuals. This scaffold learning leads to discussions that are deeper and more nuanced in their understanding of poverty and its impact on society.

How Do I Want Them to Feel?

For students, multicultural initiatives are often uncomfortable as they feel a variety of emotions from guilt to sadness to anger. It is important for me to check what conclusions students are drawing as they work within their small groups. I help them assess those conclusions as the unit proceeds, remembering to argue the alternative, when appropriate. In this way, they reflect on what they are thinking and communicate about what they have learned. I seldom know, for sure, what to expect with students' communications about their learning. A common theme is shown by this student from the Spring 2014 semester:

> In analyzing my own background, I realize that graduating from a class of 17 white, middle class students made me extremely unaware of what

else was out there. . . . I wanted to believe everyone lived and learned like me. . . . I believed children in poverty stricken areas had the same education and technology that my school provided. . . . I am [now aware of my ignorance to other people's situations]. . . . I now understand that there is more out there than what I have experienced and it is my responsibility to allow myself to see how people's situations affect . . . the way they live their lives.

Our discussions centered around "big" fixes that could occur if there was social and political will, but the students didn't believe that sort of change was likely. So, accepted solutions became those that could be done at the more local level through social programs and job creation that would put a "Band-Aid" (their word for it) on the problem instead of challenging the inequity in wealth distribution that they saw no way around. It is my sense that the students' privilege often plays into this notion of impotence. There is a reticence on their part to alter wealth distribution in meaningful ways. Although there is a feeling of frustration and anger at the injustice of class division, there is still a protection of the status quo. Students feel more comfortable working to change local conditions where they can see immediate results in children for whom they cared.

I made note of solutions they proposed and I continued to ask them to consider further plans of action. Students can become overpowered by problems they perceive as too big and any action they take too small and insignificant. We fought this by brainstorming smaller, local solutions available to them upon graduation as they enter communities and work with families. This was meaningful to them because they felt very strongly that it was "not fair" for children to be saddled with poverty. We processed the continuum of emotions as a group, because although I want the students to feel something, I want it to be an appropriate and positive emotional connection. I ultimately want them to experience resolve.

We must challenge our students to take action upon finishing a multicultural initiative. This will help students feel part of the solution and empowered. In this case, those actions will be further down the road. Action brings the multicultural initiative full circle as students take what they have learned and felt and apply it to their circumstances.

What Do I Hope They Will Do?

The best learning is authentic and experiential. Unfortunately, due to resource restraints we can seldom transport our participants to experience some of what we are trying to get them to understand. For example, students would make very real connections to race, poverty, and class if they could experience the inequity of K–12 school funding firsthand. Yet, it is impossible in a four-hour workshop and nearly so in a semester-long class. This presents a unique challenge for facilitators of multicultural initiatives who are striving to change minds, attitudes, and behaviors.

The dilemma is what can be done to attain the same effects that experience would provide—how to get participants to reach a level that is something beyond the intellectual. I want my participants to feel something because, in my experience, feelings spur action much more quickly than an intellectual exercise. Part of the solution is to allow time for thinking, processing, making connections, and getting to the feeling. In my example, I asked students to complete a variation of the SNAP Challenge (Feeding America, 2014). This challenge requires them to live on the food stamp amount given to an individual for one week. The added burden was to do so healthfully and determine any effects that might come with long-term dependence on the subsidy. Students actually experienced, as much as possible through an artificial activity, what it is like for some of the families we were studying.

As a finale to the experience, I showed a video that describes poverty from the perspective of local children. Disbelief was the most common reaction to the statistics and experiences of the children despite all the information the students had previously gleaned historically and statistically. The discussion that followed the video showed clearly that, for the first time, many of the students were able to put everything together and integrate all they had experienced over the other three sessions. Reactions included anger, frustration, determination, and powerlessness. I allowed time for small group discussion to brainstorm smaller, more manageable strategies that they could implement within a school district; we then processed those ideas within the large group. I ended the final session with a challenge for all to continue to learn about the topic and gave them ideas for blogs and readings that would help them to do so. We ended the unit at that point.

As proof that this was a valuable experience for the students, I continue to receive video suggestions and Facebook postings that deal with the topic long after the students have gone on to the next semester and out from under my educational care. It matters to me that they remember so deeply the experience and care enough to pass along wonderful suggestions. I believe without a mix of knowledge and emotion, students cannot reach the deeper commitment needed to act on perceived inequities.

All students are not deeply impacted every semester, of course. I constantly seek out new teaching strategies that might be more powerful. Some of these have included art, poetry, and literature, as well as music and videos. I have had luck with gallery walks where students explore and respond to text or images placed around a room. I have also asked students to create poems about themselves and the experiences they bring to the topic. These personal revelations are some of the most powerful tools in prompting participants to think from multiple perspectives.

I know that not everyone arrives at the end of the sessions in a place where I think they should be, and that is okay. My objective is to provide an opportunity for them to think through the information I provide and arrive at their own conclusions. Their conclusions do not often match mine, but there is almost always a change of some kind. Where my students go from that point is their journey. I have been lucky to be a part of it and I am always thankful to my students for letting me take the journey with them. Multicultural experiences are not about forcing someone to change, but lighting a path for them to follow. I often remind myself to celebrate those who come along and let go of those who do not.

Conclusion

Topics of equity and opportunity have always been important to me. As a sixth-grade girl, I was tired of always reading in third-person masculine. I wrote an essay in third-person feminine. I failed that paper, argued my case, and still failed the paper, but carried a resolve to see change over my lifetime. Some of that change has happened; much has not. That failure to change, more than anything, drives my teaching style. I want my students to exit my class changed people. I want them to have learned something, to have felt some emotions, and then resolve to carry that forward into their own teaching. It is an emotional experience for me as I go through it with my students. We discuss and argue important points. We get emotional together and we plan and plot together, too. I honor my freshmen for who they currently are and for who they can become. If I can positively facilitate a change that will further help the students they will touch as teachers, then my eternity is ensured.

I get many thoughtful e-mails from current and past students. None has summed up why I teach—or more importantly, why I teach the way I do—better than a certain e-mail about class that I received from a current student. In part, this is what he said:

> I don't know if I have learned more from any other course I have ever taken than what I have learned so far in this class. My head throbs every time I leave class but I love the feeling of throbbing. I try to soak in as much knowledge from you and our readings as mentally possible. You are touching the lives of thousands of children you will never meet. The way you teach and the content we have and will study will hopefully do many wonderful things for our future students. Those students will be getting

great teachers because of instructors like you. I am sure you have thought about stuff like this over and over again. I just wanted to let you know that there is always a chance that you could be the spark to the next big education reform.

That is a very powerful message, one that is humbling and affirming all at once. It is exactly why I do what I do.

Reference

Feeding America. (2014). *Taking the SNAP challenge.* Retrieved from http://feedingamerica.org/get-involved/hunger-action-month/snap-challenge.aspx

17

DARING GREATLY

A Reflective Critique of the Authentic, Action-Oriented, Framing for Environmental Shifts (AAFES) Method

Tracy L. Robinson-Wood and Sherry K. Watt

It is not the critic who counts; not the man who points out how the strong man stumbles, or where the doer of deeds could have done them better. The credit belongs to the man who is actually in the arena, whose face is marred by dust and sweat and blood; who strives valiantly; who errs, who comes short again and again, because there is no effort without error and shortcoming; but who does actually strive to do the deeds; who knows the great enthusiasms, the great devotions; who spends himself in a worthy cause; who at the best knows in the end the triumph of high achievement, and who at the worst, if he fails, at least fails while daring greatly, so that his place shall never be with those cold and timid souls who neither know victory nor defeat.
— Theodore Roosevelt, 1910

My theoretical and conceptual approach to multicultural initiatives has developed over my 20-year career of participating in and facilitating difficult dialogues on cultural issues. As my ideas culminated into this book, I talked with many friends, mentors, colleagues, and students about the fundamentals of my approach to engaging Difference.

In Chapter 2, I describe the essential elements to my approach entitled the *authentic, action-oriented, framing for environmental shifts (AAFES) method.* The AAFES method describes the process qualities that I believe are essential to transformational multicultural initiatives. Those qualities include multi-cultural initiatives that focus on being **authentic,** which focuses on how you engage with difference rather than concentration on dissecting the difference; being **action-oriented,** which emphasizes thoughtful balance between dia-logue and taking action to deconstruct and create social change; and **framing for environmental shifts,** which appeals to shifting the environment toward inclusion of Difference rather than focusing on ways the marginalized mem-bers of a community can survive dehumanization.

In my conversations about this approach, I have received some tough questions. The most troubling questions: Is it possible for this approach to influence change in the "real" world? Is the AAFES method just academic and not practical? I ponder whether this approach can transform the interac-tions between a healthcare provider and a patient or an elementary teacher and a student. I question whether the AAFES approach can transform how institutions of higher learning involve students in campus life. Is it realistic to expect people to invest emotionally in environments where intellect is most highly valued? I wonder if it can have any influence over how I raise my children to live in a diverse society. Is it possible that AAFES could begin to uproot the institutional structures that result in particularly marginalizing and demeaning those who are not part of the dominant group (i.e., White, heterosexual, male, and affluent)?

I asked my friend and colleague Tracy Robinson-Wood to write a response to this approach to multicultural initiatives for two reasons. First, I know that Tracy dares greatly as quoted by Theodore Roosevelt. By that I mean, she teaches multicultural courses and advocates for social change. Moreover, she is one of those rare people who unfailingly commits to telling you the truth under any and all circumstances. I have known Tracy since I was a graduate student at North Carolina State University. She taught the required cross-cultural counseling course that I took as a master's student. Truthfully, I felt intimidated by her decisive and commanding presence. She was the only African American faculty member in the department, unten-ured at the time, now a full professor. Many of the students had limited or no experiences with having an African American professor lead the class-room, including myself. She asked searing questions and demanded I face truths about social oppression that even as an African American woman I did not want to accept fully. Her commitment to living authentically is pal-pable when you are in her presence. I find her as a teacher, a mentor, and a friend to be willing to see and speak the truth whether it is the type of reality that is good, bad, or ugly. She is completely committed to being in the arena with you as you work through ideas. As my dissertation chair, Tracy was a fierce advocate. Simultaneously, asking tough questions about the research to me as a student, appropriately demanding her colleagues to think broadly to invite cutting-edge ideas from me as a young scholar, all while expecting everyone involved to bring their highest quality work to the project. Hence, I asked Tracy to respond to this approach because she dares greatly, is committed to truth, is unconditionally honest, and is a fierce advocate.

Second, I asked Tracy to respond to this approach because we have very different approaches to teaching multicultural initiatives. We both want our students to have increased awareness of Difference and we want them to be ethical and culturally skilled counseling or student affairs practitioners. However, we take different routes to reach that end goal. In Tracy's class, I recall examining social oppression primarily from an intellectual location and secondarily from an emotional space. On the other hand, I lean more to a balance between the head, heart, and hands in classroom settings. I lead students into intellectual exploration first through their emotion. I would sum it to say that I take an indirect route by inviting participation and self-exploration whereas Tracy takes a more direct route by requiring those things and depending on intellectual acuity. We have talked numerous times about the benefits and consequences of each other's approach. We are both concerned that in my approach to teaching students, they can avoid taking the invitation to learning that is transforming and use emotion inappropriately. In Tracy's approach with students, we fear that students can perform competency or shutdown and disengage from the process, but not necessarily transform. I chose Tracy to respond to the AAFES method because our approaches to multicultural initiatives are different.

Ultimately, I learned that Tracy is one of those people who dares greatly. I am grateful that she accepted the invitation to respond to the approach described in the opening chapters. Next you will find Tracy's response. I hope that the questions raised in Tracy's letter will inspire further adaptations and development of the AAFES method. Ultimately, I am seeking a way to engage Difference with integrity, authenticity, and respect. I hope that the AAFES method presents an opportunity for a shift away from surface-level change and provides some steps toward transforming organizations for inclusion of marginalized voices.

Dearest Sherry:

I thought I would write you a letter concerning my thoughts about the AAFES method. I am honored that you asked me to respond to your scholarly work. I write with a mixture of positive emotions which speaks to the reflexive process of the reader who is reading a writer's words where both are framed and shaped by multiple and simultaneous forces, histories, contemporary realities, and personal experiences.

Gratitude: I am grateful for your belief in humanity and gracious commitment to diversity, which are not born from untested naiveté. More than anyone I know, you have been through the fire and the rain. There is not a sector of your life that has been immune from loss, pain, delay, dreams deferred, trauma, and involuntary change. You, more than anyone I know, have maintained your laser focus on core values and honored your life and living with choices that reflect love, faith, hope, community, and joy. I love you Sherry Kay and am so proud of you.

Fascination: There are tenets associated with the AAFES Method. As I reflected on your important work, I had questions: (1) Participation in AAFES requires ample time. How will you accommodate those who do not have time and control over their calendar but would like to actively participate? (2) AAFES requires critical thinking. Do people need to be at conceptually rich levels of ethnic, racial, conceptual, and spiritual identity development or is commitment to participate in the difficult process of deconstruction the primary characteristic for AAFES? (3) The university is a site for the reproduction of inequity. How will you help people with more vulnerability and less power feel safe enough to speak freely given that AAFES honors Difference?

Because of your willingness to name histories, power, and vulnerability, I envision that AAFES could encourage resistance. Resistance is needed to read, name, and confront systems that marginalize and silence people across dominant and marginalized identities. That said consider creating a video that could instruct people on how to apply the AAFES Method. People will be galvanized to see the AAFES Method in action with you as the instructor, coach, and Goddess that you are. Maybe you could put out a call to programs, departments, colleges, and institutions that you perceive capable of implementing AAFES and request their participation. You could also secure a grant to record the vivid and reflexive processes of learning, unlearning, demolition, and rebuilding while offering stipends to people for their time and work.

The AAFES Method does not call for tinkering with the status quo but for a full-scale overhaul. I wonder how you will educate people about the benefit or purpose of transformation considering that the dominant paradigm works for so many within the academy. Your work honestly acknowledges that an elevation of dominant cultural beliefs (e.g., Whiteness, patriarchy, Christianity) and stigmatized identities (non-Whiteness, gender fluidity, and non-Christianity) is oppressive and pathological. You have courageously named and confronted the pathology and oppression of racism within society yet,

I am curious to learn how the AAFES Method can address nuanced "third things" that normalize Whiteness and undervalue Blackness. In class recently, I was discussing the 2010 Census where more than half of Latinos identified as White, perhaps irrespective of skin color. One of my White students asked, "Why would someone who does not have white skin want to claim a White identity?" Increasingly, the Census defines and counts people as White even in the presence of non-white skin. The scope of White incumbency is fluid and broadening. It is important to query why this dynamic exists and what it means. AAFES supports initiatives that ask these and other searing questions.

I am concerned that multiculturalism has become both an umbrella term and a marketing tool in higher education. Clearly, culturally diverse groups, including the White LGBT community; White ethnics; international faculty; and Asians, particularly those who are in STEM disciplines, are valued members of the academy and valid representations of diversity. Yet so many institutions avow a commitment to inclusion but have alarmingly few high-ranking Black American, Latino, and Native American administrators or full tenured professors. Globalization is essential but it is not synonymous with domestic multicultural initiatives. How would AAFES encourage participants to consider their positionality within a capitalistic and patriarchal system amidst pressing demands on universities to stay solvent and remain competitive?

Frustration: I am inclined to believe that AAFES could have traction in grassroots community groups where *off the grid White people* and people of color are willing to co-exist with their feelings—fatigue, frustration, sadness, and anger—as White people newly encounter the daunting process of learning about racial injustice and inequality (remember the '60s and '70s). The few people who prevail will be changed at depth by the head, hand, and heart work tackled within these environments where trust is cultivated, but is such transformation rooted in the strategic goals of most institutions? I question how White people will co-exist with the swell of emotions from people of color as they reflect on overt and covert acts of daily racism. I wonder if AAFES requires the presence of clinicians to help people deal with a host of big emotions that will arise in the process of environmental shifts? Do you think in our lifetimes we will see racism receive a code in the Diagnostic Statistical Manual (DSM)? Once this happens, psychological and educational communities will be better positioned to help people, as you so aptly say, "survive the dehumanization."

Anticipation: The AAFES method calls for the reflexive process of engaging in perpetual dialogue between people with and without white skin color, privilege, and power. You do not look away from race as having grand master status and its effect on the dialogue space. I could see the AAFES

Method creating a space to systematically prepare newly minted and sea-soned PhDs with skills for survival and success given how commonplace race, gender, and sexual microaggressions are in the academy.

With your understanding of and respect for how people are positioned by race, gender, and other identities, I anticipate that the AAFES method can create the dialogue space to honor Difference between and within groups where power, privilege, vulnerability, and marginalization are occurring. However, it is important to ask, do certain types of Difference place real constraints on the efficacy of AAFES? The AAFES Method gives voice to marginalized and dominant identities yet needs to continue to interrogate intersectionality. In this way, your powerful model will become even stronger.

Inspiration: AAFES inspires me to stay in the arena. It is clear that the change you envision for institutions should be reflected in strategic goals and mission statements. Due to the process orientation of the method, I wonder if large, PhD granting, research intensive institutions, in the top 50 schools nationwide, where so much emphasis is placed on receiving federal grant money, are structured for prolonged participation in AAFES? As challenging as the issues are, I will continue to search for and endeavor to cultivate spaces that honor your lovely work. While writing my letter to you, the number of states allowing same-sex marriage has increased. For our children, we dream of a world where people across sources of difference work collaboratively to share the burden of creating solutions to inequity. This dream compelled many of us to enter higher education. When you receive your genius award, deserved notoriety, and fiscal prosperity from your scholarly work inspired by devotion and courage, know that I will be transforming with you and offer my head, heart, and hand in a spirit of collegiality and sisterhood.

Sincerely,
Tracy L. Robinson, Professor, Northeastern University

Conclusion

After reading Tracy's response to the AAFES method, I see many valid points and welcome the opportunity to improve the articulation of this approach based on her feedback. I wonder what the influence of my research on privi-leged identities has on the conception of the AAFES method. In other words, I wonder if this approach privileges the dominant paradigm and asks permis-sion from institutional structures rather than demands deconstructing the marginalization and revolts against the inequities. Does using this approach serve to transform systems or reinforce the dominant paradigm and pre-vent transformation? I question how my lived experiences and my personal capacity for forgiveness shape my openness to this approach to multicultural initiatives. In situations where grave social injustices (cases of over-aggressive police tactics, hate crimes, etc.) have occurred, is it reasonable to expect participation in the way that the AAFES method invites? As I prepare to apply this approach more intentionally in practice, these are important considerations.

On the other hand, I also reflect back on times that I practiced the principles of the AAFES method and I recall remarkable moments of transformation. There are moments in the classroom when it astounded me to see how people exist within the darkness associated with social oppression and have productive dialogue. I recently recited in a blog a remarkable classroom exchange where students discussed and attended the pain associated with the Christian church's stand on same-sex relationships (Courage & Renewal, Blog Post, September 25, 2014). It was transformative for me to witness the power of both acknowledging the pain and reaching for a different way to communicate about Difference. I have had success with the AAFES method with faculty, staff, and administrators as well. For instance, I recall co-facilitating a workshop for a small community college with concerns about their diversity climate. The workshop included faculty, staff, and administrators. I used the principles of AAFES to guide the workshop structure and content. Early in the workshop, I asked everyone in the room to write a poem about their upbringing. I recall looking toward the far right of the room and seeing the facilities service workers all together at one table. The majority of the people in the room were White. The facilities service workers seemed to differ outwardly only by social status. These five men seemed to gather purposely at this one table to be away from the faculty and the administrators. When I asked if anyone would like to share their poem, one of those facilities service workers stood up, shared his poem, and told his story. It was profound and applauded by the group. I noticed how the interactions during break shifted. Many came over to that one table and talked to those men. I noticed that after he shared his story, he joined the dialogue about how to improve the climate on the campus and the others in the room listened intently. The environment invited authenticity, intentionally encouraged personal reflection on positionality, and offered a space for a different voice. Although I am completely open to feedback and recognize there are ways to improve the approach, I believed in it. Using these process-oriented qualities of the AAFES method, I am able to co-exist in productive ways in environments where the complexities of social oppression can bind others and me.

I am grateful to Tracy for her insights and for how nobly she has examined the AAFES method and the spirit behind it. It seems ironic to paraphrase

Theodore Roosevelt, a politician whose solution to America's race problem was racist and aimed to maintain the status of Whites. At the same time, I see this as an exchange that reveals that Tracy and I are in the ring, slugging it out, marred by dust, sweat, blood, striving valiantly "who err and come short again and again" while we attempt to unpack this legacy of racism and other social oppressions that we have all inherited. Tracy and I embrace the possibility in the AAFES method. I am eager for opportunities to apply these ideas within higher education.

Reference

Roosevelt, T. (1910, April 23). The man in the arena [Speech at the Sarbonne, Paris]. Retrieved from http://www.theodore-roosevelt.com/images/research/speeches /maninthearena.pdf

ABOUT THE EDITOR AND CONTRIBUTORS

Editor

Sherry K. Watt is an associate professor in the Higher Education and Student Affairs program at the University of Iowa. Her research explores the reactions individuals have to difficult dialogues on race, sexual orientation, and disability. Currently, she is working on an instrument development study that expands on her research on the Privileged Identity Exploration model (2007). She has received several awards in recognition of her teaching and scholarship, including Radford University's Chi Sigma Iota Outstanding Teacher Award. In addition, she is an Annuit Coeptis award recipient, and an Emerging Scholar and a Senior Scholar within the American College Personnel Association (ACPA). She received three prestigious awards honoring both her service related to diversity efforts as well as her teaching, namely, the 2006 College of Education's Audrey Qualls Commitment to Diversity Award, and the University of Iowa's Collegiate Teaching Award in both 2006 and 2013. She is a facilitator prepared by the Center for Courage and Renewal. She has almost 20 years of experience in designing and leading educational experiences that involve effective strategies for engaging Difference authentically.

Contributors

Richard Barajas is currently a doctoral candidate in the Higher Education and Student Affairs program at the University of Iowa. He also serves in the role of director of admissions at the College of Pharmacy. He focuses on higher education administration with particular interests in access to higher education for minoritized populations as well as the role education can play in reducing health disparities. Prior to his current role he worked at the Office of Multicultural Student Affairs at Iowa State University, where he oversaw a variety of programs including scholarship coordination, summer bridge programs, and student identity development.

John P. Dugan currently serves as an associate professor in the Higher Education graduate program at Loyola University Chicago where he teaches courses on leadership, student development theory, and multiculturalism for social justice. He received both his PhD and MEd from the University of Maryland in counseling and personnel services, and his BA in communications and Spanish from John Carroll University. John's research focuses on the influences of higher education in shaping college students' involvement and leadership development with a specific emphasis on marginalized voices and ideas. John currently serves as the principal investigator for the Multi-Institutional Study of Leadership, an international research program examining the influences of higher education on socially responsible leadership and other educational outcomes (e.g., efficacy, resilience, social perspective-taking). To date, more than 300 institutions in Australia, Canada, Jamaica, Mexico, and the United States have participated in the study, yielding over 300,000 participants. John is also the principal investigator on a qualitative study using critical narrative inquiry to explore the ways in which social identity influences individuals' understanding of, enactment of, and experiences with leadership. John's research has generated 24 printed or in-press publications and more than 60 presentations at national and international conferences.

Sherri Edvalson Erkel is director of First Year Experience at St. Ambrose University in Davenport, Iowa. She earned her PhD in student affairs administration and research at the University of Iowa. Her research interests include applying Critical Race Theory to college student dialogues and creating positive campus climates for diversity.

Ellen E. Fairchild is currently a senior lecturer in the Teacher Preparation Program within the School of Education at Iowa State University. She previously was director of the Office of Adult Learner and Commuter Students at Iowa State University. Dr. Fairchild has written and presented on a variety of topics including homeschooling; adult student needs; and, more recently, Christian privilege. She is currently interested in how particular ways of teaching impact student learning.

Lacretia Johnson Flash is the senior advisor and chief of staff to the vice president for Human Resources, Diversity and Multicultural Affairs at the University of Vermont (UVM), where she helped establish the university's

President's Commission for Inclusive Excellence. Dr. Flash served as the assistant dean for conduct, policy, and climate for the Division of Student Affairs at UVM, where she created and led the division's Diversity Council, providing leadership for major initiatives, including a nationally recognized diversity professional development program and a multicultural competencies assessment process. Lacretia earned a doctorate from the Educational Leadership and Policy Studies program at UVM. Her dissertation was entitled Developing a Measure of Multicultural Competence in Student Affairs Organizations. She has presented nationally on her work, including the presentations "From Ambivalence to Action: Institutional Steps Towards Becoming a Multiculturally Affirming Campus" and "Innovative Strategies and Tools for Assessing Multicultural Competence in Student Affairs Organizations," and a model of organizational multicultural competence. Lacretia was awarded the Susan Hasazi ALANA Award for Outstanding Academic Achievement in Doctoral Education from the College of Education and Social Services at UVM, and has received research grants from the American College Personnel Association and the National Association of Student Personnel Administrators.

Joy Gaston Gayles is an associate professor of higher education in the Department of Leadership, Policy and Adult and Higher Education at North Carolina State University. Dr. Gayles's research agenda focuses on college student access and success, particularly for student athletes and women and underrepresented minorities in STEM fields. Equity and diversity are themes that cut across all areas of her research agenda. Her research has been published in outlets including the *Journal of Higher Education*, *Research in Higher Education*, *Journal of College Student Development*, and *Innovative Higher Education,* to name a few. In 2014 Dr. Gayles received the Diamond Honoree Award from ACPA for her contributions to the field of higher education and student affairs.

Paulette Granberry Russell is senior advisor to the president for diversity and is the director of the Office for Inclusion and Intercultural Initiatives (OCIII) at Michigan State University (MSU). Ms. Granberry Russell plays a vital leadership role on all campus inclusion and intercultural support committees. As Director of the OCIII, Ms. Granberry Russell leads efforts in four functional areas: institutional equity, education and development, community outreach and research and assessment. A CIC Academic Leadership Fellow (2000–2001), Ms. Granberry Russell is a sought-after presenter concerning inclusion, diversity, and equal opportunity in higher education. In 2002, she presented workshops on affirmative action and diversity programming for post-apartheid merged higher education institutions at Durban Institute of Technology in South Africa. She was a panelist on diversity initiatives in U.S. higher education in Rio de Janeiro, Brazil, in 2005; and in 2012 and 2014, traveled to the countries of Burkina Faso, Senegal, South Africa, and Tanzania as a member of two separate delegations on economic development and civil society, and women's empowerment. Ms. Granberry Russell is a graduate of MSU, earned a juris doctor degree from the Thomas M. Cooley Law School, and is a licensed attorney in the state of Michigan.

Mary F. Howard-Hamilton is a professor and coordinator of the Higher Education Leadership Program in the Bayh College of Education's Department of Educational Leadership. She was a recipient of the Indiana State University Presidential Medal for Exemplary Teaching and Scholarship and the Theodore Dreiser Distinguished Research and Creativity Award in 2015. She also received the Bayh College of Education, Holmstedt Distinguished Professorship Award for 2012–2013. Dr. Howard-Hamilton received her BA and MA degrees from the University of Iowa and her EdD from North Carolina State University. She has served as a higher education student affairs administrator for 15 years and a full-time faculty member for 23 years. Dr. Howard-Hamilton has published over 90 articles and book chapters. Her most recent coedited books include *Diverse Millennial Students in College* (with Fred A. Bonner and Aretha F. Marbley; Stylus, 2012), *Multiculturalism on Campus: Theories, Models, and Practices for Understanding Diversity and Creating Inclusion* (with Michael J. Cuyjet and Diane L. Cooper; Stylus, 2011), and *Standing on the Outside Looking In: Underrepresented Students' Experiences in Advanced Degree Programs* (with Carla L. Morelon-Quainoo, Susan D. Johnson, Rachelle Winkle-Wagner, and Lilia Santiague; Stylus, 2009). Dr. Howard-Hamilton serves on the Association for the Study of Higher Education, is a member-at-large on the Board of Directors, and is an American College Student Personnel Association Senior Scholar. She has received the Champion of Diversity Award from the Indiana Minority Business and the Terre Haute Human Rights Commission Diversity Award.

Wayne Jacobson is assessment director in the Office of the Provost at the University of Iowa (UI), and also holds an adjunct faculty appointment in Educational Policy and Leadership Studies. He is responsible for coordinating learning outcomes assessment in academic programs at UI, engaging departments in evidence-based examination of student experience and success in their programs, and coordinating campus surveys that provide opportunities to bring student voices into institutional assessment and decision making. Before coming to UI, he was director of the Center for Instructional

Development and Research at the University of Washington. He holds degrees in counseling (MS) and adult education (PhD) from the University of Wisconsin–Madison.

Bridget Turner Kelly is associate professor of higher education at Loyola University Chicago. Dr. Kelly's scholarship is focused on marginalized populations in higher education; more specifically, she studies the experiences of students of color on predominantly White campuses, women and faculty of color at research universities, and how all students can become socially just educators. She has authored articles in peer-refereed journals of high national reputation and also presented numerous refereed papers at national conferences. She won the Distinguished Faculty Award for Excellence in teaching from the School of Education at Loyola University Chicago in 2014; was named a 2013 Diamond Honoree for ACPA; was awarded the NASPA IV-East Outstanding Contribution to Student Affairs through Teaching in 2011; was recognized as an Emerging Scholar by ACPA in 2005; and received the Peggy R. Williams Emerging Professional Award in 2004 from the Office on Women in Higher Education, a division of the American Council on Education.

Shelly Kerr is a licensed psychologist and the director of the University of Oregon's Counseling and Testing Center. Dr. Kerr earned her doctorate in counseling psychology from Washington State University and her master's degree in college student personnel from Western Illinois University. She previously coedited *Preventive Health Measures for Lesbian and Bisexual Women* (with Robin Mathy; Haworth Press, 2006) and *Lesbian and Bisexual Women's Mental Health* (with Robin M. Mathy; Haworth Press, 2003). Her professional interests include multicultural organizational development, college mental health, and violence prevention.

Cindy A. Kilgo is a doctoral candidate in the Higher Education and Student Affairs program at the University of Iowa. They* also currently serves as a research assistant in the Center for Research on Undergraduate Education. Prior to this role, they served as the graduate assistant for research, grants, and assessment for the National Resource Center for the First-Year Experience and Students in Transition at the University of South Carolina. Cindy has a master's degree in higher education and student affairs from the University of South Carolina, and a bachelor's degree in psychology from Georgia Southern University. Their research interests include high-impact

---

* Cindy Ann Kilgo's preferred pronouns are *they*, *them*, and *theirs*.

educational practices—specifically, undergraduate research and service learning; student success and college impact for LGBTQ+ identified students;
and the link between campus environment and climate and college student
involvement and engagement.

Lucy A. LePeau is an assistant professor of higher education and student affairs at Indiana University Bloomington. Her research, teaching,
and service activities have focused on academic affairs and student affairs
partnerships promoting diversity and social justice initiatives on campus,
organizational change, and improved student affairs practice. She joined the
faculty at IU after completing her PhD in college student personnel at the
University of Maryland College Park (UMCP). She was a recipient of the
Emerging Scholar and Annuit Coeptis awards from ACPA–College Student
Educators International in 2015 and the Melvene D. Hardee Dissertation
of the Year from NASPA–Student Affairs Administrators in Higher Education in 2013. Prior to doctoral study Lucy served as an assistant dean of
students for new student programs at the University of North Carolina at
Charlotte. She has been a student affairs educator as a faculty member and
practitioner in the field for over 10 years. She earned her BA in psychology
from Marquette University and her MS in higher education and student
affairs from Indiana University.

Jodi L. Linley is a visiting faculty member of the University of Iowa's
Higher Education and Student Affairs program and is earning her doctorate in higher, adult, and lifelong education at Michigan State University.
Jodi's longstanding career in student affairs and her research agenda center on
issues of multiculturalism, leadership, socialization, and equity.

Melissa McDaniels is assistant dean of the Graduate School and director
of the Teaching Assistant Program at Michigan State University. McDaniels has over 20 years of experience in graduate student and faculty development, undergraduate and graduate teaching and learning, and organizational
change. From 2008 to 2012, McDaniels served as director of Michigan State
University's National Science Foundation ADVANCE grant (in the Office
of the Provost) where she spearheaded the institution's efforts to diversify
the faculty in science, technology, engineering, and mathematics (STEM)
fields. Prior to 2008, she held full-time positions at Northeastern University,
Boston College, and the National Geographic Society. She has had the plea-
sure of consulting domestically and internationally (Nelson Mandela Met-
ropolitan University, Purdue University, MSU Center for the Scholarship of

Teaching, the Association for the Study of Higher Education, and the University of Wisconsin–Madison) on topics related to organizational change, programmatic/learning assessment in higher education, graduate student research capacity development, and graduate student and faculty teaching development. She has authored papers and book chapters on topics related to diversity, organizational change, and graduate student and faculty teaching development. She holds degrees from Michigan State University (PhD), Boston College Graduate School of Education (MA), and the University of Michigan (BA).

John A. Mueller is a professor in the department of Student Affairs in Higher Education at Indiana University of Pennsylvania. He has worked in higher education for over 25 years with practitioner and teaching experience at multiple institutions. Mueller is an active member and leader in the American College Personnel Association. His publications, presentations, and service activities have focused primarily on issues of diversity, multiculturalism, and inclusion. He is coauthor of Jossey-Bass publications' *Multicultural Competence in Student Affairs* (Pope, Reynolds, & Mueller, 2004) and *Creating Multicultural Change on Campus* (Pope, Reynolds, & Mueller, 2014).

Kathy Obear is an organizational development consultant who worked in student affairs and is a faculty member of the Social Justice Training Institute. For 30 years she has facilitated workshops on diversity, equity, and inclusion for campuses across the United States *and internationally, and has consulted with top leaders and members of change teams to create inclusive campus environments that support the success of the full breadth of students, staff, and faculty on campus.*

Craig Pickett is the coordinator for Student Life and Diversity at the University of Tennessee, College of Agricultural Sciences and Natural Resources. He earned his bachelor's degree in political science from Davidson College (2008) and his master's degree in student affairs in higher education from Indiana University of Pennsylvania (2010). With a focus on holistic student development, Pickett holds several years of student affairs experience within a wide range of functional areas, including career development, first year programming, student activities, multicultural initiatives, recruitment, and student retention.

Tracy L. Robinson-Wood is is a professor in the Department of Applied Psychology at Northeastern University. She is author of *The Convergence of Race, Ethnicity, and Gender: Multiple Identities in Counseling.* The fifth edition, to be published by SAGE, is anticipated in 2016. Her research interests focus on the intersections of race, gender, sexuality, and class in psychosocial identity development. She has developed the resistance modality inventory (RMI), which is a psychometrically valid measure of resistance, a theory she code-veloped for Black girls and women to optimally push back against racism, sexism, classism, and other forms of oppression. Her research is also focused on parents' racial socialization messages within interracial families; and the relational, psychological, and physiological impact of microaggressions on highly educated racial, gender, and sexual minorities.

Daviree L. Velázquez currently serves as the assistant director for diversity programs in the Center for Multicultural Equity and Access at Georgetown University, where she oversees initiatives illuminating the importance of intergroup dialogue, justice and solidarity work, and the leadership devel-opment of students with marginalized identities. Prior to her current role, Daviree oversaw Student Staff Training and Development in the Office of Student Life at Loyola University Maryland. She received her MEd from Loyola University Chicago in higher education administration, and her BA in psychology with a minor in sociology from DePaul University. Daviree's research interests include leadership efficacy and capacity building initiatives for students of color, and developing cultural competency in student affairs practitioners and graduate programs. She has facilitated over 100 dialogues around student leadership and social justice, attended numerous social jus-tice institutes, and has established two conferences supporting the leadership development of women of color.

The Nigger in You

Challenging Dysfunctional Language, Engaging Leadership Moments

Dr. J. W. Wiley

"Employing arguably the most polarizing epithet in American history, *nigger*, Dr. J. W. Wiley grabs the attention of those who understand the castigation of racism, but who may not grasp the multiple ways that otherness beyond race is treated in contemporary American culture. *The Nigger in You* is a spellbinding book that will challenge both the newcomer to diversity studies as well as the veteran of social justice."

—***Thomas Keith***, *Professor, California State Polytechnic University–Pomona, and Filmmaker (*Generation M: Misogyny in Media & Culture *and* The Bro Code*)*

"This book is inspiring, challenging, informative, and a timeless resource for educators, parents, and community leaders. It's the real deal. You'll learn something every time you read it."

—***Eddie Moore, Jr.***, *Founder/Director, The White Privilege Conference*

Sty/us

22883 Quicksilver Drive
Sterling, VA 20166-2102

Subscribe to our e-mail alerts: www.Styluspub.com

Also available from Stylus

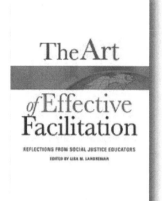

The Art of Effective Facilitation

Reflections From Social Justice Educators
Edited by Lisa M. Landreman
This book is intended for the increasing number of faculty and student affairs administrators—at whatever their level of experience—who are being asked to become social justice educators to prepare students to live successfully within, and contribute to, an equitable multicultural society.

It emphasizes the need to prepare by taking into account such considerations as the developmental readiness of the participants, and the particular issues and historical context of the campus, before designing and facilitating a social justice training or selecting specific exercises.

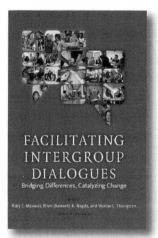

Facilitating Intergroup Dialogues

Bridging Differences, Catalyzing Change
Kelly E. Maxwell, Biren Ratnesh Nagda, and Monita C. Thompson
Foreword by Patricia Gurin
"This book is a treasure trove of theory, research, and personal narratives of both successes and challenges. Anyone interested in developing an intergroup dialogue program, or using the intergroup dialogue method in other courses, campus organizations, research labs, or other educational settings composed of people from diverse backgrounds will find this book their most important resource. So, too, will practitioners who work with diverse groups of people in communities and in state, national, and international organizations."

—*Patricia Gurin*, *Nancy Cantor Distinguished University Professor Emerita of Psychology and Women's Studies, University of Michigan*

Continues on preceding page